**Christoph Angerer**

**Exploiting Task-Order Information**

Christoph Angerer

# Exploiting Task-Order Information
## in Compilers for Shared-Memory Parallel Programs

Südwestdeutscher Verlag für Hochschulschriften

**Impressum/Imprint (nur für Deutschland/only for Germany)**
Bibliografische Information der Deutschen Nationalbibliothek: Die Deutsche Nationalbibliothek verzeichnet diese Publikation in der Deutschen Nationalbibliografie; detaillierte bibliografische Daten sind im Internet über http://dnb.d-nb.de abrufbar.
Alle in diesem Buch genannten Marken und Produktnamen unterliegen warenzeichen-, marken- oder patentrechtlichem Schutz bzw. sind Warenzeichen oder eingetragene Warenzeichen der jeweiligen Inhaber. Die Wiedergabe von Marken, Produktnamen, Gebrauchsnamen, Handelsnamen, Warenbezeichnungen u.s.w. in diesem Werk berechtigt auch ohne besondere Kennzeichnung nicht zu der Annahme, dass solche Namen im Sinne der Warenzeichen- und Markenschutzgesetzgebung als frei zu betrachten wären und daher von jedermann benutzt werden dürften.

Coverbild: www.ingimage.com

Verlag: Südwestdeutscher Verlag für Hochschulschriften GmbH & Co. KG
Heinrich-Böcking-Str. 6-8, 66121 Saarbrücken, Deutschland
Telefon +49 681 37 20 271-1, Telefax +49 681 37 20 271-0
Email: info@svh-verlag.de

Approved by: Zürich, ETH, Diss., 2011

Herstellung in Deutschland:
Schaltungsdienst Lange o.H.G., Berlin
Books on Demand GmbH, Norderstedt
Reha GmbH, Saarbrücken
Amazon Distribution GmbH, Leipzig
**ISBN: 978-3-8381-3174-0**

**Imprint (only for USA, GB)**
Bibliographic information published by the Deutsche Nationalbibliothek: The Deutsche Nationalbibliothek lists this publication in the Deutsche Nationalbibliografie; detailed bibliographic data are available in the Internet at http://dnb.d-nb.de.
Any brand names and product names mentioned in this book are subject to trademark, brand or patent protection and are trademarks or registered trademarks of their respective holders. The use of brand names, product names, common names, trade names, product descriptions etc. even without a particular marking in this works is in no way to be construed to mean that such names may be regarded as unrestricted in respect of trademark and brand protection legislation and could thus be used by anyone.

Cover image: www.ingimage.com

Publisher: Südwestdeutscher Verlag für Hochschulschriften GmbH & Co. KG
Heinrich-Böcking-Str. 6-8, 66121 Saarbrücken, Germany
Phone +49 681 37 20 271-1, Fax +49 681 37 20 271-0
Email: info@svh-verlag.de

Printed in the U.S.A.
Printed in the U.K. by (see last page)
**ISBN: 978-3-8381-3174-0**

Copyright © 2012 by the author and Südwestdeutscher Verlag für Hochschulschriften GmbH & Co. KG and licensors
All rights reserved. Saarbrücken 2012

Exploiting Task-Order Information in Compilers for Shared-Memory Parallel Programs

Christoph Angerer

Diss. ETH No. 20022

# Exploiting Task-Order Information in Compilers for Shared-Memory Parallel Programs

*A dissertation submitted to*
ETH ZURICH

*for the degree of*
Doctor of Sciences

*presented by*
Christoph Angerer
Dipl.-Inf. Univ. TU München
born August 18, 1977
citizen of Germany

*accepted on the recommendation of*
Prof. Dr. Thomas Gross, examiner
Prof. Dr. Abraham Bernstein, co-examiner
Dr. Evelyn Duesterwald, co-examiner

2011

*For my baby girl Sophia!*

# Abstract

With the arrival of multicore systems, parallel programming is becoming increasingly mainstream. Writing correct parallel programs, however, has turned out to be difficult and prone to errors without proper support from the employed programming languages, compilers, and runtime systems. Over the last years, researchers and engineers have developed numerous abstractions and programming models that make developing parallel programs easier, safer, and more efficient.

Despite the advances made in parallel programming models, libraries, and runtime systems, the corresponding compilers still remain largely ignorant of the parallelism exhibited by the program execution. In particular, current compilers do not have any knowledge about *what* tasks are scheduled *when* in the program and *how* they are ordered—even though many higher-level parallel programming models and libraries contain a wealth of task-order information that can be exploited by the compiler. Without task-scheduling knowledge, however, compilers are missing important optimization and verification opportunities.

This dissertation explores how compilers for parallel programs with shared memory can gather and exploit knowledge about the scheduling of tasks at runtime. By analyzing potential orderings between tasks, the compiler can decide whether accesses to shared memory by different tasks may conflict and thus result in data races. We present a concrete *schedule analysis* that can extract task-ordering information from real-world programs. The schedule analysis can be combined with standard program analyses such as points-to and escape analyses to improve the precision of known optimizations as well as enable new optimizations.

We present two case studies to evaluate the effectiveness of the schedule analysis. The first case study is an optimizing compiler for a version of Java that uses *sequential consistency* as its memory model. Sequential consistency solves many inconsistencies of the Java Memory Model. However, it comes at the cost of large runtime overhead, because it prevents many of the standard optimization techniques. Our compiler exploits task-order information to decide whether or not a program operation may conflict with a parallel task. If not, the compiler is allowed to aggressively apply all standard optimizations to this program part.

The second case study is an optimizing compiler for a system with *dynamic fractional permissions*. In this system, every object is associated with a list of tasks that have read and/or write permission for the object. Tasks can grant read permission to subtasks by splitting their own permission into fractions and later collect those fractions back to re-gain the original permission. The overhead of checking permissions is reduced by an optimizing compiler that uses task-ordering information to minimize the places where permission checks must be inserted.

In addition to the two case studies, we describe multiple smaller optimization and verification techniques that benefit from task-order information. While we do not present a thorough evaluation of those techniques, we do report anecdotal evidence where we have data available.

# Kurzfassung

Durch die wachsende Verbreitung von Mehrkernprozessoren wird der nebenläufigen Programmierung ein immer höherer Stellenwert beigemessen. Die Erfahrung hat jedoch gezeigt, dass die Entwicklung korrekter paralleler Programme schwierig und fehleranfällig ist. Dies ist insbesondere der Fall, wenn der Entwickler nicht auf die Unterstützung der eingesetzten Programmiersprache, des Compilers und des Laufzeitsystems zählen kann. Aus diesem Grund wurden über die letzten Jahre zahlreiche neuartige Abstraktionen und Programmiermodelle entworfen, die das Erstellen nebenläufiger Programme einfacher, sicherer und effizienter gestalten sollen.

Ungeachtet der Fortschritte, die die Forschung in parallelen Programmiermodellen, Bibliotheken und Laufzeitumgebungen vorweisen kann, haben die meisten zugehörigen Compiler kein Konzept von der in Programmen auftretenden Nebenläufigkeit. Moderne Compiler haben im Allgemeinen keine Information darüber, *wann* welche Tasks im Programm disponiert und in *welcher Reihenfolge* sie ausgeführt werden. Den Compilern gehen dadurch wertvolle Möglichkeiten zur Programmoptimierung und -verifikation verloren, obwohl viele parallele Programmiermodelle und -bibliotheken eine Fülle von Informationen bezüglich der Ausführungsreihenfolge von Tasks beinhalten, die der Compiler zur Effizienzsteigerung einsetzen könnte.

Diese Dissertation behandelt das Thema, wie ein Compiler Informationen über die Ausführungsreihenfolge von Tasks autonom und automatisiert aus nebenläufigen Programmen mit gemeinsam genutztem Hauptspeicher extrahieren und ausnutzen kann. Indem der Compiler die partielle Ordnung der Tasks analysiert, kann er potentiell konkurrierende Zugriffe auf den gemeinsamen Hauptspeicher und die daraus resultierenden Wettlaufsituationen erkennen. Wir präsentieren einen Algorithmus, genannt *Schedule Analyse*, welcher eine partielle Task-Ordnung automatisiert aus anwendungsnahen Programmen extrahiert. Die Kombination der Schedule Analyse mit weiteren Standardanalysen aus dem Compilerbau resultiert in einer erhöhten Präzision und damit Effizienzsteigerung bekannter und neuartiger Optimierungen gleichermassen.

Wir evaluieren die Effektivität der Schedule Analyse anhand zweier Fallbeispiele. Das erste Fallbeispiel beschreibt einen optimierenden Compiler für eine Javaversion mit einem sequentiellen Konsistenzmodell. Der Einsatz sequentieller Konsistenz als Speichermodell löst viele Inkonsistenzen des Java Speichermodells, resultiert jedoch aufgrund der zusätzlich notwendigen Speicherverwaltung und der Verunmöglichung vieler Optimierungen in einer erhöhten Laufzeit. Der beschriebene Compiler nutzt Informationen über die Ausführungsreihenfolge von Tasks, um zu entscheiden, ob eine gegebene Programmoperation mit einem nebenläufigen Task potentiell in Konflikt steht. Falls nicht, kann der Compiler die Kosten für die Speicherverwaltung reduzieren und den entsprechenden Programmteil aggressiv optimieren.

Das zweite Fallbeispiel behandelt einen optimierenden Compiler für ein System mit dynamischen partiellen Zugriffsrechten. In diesem System ist jedes Objekt mit einer Liste zugriffsberechtigter Tasks assoziiert. Ein Task, dem zumindest Lesezugriff gewährt wurde, kann sein

Zugriffsrecht in partielle Leserechte zerteilen und diese an Subtasks weitergeben. Diese Bruchstücke können zu einem späteren Zeitpunkt wieder eingesammelt werden, um das originale Zugriffsrecht zurück zu erhalten. Da zu jedem gegebenen Zeitpunkt nur jeweils ein Task das vollständige Zugriffsrecht auf ein Objekt besitzen kann, werden konkurrierende Zugriffe auf das Objekt verhindert. Die Kosten, die mit der Überprüfung der Zugriffsrechte einher gehen, werden minimiert, indem der Compiler eine auf der Schedule Analyse basierenden Optimierung anwendet.

Zusätzlich zu den beiden Fallbeispielen beschreibt diese Dissertation eine Auswahl weiterer Optimierungen und Verifikationen, die von dem Wissen über die Ausführungsreihenfolge von Tasks profitieren. Obwohl wir für diese Beispiele aus Zeitgründen keine tief gehende Evaluation durchführen können, präsentieren wir Daten und Anhaltspunkte, die die Bedeutung der Schedule Analyse für die effektive Optimierung paralleler Programme verdeutlichen.

# Contents

**1 Introduction**   **1**
     1.1 Thesis statement . . . . . . . . . . . . . . . . . . . . . . . . . . . . 2
     1.2 Summary of the thesis and key contributions . . . . . . . . . . . . . 3
     1.3 Organization of this dissertation . . . . . . . . . . . . . . . . . . . . 4

**2 Background**   **7**
     2.1 Lamport's happens-before relations . . . . . . . . . . . . . . . . . . 7
         2.1.1 Formalism . . . . . . . . . . . . . . . . . . . . . . . . . . . . 7
         2.1.2 Example: Proving correctness of the butterfly barrier for two tasks . . . . 9
         2.1.3 Can-affect relations and Java . . . . . . . . . . . . . . . . . 12
     2.2 Task schedules . . . . . . . . . . . . . . . . . . . . . . . . . . . . . . 14
     2.3 Sources of task-order information . . . . . . . . . . . . . . . . . . . 16
     2.4 Summary . . . . . . . . . . . . . . . . . . . . . . . . . . . . . . . . . 19

**3 A generic task model with ordering information**   **21**
     3.1 Tasks with explicit scheduling constraints . . . . . . . . . . . . . . . 21
     3.2 Task objects as parameters: The *now happens-before later* pattern . . . . . . . 23
     3.3 Example: Barrier synchronization . . . . . . . . . . . . . . . . . . . 23
         3.3.1 Example with threads and barriers . . . . . . . . . . . . . . 24
         3.3.2 Example with explicit scheduling constraints . . . . . . . . 25
     3.4 Exception handling and inter-task exception propagation . . . . . . 27
     3.5 Explicit task ordering vs. lock-based synchronization . . . . . . . . 29
     3.6 Programming model or intermediate representation? . . . . . . . . 29
     3.7 Structural properties of schedules . . . . . . . . . . . . . . . . . . . 30
         3.7.1 Well-formed schedules . . . . . . . . . . . . . . . . . . . . . 30
         3.7.2 Creation trees . . . . . . . . . . . . . . . . . . . . . . . . . . 31
         3.7.3 Exclusive tasks . . . . . . . . . . . . . . . . . . . . . . . . . 31
         3.7.4 Genuine edges . . . . . . . . . . . . . . . . . . . . . . . . . 32
     3.8 Related work . . . . . . . . . . . . . . . . . . . . . . . . . . . . . . . 33
     3.9 Summary . . . . . . . . . . . . . . . . . . . . . . . . . . . . . . . . . 35

**4 Schedule analysis in optimizing compilers**   **37**
     4.1 Terminology and notation . . . . . . . . . . . . . . . . . . . . . . . 39
         4.1.1 Running example: The sor benchmark . . . . . . . . . . . . . . . . . . 42

| | 4.2 | The schedule analysis algorithm | 43 |
|---|---|---|---|
| | | 4.2.1 Step 1: Normalizing the input program | 44 |
| | | 4.2.2 Step 2: Extracting the loop-contextualized task-variable ordering graph | 48 |
| | | 4.2.3 Step 3: Computing relations between task variables | 63 |
| | | 4.2.4 Step 4: Computing unordered task-variable/task-object pairs | 64 |
| | | 4.2.5 Step 5: Computing unordered task-object/task-object pairs | 67 |
| | 4.3 | Implementation | 68 |
| | | 4.3.1 Datalog implementation | 69 |
| | | 4.3.2 Java implementation | 69 |
| | 4.4 | Related work | 70 |
| | 4.5 | Summary | 73 |
| **5** | **Case study 1: Sequentially consistent Java** | | **75** |
| | 5.1 | Sequential consistency | 75 |
| | 5.2 | An optimizing compiler for sequentially consistent Java | 78 |
| | | 5.2.1 Transforming Java into sequentially consistent Java | 79 |
| | | 5.2.2 Optimizing away volatile memory accesses | 80 |
| | 5.3 | Evaluation | 81 |
| | | 5.3.1 Setup of the experiment | 82 |
| | | 5.3.2 Benchmark characteristics and analysis performance | 82 |
| | | 5.3.3 Precision of the analysis | 84 |
| | | 5.3.4 Runtime overhead of sequentially consistent Java | 85 |
| | 5.4 | Related work | 86 |
| | 5.5 | Summary | 88 |
| **6** | **Case study 2: Dynamic fractional permissions** | | **89** |
| | 6.1 | Dynamic fractional permissions | 90 |
| | | 6.1.1 Access control lists and permissions | 90 |
| | | 6.1.2 Permission management operations | 91 |
| | 6.2 | Example: MapReduce with dynamic data-race detection | 93 |
| | 6.3 | Optimizing dynamic fractional permissions | 95 |
| | | 6.3.1 Handling Permission Operations | 96 |
| | | 6.3.2 Auxiliary Rules | 97 |
| | | 6.3.3 Optimizations | 98 |
| | 6.4 | Evaluation | 99 |
| | | 6.4.1 Setup of the experiment | 99 |
| | | 6.4.2 Runtime overhead of dynamic fractional permissions | 100 |
| | 6.5 | Related work | 101 |
| | 6.6 | Summary | 102 |
| **7** | **Other applications in optimization and verification** | | **103** |
| | 7.1 | Synchronization removal | 104 |
| | | 7.1.1 Unnecessary synchronization | 104 |
| | | 7.1.2 Removing unnecessary synchronization | 104 |

|       |       | 7.1.3 Experimental data . . . . . . . . . . . . . . . . . . . . . . . . . . 105 |
|---|---|---|

- 7.1.3 Experimental data . . . . . . . . . . . . . . . . . . . . . . . . . 105
- 7.1.4 Related work . . . . . . . . . . . . . . . . . . . . . . . . . . . 106
- 7.2 Optimizing strong atomicity in software transactional memory . . . . . . . . . 107
  - 7.2.1 Reducing strong atomicity overhead . . . . . . . . . . . . . . . . . 108
  - 7.2.2 Related work . . . . . . . . . . . . . . . . . . . . . . . . . . . 109
- 7.3 Synchronization variant selection . . . . . . . . . . . . . . . . . . . . . 110
  - 7.3.1 Code duplication in Java libraries . . . . . . . . . . . . . . . . . . . 110
  - 7.3.2 Compiler selected synchronized/unsynchronized variants . . . . . . . . 111
  - 7.3.3 Experimental data . . . . . . . . . . . . . . . . . . . . . . . . . 112
- 7.4 Happens-before order relaxation . . . . . . . . . . . . . . . . . . . . . . 113
  - 7.4.1 Example: Parallel continuation passing style . . . . . . . . . . . . . 114
  - 7.4.2 Removing unnecessary ordering . . . . . . . . . . . . . . . . . . . 115
  - 7.4.3 Related work . . . . . . . . . . . . . . . . . . . . . . . . . . . 116
- 7.5 Verifying programmers' sharing intentions . . . . . . . . . . . . . . . . . 117
  - 7.5.1 Experimental data . . . . . . . . . . . . . . . . . . . . . . . . . 117
- 7.6 Summary . . . . . . . . . . . . . . . . . . . . . . . . . . . . . . . . 119

**8 Future directions**     **123**
- 8.1 Task model extensions . . . . . . . . . . . . . . . . . . . . . . . . . . 123
- 8.2 Improving schedule analysis precision . . . . . . . . . . . . . . . . . . . 124
- 8.3 Task-aware program analyses and wellformed-ness checks . . . . . . . . . . 125
- 8.4 Integration with just-in-time compilers . . . . . . . . . . . . . . . . . . . 126

**9 Conclusions**     **129**

**A Datalog implementation**     **141**
- A.1 Extensional database . . . . . . . . . . . . . . . . . . . . . . . . . . 142
- A.2 Rules for the task-sensitive points-to analysis . . . . . . . . . . . . . . . . 143
- A.3 Rules for the task-sensitive escape analysis . . . . . . . . . . . . . . . . . 147
- A.4 Rules for the schedule analysis . . . . . . . . . . . . . . . . . . . . . . 149
- A.5 Rules for the synchronization removal optimization . . . . . . . . . . . . . 152

# List of Figures

2.1   Butterfly Barrier for Two Tasks. .......................... 10
2.2   Initial relations for the correctness proof of the Butterfly barrier. .......... 11
2.3   Types of relations between two operations. ...................... 13
2.4   Higher-level view of the butterfly barrier from Figure 2.2. Internal details of the barrier have been abstracted into distinct *Arrive* operations. The original low-level operations and happens-before relations are shown in white. ...... 15
2.5   Task schedule of the butterfly barrier from Figure 2.2. ................ 16
2.6   Comparison of fork/join constructs using different languages and parallelism mechanisms. After the sequential phase /*A*/, three parallel tasks /*B*/ are spawned and joined before the sequential phase /*C*/. ............... 18

3.1   Simplified version of the sor benchmark using threads and barriers. ....... 24
3.2   One main and three worker threads w1, w2, and w3 while executing the example from Figure 3.1. Dashed lines depict periods where a thread is blocked. ..... 25
3.3   The sor benchmark from Figure 3.1 using explicit scheduling constraints. .... 26
3.4   Schedule statically extracted from task Round() from Figure 3.3. Double-headed arrows indicate implicit creation edges, gray boxes indicate schedule sites inside loops. ..................................... 27
3.5   Marking tasks in the creation tree to test if $\mathcal{A} \rightarrow \mathcal{B}$ is genuine. The fence is circled by the dotted line, marks are shown as stars. Arcs denote exclusive tasks. 32

4.1   The three cases where two program points $P$ and $Q$ *commute*. .......... 38
4.2   A generic optimization. ................................. 39
4.3   Control-flow graph for the Round() task method of the Sor class from Figure 3.3  42
4.4   Steps of the schedule analysis and the intermediate products. ........... 44
4.5   A small example in SSA form. ............................. 45
4.6   Control-flow graph with exception edges representing uncaught exceptions. ... 47
4.7   Example with happens-before edges between tasks that were scheduled in different loop iterations. The diagram on the right depicts the schedule for the case numRounds = 3. .................................... 59
4.8   Control-flow graph for the Start() task method of the ChainedSteps class from Figure 4.7 ..................................... 60
4.9   The relation *REL* between the task variables computed from the loop-contextualized task-variable ordering graph for the running example from Table 4.1. ............................................ 64
4.10  Illustrations for computing the *taskNotOrdered* relation. ............... 65

| | | |
|---|---|---|
| 4.11 | Rules for computing unordered variable/task pairs . . . . . . . . . . . . . . . . . . | 66 |
| 4.12 | Computing parallel tasks . . . . . . . . . . . . . . . . . . . . . . . . . . . . . . . | 68 |
| 5.1 | Execution semantics for sequentially consistent programs. . . . . . . . . . . . . | 76 |
| 5.2 | Dekker's mutual exclusion algorithm for two tasks. flag0 and flag1 are shared variables; r0 and r1 are thread-local registers. . . . . . . . . . . . . . . . . . . . | 76 |
| 5.3 | Some executions of Dekker's algorithm from Figure 5.2 . . . . . . . . . . . . . | 77 |
| 5.4 | Redundant read elimination is permitted by the JMM but violates sequential consistency (example adapted from [2]). . . . . . . . . . . . . . . . . . . . . . . | 78 |
| 5.5 | Phases of the optimizing compiler for sequentially consistent Java. . . . . . . . | 80 |
| 5.6 | Computing required **volatile** memory accesses for sequentially consistent Java. Variable $f$ ranges over all fields. For array accesses, $f$ is a synthetic field elements representing the contents of the array. . . . . . . . . . . . . . . . | 81 |
| 5.7 | Relative number of instrumented field and array accesses. . . . . . . . . . . . . | 84 |
| 5.8 | Runtime overhead of unoptimized and optimized sequential consistency compared to Java's relaxed memory model. . . . . . . . . . . . . . . . . . . . . . . . | 85 |
| 6.1 | Implementation of the MapReduce pattern using dynamic fractional permissions for data-race detection. . . . . . . . . . . . . . . . . . . . . . . . . . . . . . | 94 |
| 6.2 | Auxiliary functions used for optimizing dynamic fractional permissions. The NEEDSREADCHECK and NEEDSWRITECHECK rules start with marking local variables that may be accessed concurrently and propagate this information inter-procedurally. . . . . . . . . . . . . . . . . . . . . . . . . . . . . . . . . . . | 98 |
| 6.3 | Rules used by the compiler to remove unnecessary permission operations and to decide where read and write checks must be inserted. . . . . . . . . . . . . . | 99 |
| 6.4 | Runtime overhead of different optimization levels for dynamic fractional permissions compared to the original version without a dynamic fractional permission system. . . . . . . . . . . . . . . . . . . . . . . . . . . . . . . . . . . . . . . | 100 |
| 7.1 | Computing required monitorenter bytecodes for synchronization removal. The *parallel*() relation is computed by the schedule analysis. . . . . . . . . . . | 105 |
| 7.2 | Number of monitor enter statements that are required. . . . . . . . . . . . . . . | 106 |
| 7.3 | Weak versus strong atomicity (example from [105]): Under weak atomicity, task 1 can observe an odd value in r. Under strong atomicity, r is always even. | 108 |
| 7.4 | Rules deciding for each read bytecode $R$ and write bytecode $W$ whether they must follow transactional semantics in order to guarantee strong atomicity. . . . | 109 |
| 7.5 | Safe variant selection optimization with class-level and method-level granularity. | 111 |
| 7.6 | Number of allocation sites that may result in shared objects. . . . . . . . . . . . | 112 |
| 7.7 | Number of methods that may conflict in a parallel context. . . . . . . . . . . . . | 113 |
| 7.8 | Fibonacci numbers translated from CPS to pCPS. . . . . . . . . . . . . . . . . . | 115 |
| 7.9 | Fixing the transitive ordering in the fib() schedule after removing the edge f. | 116 |
| 7.10 | Rules to check what classes, fields, and **new**-statements should be annotated as being shared. . . . . . . . . . . . . . . . . . . . . . . . . . . . . . . . . . . . . . | 118 |
| 7.11 | Number of pairs of static field accesses that may interfere. . . . . . . . . . . . . | 118 |
| 7.12 | Number of pairs of instance field accesses that may interfere. . . . . . . . . . . | 119 |

A.1 The Datalog domains. . . . . . . . . . . . . . . . . . . . . . . . . . . . . 141

# List of Tables

4.1 Extracting the loop-sensitive task-variable ordering graph from the `sor` example.  50
4.2 Task-scheduling and task-ordering effect analysis of the `ChainedSteps` example.  62
5.1 Complexity and performance of the analysis. . . . . . . . . . . . . . . . . . . . . 83
7.1 Running time of the sharing intention verification analysis. . . . . . . . . . . . . 121

# 1

# Introduction

The widespread adoption of multicore processors in both high-end and commodity computer systems over the last years made parallel programming become increasingly mainstream. As an answer to this trend, researchers and engineers have developed new abstractions and programming models for concurrent programming. Despite the advances in parallel programming models, libraries, and runtime systems, however, the corresponding compilers still remain largely ignorant of how and when tasks are scheduled and how they relate to one another. This dissertation shows that it is valuable for a compiler to compute scheduling information in the form of $Task \times Task \rightarrow Relation$ mappings where $Relation$ answers the question of how two program tasks relate to each other:

**Sequential:** Two tasks are sequential if their execution is strictly ordered.

**Exclusive:** Two tasks are exclusive if they can never co-exist in a single run of the program (e.g., they are scheduled in different branches of a conditional statement).

**Parallel:** If two tasks are neither sequential nor exclusive, they are considered (potentially) parallel.

Scheduling information can, for example, enable a compiler to apply more aggressive optimizations to program parts that do not interfere with any task that may execute concurrently. Without knowledge about task scheduling, compilers are missing important optimization and verification opportunities.

The quality of the scheduling information that a compiler can extract from a program highly depends on the parallel computation model that the program uses. In a traditional thread model, such as the threads used in the Java language, for example, the lifetime of a thread and its dependencies on other threads are not stated explicitly; rather, they come about as a side effect of executing low-level primitives such as signals, barriers, and locks. While making for an efficient and reasonably easy to use system, compilers have a hard time extracting high-level execution behavior from such low-level operations.

Experience has shown that not only compilers have difficulties with analyzing threaded programs. Even programmers often reason incorrectly about the execution behavior of their program and thus inadvertently introduce errors that are related to incorrect thread ordering and synchronization [26, 37, 73]. The exponential growth of possible program-operation interleavings makes manual reasoning difficult for small programs, and intractable already for medium-sized applications.

To help programmers with designing and implementing correct and efficient parallel programs, researchers therefore have come up with safer approaches. In general terms, those approaches reduce the unbound flexibility provided by standard threads and introduce restrictions in the form of specialized syntactic language features, libraries, and programming models. By taking away flexibility and adding restrictions on how and when tasks can execute and what memory each task can access, reasoning about the program behavior and writing correct code becomes easier.

**Structured parallelism** Programming models that support structured parallelism provide high-level concurrency constructs that are sufficiently expressive for a wide range of parallel computation patterns. Lexically scoped fork/join constructs, for example, make it easier to identify the context an operation is executed in and helps with finding other program points that may execute in parallel with it. The syntactic restrictions imposed on the programming model simplify manual and automatic reasoning about the program, resulting in more robust and often more efficient programs [97].

Examples for systems with structured parallelism are Cilk [16, 98], X10 [27], Habanero Java [52], or OpenMP [93]. Because those systems replace ad-hoc threads with fork/join style parallelism, a compiler can extract meaningful task scheduling information much more easily from a program written in one of those languages than from a functionally equivalent Java program. For example, the fork/join pattern guarantees that the forked sub-tasks have all been executed and finished before the joining task starts.

**Task parallelism** Structured fork/join style parallelism is a relatively restrictive model and comes at the cost of flexibility, making it difficult to model some common patterns such as futures or producer-consumer. In recent years, various parallel programming libraries have been developed that allow a programmer to specify task orderings in the program with varying degrees of explicitness.

Examples for libraries with explicit task ordering are Intel's Threading Building Blocks [99], Apple's Grand Central Dispatch [12], Microsoft's Task Parallel Library [68], or Intervals [81]. By allowing the programmer to explicitly define happens-before relations between task objects in the program source, those systems avoid the limitations of lexically scoped parallelism while addressing many of the problems resulting from unrestricted threads.

This dissertation describes *schedule analysis* as a fully automated approach for extracting task-ordering information from programs and explores how compilers can effectively exploit the computed scheduling information in optimizations.

## 1.1 Thesis statement

The primary goal of this thesis is to explore how optimizing compilers for parallel programs with shared memory can benefit from the knowledge about the scheduling of tasks at runtime. By analyzing what tasks may execute concurrently and whether they access the same memory, a compiler can better optimize programs and apply program transformations that could not be safely applied otherwise. This motivates the following thesis statement:

> *"In order to be effective, compiler optimizations for shared-memory parallel programs must exploit task-ordering information: information about whether two tasks are potentially executed in parallel or whether they are always ordered. Schedule analysis is one approach that can extract task-ordering information from real-world programs; the extracted ordering information is sufficient to improve existing compiler optimizations as well as enable new ones."*

To establish this thesis I proceed in three steps. The first step is to define a programming model that is expressive and flexible enough to represent task-ordering in many current programming languages and libraries while containing enough information to be useful for static analysis. The second step is to develop an algorithm for extracting scheduling information from programs that use this programming model. In a third step, I compare different optimizations that are written with and without scheduling information. The evaluation suggests that knowledge about task scheduling is important for effective optimization and the proposed schedule analysis is one way how such information can be gathered.

## 1.2 Summary of the thesis and key contributions

This dissertation investigates how compiler optimizations can benefit from knowledge about the (partial) ordering of tasks. The goal is to design a system for analyzing and optimizing parallel programs. The presented approach preserves both flexible, unstructured control flow and static analysis of the program schedule. To summarize, this thesis makes the following key contributions:

**A programming model with explicit ordering constraints:** We define a representation and execution model for parallel programs that is based on tasks. As program-level objects, task objects can be kept in local variables, passed around as parameters, and stored in fields. Programmers can explicitly add happens-before ordering constraints between two task objects. At runtime, a scheduler constantly chooses tasks that are eligible for execution and starts them. Tasks and happens-before relations provide a minimalist model that is expressive enough to model the behavior of current state-of-the-art parallel libraries and language constructs while providing enough information to statically extract meaningful task-order information from real-world programs.

**Schedule analysis:** We describe an analysis that extracts an abstract schedule from a program that was written in or transformed into our task representation. The analysis abstracts a potentially infinite number of runtime task objects into a finite set of analysis-time objects. By analyzing the effects of the explicit happens-before constraints present in the source program, the analysis computes a relation for each pair of abstract task objects.

**Evaluation:** We present two detailed case studies. In the first case study we have developed an optimizing compiler for a version of Java that uses sequential consistency as its memory model. The second case study is an optimizing compiler for a system that uses dynamic fractional permissions to detect data-races at runtime. Each case study is evaluated with multiple benchmark programs and show that optimizations based on scheduling information significantly improve execution performance. Besides the detailed case studies we describe additional uses of task-schedule information in compilers that have been implemented as prototypes but not evaluated in detail.

## 1.3 Organization of this dissertation

This dissertation is organized as follows:

Chapter 2 provides some background on Leslie Lamport's approach to proving correctness of parallel programs and explains the two fundamental operation relations, *happens-before* and *can-affect*. Being familiar with how program correctness can be proven in Lamport's framework is important for developing compiler optimizations because in essence a compiler optimization is a proof that a given program transformation does not violate the observable program semantics. This chapter also expands Lamport's model to include the notion of happens-before relations not only between individual operations but between whole tasks.

Chapter 3 introduces a programming model for fine-grained parallelism based on lightweight tasks with explicit happens-before relations. This model is general enough to express a wide variety of existing concurrency patterns: structured fork/join style parallelism, semi-structured tasks with ordering information, and unstructured threads. For representing concurrent programs, we introduce two new primitives to a Java-like language. One primitive schedules a new task and the other explicitly adds a happens-before relation between two task objects. Furthermore, this chapter discusses some general properties of task schedules that aid the understanding of the program behavior.

Chapter 4 presents a compiler framework for parallel programs that exploits task-order information in its optimizations. When executing a program with explicit scheduling, the runtime keeps track of the task objects and their happens-before relations. At compile-time, the runtime schedule is approximated by an abstract schedule. We describe an algorithm that autonomously extracts the abstract schedule from the input program and present a *schedule analysis* that can compute from the abstract schedule what tasks may be executed in parallel and what tasks are ordered.

The case study in Chapter 5 presents and evaluates an optimizing compiler for a Java version with a sequentially consistent memory model. Because the compiler is a bytecode-to-bytecode translator, the programs can run on an unmodified standard Java Virtual Machine. The compiler uses the task-ordering information gathered by the schedule analysis to compute the minimal set of field and array accesses that must be protected with memory fences in order to guarantee sequential consistency semantics. The evaluation shows that scheduling information significantly improves the effectiveness of the optimizations. For our set of multi-threaded benchmarks the overhead of sequentially consistent Java compared to standard Java is reduced from 136% on average for the unoptimized version to 11% on average for the optimized version. The results indicate that with appropriate optimizations, sequential consistency can be a feasible alternative to the Java Memory Model.

The second case study, presented in Chapter 6, is an optimizing compiler for a language with dynamic fractional permissions, a dynamic variant of fractional permissions. In this programming model, objects are associated with access control lists (ACLs) that define what access rights a given task has on the object. ACLs guarantee data-race freedom by asserting that if a task has write access to an object, no other task can read the object. In the general case, the

## 1.3. ORGANIZATION OF THIS DISSERTATION 5

compiler must guard all object accesses with checks of the objects' ACLs. However, by exploiting task-order information, the compiler can remove ACL checks for those operations that are not conflicting with any parallel task.

Chapter 7 describes further uses of how task-order information can be used in optimizing compilers. By comparing results from the schedule analysis with programmer provided annotations, for example, the compiler can warn the programmer when objects he intended to be task-local may be accidentally shared. We also present additional optimizations that we have implemented but not systematically evaluated. Optimizations presented in this chapters include synchronization removal, reducing strong atomicity overhead in software transactional memory, synchronization variant selection, and happens-before order relaxation.

Chapter 8 discusses open issues and future work before Chapter 9 summarizes and concludes the dissertation.

# 2

# Background

The theory behind this work is based on the happens-before relation formulated by Leslie Lamport [59]. The happens-before relation (denoted: →) is a strict partial ordering of operations in a concurrent system such that two operations A and B are ordered, written A→B, if there is a causal relationship between them. Lamport's model does not require the operations to be indivisible atomic events but allows for complex operations. Therefore, the same formalisms and axioms can be applied on different abstraction levels of the system.

This chapter introduces the idea to raise the abstraction level of operations from relatively low-level events to the level of whole tasks. Merging all operations that are executed by the same task into a single operation and adapting the happens-before relations and can-affect relations accordingly results in a *task schedule*: a set of tasks that are partially ordered by happens-before relations.

After providing some background on Lamport's happens-before relations, this chapter then introduces task schedules and discusses sources for task-ordering in programs using different parallel models, languages, and libraries.

## 2.1 Lamport's happens-before relations

In "A New Approach to Proving the Correctness of Multiprocess Programs" [60], Leslie Lamport presented a formalism for proving the correctness of parallel algorithms which he developed further in subsequent years [62]. Lamport's model proved to be useful in many different areas because it avoids making any assumptions about the atomicity of operations and only few assumptions about the interaction of concurrent memory reads and writes. [9] Because Lamport's method does not require operations to be atomic, it allows for analyzing systems at different levels of detail: multiple low-level operations can simply be aggregated into higher-level operations and analyzed with the same basic formalism.

### 2.1.1 Formalism

Lamport defines programs as collection of *operations*. Each operation is ultimately composed of a set of indivisible *events* such as memory reads/writes, jumps, or arithmetic calculations. A program execution is a partial order over operations defined by two distinct types of relations: *happens-before* relations (→) and *can-affect* relations (⇾, also called "can causally affect").

For two operations A and B that are ordered by a happens-before relation A→B, all events in B happen only after all events in A have been completed. If we think of the execution of an operation as the time interval it takes to execute all its contained events, the happens-before relation A→B can be graphically depicted as follows (where time is running from left to right):

$$\underset{\phantom{A}}{\overset{A}{\vdash\!\!-\!\!\dashv}} \rightarrow \underset{\phantom{B}}{\overset{B}{\vdash\!\!-\!\!\dashv}}$$

Two operations A and B that are not ordered by a →-relation can affect each other, written as A-↠B, if at least one event a ∈ A precedes at least one event b ∈ B; that is, operation A has begun before operation B is completed. Graphically, the can-affect relation is presented as:

$$\begin{array}{c} \overset{A}{\vdash\!\!-\!\!\dashv} \\ \downarrow \\ \underset{B}{\vdash\!\!-\!\!\dashv} \end{array}$$

Note, that A-↠B only relates the start-point of A's interval to the end-point of B's interval. Specifically, it does not order the two start-points with each and it does not order the two end-points. Therefore, it is undefined whether A or B starts first and it is undefined whether A or B finishes first. However, it is known that interval A has started before B ends. As an example for such a program behavior, consider the case where operation A contains an event that sets a shared flag and operation B is a loop that waits for that flag to be set. While it is unimportant whether during the program execution interval A or B started first, it is clear that B will only end after A has set the flag.

From the definitions for operations, happens-before relations, and can-affect relations, Lamport derives the following five basic axioms:

**A1.** → is transitive (A→B→C implies A→C) and irreflexive (A↛A).

The →-relation is a partial order on the operations: if operation A happens before operation B then A also happens before all operations that are preceded by B. Because an operation execution can never precede itself, the →-relation is irreflexive.

The -↠-relation is not an order relation, however, because two interfering operations can affect each others execution. If two operations A and B overlap, it is possible that A-↠B and B-↠A at the same time. Further, the -↠-relation is not transitive. The following drawing (adopted from [9]) illustrates a case where A-↠B-↠C but A-↛C:

**A2.** A→B implies A-↠B and B-↛A.

Intuitively, → is stronger than -↠. If A has finished before B starts then all events a∈A precede all events b∈B, which matches the definition of the -↠-relation. In the other direction, because operation B cannot affect an operation A that has already executed earlier, B-↛A.

**A3.** A→B-↠C or A-↠B→C implies A-↠C.

The first part of this axiom, also depicted in the following drawing, states that if at least one event b ∈ B precedes at least one event c ∈ C then the events of operation A happening before B also precede at least this one event c ∈ C. The second clause can be justified accordingly.

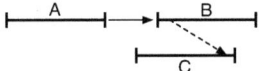

**A4.** A→B-→C→D implies A→D.

This axiom allows us to assume a stronger →-relation between A and D for a chain A→B -→C→D containing a weak -→-relation. As shown in the following drawing, if at least one event b ∈ B happens before at least one event c ∈ C then knowing that all events in A happen before b and all events in D happen after c lets us deduce that A→D.

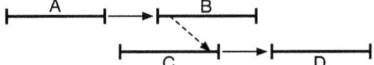

**A5.** For any A there are only a finite number of B such that A↛B.

This axiom essentially asserts a system execution must begin at some point in time and that all operations executions eventually terminate. Non-terminating operations can be modeled with a different set of axioms [62].

Axioms A1 to A4 are used for proving safety properties whereas Axiom A5 is useful for proving liveness properties. To complete the axiom system of the five original axioms described by Lamport, Anger [9] introduced the following additional axiom:

**A6.** A-→B→C-→D implies A-→D.

This axiom can be intuitively understood by following the arrows from A to D in the following diagram. If some event a ∈ A precedes some event b ∈ B, and B happens before event c ∈ C which precedes event d ∈ D then at least the one event a ∈ A precedes at least the one event d ∈ D and therefore A-→D.

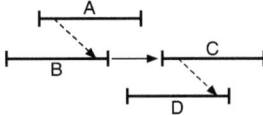

## 2.1.2 Example: Proving correctness of the butterfly barrier for two tasks

The happens-before relations and can-affect relations presented in the previous Section 2.1.1 define a framework for proving correctness of parallel programs [60]. As an example, this section presents a correctness proof of the implementation of the Brooks *butterfly barrier* [22] for two tasks.[1]

---
[1] A barrier for more than two tasks can be realized by chaining multiple of those two-task barriers.

|   | **Task 0** | **Task 1** |   |
|---|---|---|---|
| 1 | \\before barrier | \\before barrier | //phase #n |
| 2 |   |   |   |
| 3 | inBarrier0 = **true**; | inBarrier1 = **true**; | //announce arrival of this task |
| 4 | **while**(! inBarrier1); | **while**(! inBarrier0); | //wait for other task to arrive |
| 5 | inBarrier1 = **false**; | inBarrier0 = **false**; | //release other task |
| 6 | **while**(inBarrier0); | **while**(inBarrier1); | //wait for other task to release this |
| 7 |   |   |   |
| 8 | \\after barrier | \\after barrier | //phase #n+1 |

Figure 2.1: Butterfly Barrier for Two Tasks.

The butterfly barrier is an algorithm for barrier synchronization that requires no primitive operations other than reads and writes to shared memory. Informally, when a task approaches a barrier, it must wait until all participating tasks arrived at the same barrier; only then are the tasks allowed to proceed. A barrier thus separates the multiprocess computation into separate *phases* per task that are synchronized with each other.

Figure 2.1 shows a version of the basic butterfly barrier for two tasks that has been adapted slightly from the original code in [22] to make it easier to understand. This implementation uses two shared memory locations inBarrier0 and inBarrier1 through which the two processes communicate. The algorithm is symmetric under interchange of the two tasks. Therefore, we explain the code from the perspective of task 0.

Assume that task 0 has finished phase $n$ on line 1 and enters the barrier. Task 0 announces its arrival at the barrier by setting its own flag inBarrier0 to **true** on line 3. In the busy loop on line 4, task 0 then waits for its partner to enter the barrier by observing task 1's inBarrier1 flag. Once the other task has entered the barrier by arriving on line 3, task 0 proceeds by resetting its partner's inBarrier1 flag to **false** on line 5. By resetting the flag, task 0 acknowledges that it has noticed task 1's arrival at the barrier. On line 6, task 0 then waits for task 1 to acknowledge that is has noticed task 0's arrival, too. After task 1 has reset the inBarrier0 flag on line 5, task 0 can exit the barrier and continue with phase $n+1$ starting on line 8.

The purpose of the presented barrier synchronization is to separate the different computation phases across the two tasks. More formally, the barrier implementation is considered *correct* if for any two tasks 0 and 1 the $n^{th}$ phase $phase(n)$ is finished before the next phase $phase(n+1)$ starts: $\forall t, s \in \{0,1\} : phase_t(n) \to phase_s(n+1)$.

To prove the correctness of the barrier implementation, we name the following operation executions that occur during the $n^{th}$ call to the barrier by task $t$:

$P_t^n$ The execution of the last statement $p$ (line 1) in the body of p̲hase $n$ by process $t$ before entering the barrier.

$A_t^n$ In the $n^{th}$ call to the barrier, task $t$ a̲nnounces its arrival by setting its corresponding inBarrier-flag to **true**. This corresponds to line 3 in the example.

$WA_t^n$ In the $n^{th}$ call to the barrier, task $t$ w̲aits for the a̲rrival of the other task on line 4.

$R_t^n$ In the $n^{th}$ call to the barrier, task $t$ r̲eleases the other task's flag on line 5.

## 2.1. LAMPORT'S HAPPENS-BEFORE RELATIONS

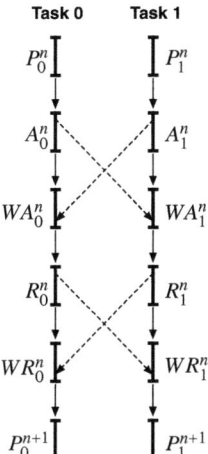

Figure 2.2: Initial relations for the correctness proof of the Butterfly barrier.

$WR_t^n$ In the $n^{th}$ call to the barrier, task $t$ waits for the partner task to release $t$'s inBarrier flag. The last read of the loop obtains the value **false**. This operation is implemented on line 6.

On most systems, a statement such as while(inBarrier0) will be translated into multiple smaller operations that load the current value of inBarrier0, compare the value with **true**, and perform a jump depending on the outcome. In a system with preemptive multitasking, the current task can be interrupted at any time. Therefore, it can happen that task 1 changes the value of inBarrier0 on line 5 after task 0 read the value of inBarrier0 but before it performed the comparison. If such interleaving can happen on a sub-statement level the operations are said to be *non-atomic*. Because Lamport's model allows for non-atomic operations, we can model even complex statements such as the busy loops on lines 4 and 6 as single operations $WA_t^n$ and $WR_t^n$.

The correctness proof of the Butterfly barrier uses axioms A1–A4 and the initial relations shown in Figure 2.2. The $\rightarrow$-relations in Figure 2.2 specify the original program order for each task. Operations $WA_t^n$ and $WR_t^n$ of task $t$ are affected by the execution of $A_s^n$ and $R_s^n$ respectively executed by the partner task $s$. Because we know that the last operation of each loop—exiting the loop through a jump—comes after the corresponding write to the flag by the other thread, we can state that the write event precedes at least the jump event of the corresponding loop. This correlation allows us to add the four inter-task $\rightarrow$-relations to the set of initial relations.

*Proof.* Proving the basic correctness property $\forall t, s \in \{0, 1\} : P_t^n \rightarrow P_s^{n+1}$ is done for each combination of tasks separately:

**Case A:** $P_0^n \rightarrow P_0^{n+1}$. Directly from transitive program-order (Axiom A1).

**Case B:** $P_1^n \rightarrow P_1^{n+1}$. Symmetric to the previous case.

**Case C:** $P_0^n \to P_1^{n+1}$. By applying Axiom A4, we get $P_0^n \to R_1^n$; therefore, transitively $P_0^n \to P_1^{n+1}$ (Axiom A1).

**Case D:** $P_1^n \to P_0^{n+1}$. Symmetric to the previous case.

□

This proof verifies the basic correctness property for a single invocation of the barrier. For separating two phases in two tasks, the simple signaling mechanism via shared flags on lines 3, 4, and 5 is sufficient. Therefore the proof did not need to take the $WR_t^n$ operation into account. However, a full correctness proof must additionally show that a program using the barrier progresses, does not deadlock, and that the phases are actually executed in lock-step (that is, if task 0 is in phase $n$, task 1 cannot be in any phase $\neq n$).

We can proof the lock-step property by showing that a task always waits for the other task to exit the loop on line 4 before it continues.

*Proof.* Before starting the next phase $n+1$, a task $t$ always waits for the other task $s$ to exit the loop on line 4. In other words, $WA_t^n \to P_s^{n+1}$. This follows directly from axiom A4. □

### 2.1.3 Can-affect relations and Java

The proof for the butterfly barrier shows that the barrier correctly separates the individual phases across all tasks. However, it does not proof that the barrier does not deadlock. As an example, assume that the busy loop on line 6 were not present in task 0. In this case, the write to inBarrier1 by task 0 on line 5 would race with the write to inBarrier1 in the next phase of task 1 on line 3. Therefore, it can happen that task 0 overwrites inBarrier1 to **false** after task 1 has set it to **true**. In this case, task 0 will deadlock in the next call to the barrier on line 3 because the announcement of task 1's arrival got lost.

To show that the Butterfly barrier does not deadlock we would have to prove that there are no races on the updates of the flags inBarrier0 and inBarrier1 by proving that the write accesses are ordered:

1. In the same phase: $\forall t, s \in \{0, 1\} : A_t^n \to R_s^n$; and

2. Across phases: $\forall t, s \in \{0, 1\} : R_t^n \to A_s^{n+1}$.

The axioms and the initial relations we have for the butterfly barrier, however, are not sufficient to prove deadlock freedom. Take, for example, the path $A_0^n \dashrightarrow WA_1^n \to R_1^n$. Axiom A3 only allows us to deduce $A_0^n \dashrightarrow R_1^n$ but not $A_0^n \to R_1^n$. This is, because operations are not necessarily atomic and, depending on the concrete runtime environment, the update to inBarrier0 in operation $A_0^n$ may—in theory—involve multiple single steps. Assume a hypothetical (albeit very odd) system where writes to memory are visible immediately but must be additionally committed in a second step. In this system, it can happen that task 0 announces its arrival by setting inBarrier to **true**, but the write is not yet committed. Task 1 then sees the arrival of task 0, exits the loop in $WA_1^n$ and sets and commits inBarrier0 to **false** in $R_1^n$. Finally task 0 would resume and commit the write of inBarrier0. The previous write by task 1 is lost, resulting in a deadlock.

## 2.1. LAMPORT'S HAPPENS-BEFORE RELATIONS

| The *happens-before* relation | Lamport's *can-affect* relation | Java's *volatile* guarantee |

Figure 2.3: Types of relations between two operations.

A memory model where values are visible before they are committed is obviously rather exotic—but possible. A more realistic cause for a deadlock is when updates of a flag are not propagated to the other task at all. For example, without further knowledge about multiple tasks it is legal for a compiler to keep the inBarrier0 flag in a register within the scope of the method. In this case, updates to the flag would not make it to main memory at all, resulting in a deadlock in the other task. A deadlock can also occur if the update to the flag only goes into the cache of one task but is not propagated into the cache of the other task.

In Java, this deadlock problem can be solved by declaring the two fields inBlock0 and inBlock1 as **volatile**. The Java memory model [45, 75] guarantees that update operations of **volatile** fields are atomic as far as the Lamport model is concerned. This allows us to give a stronger meaning to the $\twoheadrightarrow$-relation: For a volatile read or write operation A, A$\twoheadrightarrow$B iff *all* events in A precedes *at least one* event in B.

Figure 2.3 compares the different relation types graphically. The can-affect relation in Lamport's original work states that the execution interval of one operation has started before the other operation ends. This is depicted by the arrow from the start of the one interval to the end of the other. In contrast, Java guarantees that if a task observes a specific value by reading a **volatile** field, the write operation that wrote this value has been completed.

The guarantee that a **volatile** write operation has finished if the value was observed by another task allows us to formulate the following two axioms:

**A7.** A$\twoheadrightarrow$B$\rightarrow$C implies A$\rightarrow$C.

If operation A is a write to a **volatile** field and the write was observed by B then operation C that starts after B also starts after A.

**A8.** For all other cases, $\twoheadrightarrow$ is treated like $\rightarrow$.

If the flags inBarrier0 and inBarrier1 are declared **volatile** we can now prove that the Butterfly barrier is deadlock free by proving that there are no concurrent write races on either flag:

*Proof.* The write operations to the inBarrier0 flag are ordered both within phase $n$ and between subsequent phases $n$ and $n+1$. Only operations $A_0^n$ and $R_1^n$ write inBarrier0 and it is sufficient to show the following two cases:

**Case A:** $A_0^n \rightarrow R_1^n$. Because inBarrier0 is volatile we know that $A_0^n \twoheadrightarrow WA_1^n \rightarrow R_1^n$ and therefore $A_0^n \rightarrow R_1^n$ (Axiom A7).

**Case B:** $R_1^n \rightarrow A_0^{n+1}$. Because inBarrier0 is volatile we know that $R_1^n \twoheadrightarrow WR_0^n \rightarrow P_0^{n+1} \rightarrow A_0^{n+1}$ and therefore transitively $A_0^n \rightarrow R_1^n$ (Axioms A1 and A7).

Proving the ordering of write operations to flag `inBarrier1` is analogous to the previous proof.

## 2.2 Task schedules

Because Lamport's model makes no assumptions about the atomicity of operations we can use the same principal model for analyzing a system on any level of detail: By combining multiple operations into a single operation (and updating the relations accordingly) we can abstract away detail and raise a lower-level abstraction to a higher level.

This abstraction process can be formalized as creating *higher-level views* of lower-level *system executions*. Following [61] in general and [9] in particular we establish the following two definitions.

**Definition 1.** A triple $(\mathcal{O}, \rightarrow, \dashrightarrow)$, where $\mathcal{O}$ is a (finite) set of operations satisfying Axioms A1-A5, is called a *system execution*.

The set of operations $\mathcal{O}$ is taken to be the actions performed by the program during a *particular* execution. A higher-level view of a system execution can be created by combining elements of $\mathcal{O}$ into subsets of $\mathcal{O}$ and establishing appropriate $\rightarrow$-relations and $\dashrightarrow$-relations between the new subsets.

**Definition 2.** A *higher-level view* of a system execution is a collection $\mathcal{H}$ of subsets $\mathcal{S}$ of $\mathcal{O}$ satisfying the following conditions:

**H1.** Each set $\mathcal{S} \in \mathcal{H}$ is nonempty.

**H2.** No element of $\mathcal{O}$ is in more than a finite number of the sets in $\mathcal{H}$.

**H3.** Every element of $\mathcal{O}$ is in some set $\mathcal{S} \in \mathcal{H}$.

The elements of $\mathcal{H}$ are called *higher-level operation executions*. If $\mathcal{H}$ is a higher-level view, relations $\rightarrow^*$ and $\dashrightarrow^*$ are induced on $\mathcal{H}$ by

**H4.** $\mathcal{S}_1 \rightarrow^* \mathcal{S}_2$ iff $A \rightarrow B$ for all $A \in \mathcal{S}_1, B \in \mathcal{S}_2$; and

**H5.** $\mathcal{S}_1 \dashrightarrow^* \mathcal{S}_2$ iff $A \dashrightarrow B$ or $A = B$ for some $A \in \mathcal{S}_1, B \in \mathcal{S}_2$.

It can be shown that a higher-level view $\mathcal{H}$ of a system execution together with the induced relations $\rightarrow^*$ and $\dashrightarrow^*$ is again a system execution $(\mathcal{H}, \rightarrow^*, \dashrightarrow^*)$. [9]

Figure 2.4 depicts a higher-level view of the butterfly barrier system execution from Figure 2.2 where the internal operations $A_t^n$, $WA_t^n$, $R_t^n$, and $WR_t^n$ have been combined into a single $Arrive_t^n$ operation for each task. The rules for constructing this higher-level view allow us to retain the happens-before relation between the operations of the previous phase $P_t^n$ and the subsequent phase $P_t^{n+1}$.

2.2. TASK SCHEDULES                                                                                          15

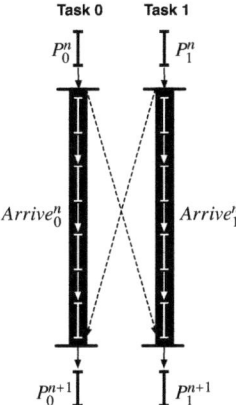

Figure 2.4: Higher-level view of the butterfly barrier from Figure 2.2. Internal details of the barrier have been abstracted into distinct *Arrive* operations. The original low-level operations and happens-before relations are shown in white.

Hiding the inner workings of the barrier can make the system easier to understand. However, by reducing the level of detail it can become be impossible to prove certain properties in a higher-level system execution. For example, while the basic correctness property $\forall t, s \in \{0, 1\} : P_t^n \rightarrow P_s^{n+1}$ of the butterfly barrier can still be proven in the higher-level view (directly by applying axiom A4), the information that the phases execute in lock-step (that is, that a task $t$ waits for the other task $s$ to exit the barrier) is lost.

In this dissertation, we are interested in exploiting task-ordering information. For this purpose, we define tasks as:

**Definition 3.** A task is a *named* single execution path through a set of program instructions that has its own execution context. [2]

A task is a named entity in the sense that it has an identity that can be referenced and compared with other tasks. In many systems, such as Java, tasks are first-class objects that can be manipulated, passed, and stored just like other objects in the language. In those cases, the task name is equal to the object identity. In other systems, for example a language with a syntactic fork/join construct, tasks may not be represented as language-level objects that are accessible by the programmer. In those cases, the task name can be thought of as the task identity maintained by the runtime.

The function *inTask* associates every operation $o \in \mathcal{O}$ of a system execution $\mathcal{O}$ with the corresponding task name $t$ of all task names $\mathcal{T}$ that executes the operation:

**Definition 4.** The function $inTask : \mathcal{O} \mapsto \mathcal{T}$ is a total, surjective function that associates each operation $o \in \mathcal{O}$ with exactly one task name $t \in \mathcal{T}$, namely the task that executes $o$.

---

[2] We use the notion of tasks to represent different but similar concepts from different parallel programming libraries and languages. Most importantly, in the case of (Java) threads, tasks and threads are the same thing.

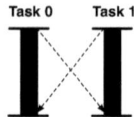

Figure 2.5: Task schedule of the butterfly barrier from Figure 2.2.

A *task schedule* is then a higher-level view $\mathcal{H}$ of a system execution $\mathcal{O}$ where all operations that are executed by the same task $t$ are grouped into a single set $S_t$.

**Definition 5.** A *task schedule* is a higher-level view $(\mathcal{H}, \rightarrow^*, \dashrightarrow^*)$ of a system execution where for every task $t \in \mathcal{T}$ there is exactly one higher-level operation $S_t \in \mathcal{H}$ containing all the operations $o$ that are executed in $t$: $S_t := \{o \in \mathcal{O} \mid inTask(o) = t\}$.

The task schedule for the butterfly barrier example is shown in Figure 2.5. All the internal operations of the tasks are abstracted away, retaining only the two high-level operations representing the tasks themselves together with two $\dashrightarrow$-relations representing the interactions through the barrier and other shared memory.

This example shows that the information contained in the task schedule is sensitive to the way how tasks are used in the program. In this example, the task schedule does not contain much useful information (other than task 0 will not end before task 1 has started and vice versa) because the butterfly barrier achieves synchronization through low-level operations. Low-level operations are difficult to analyze for a compiler, however, because of the imprecision inherent in a static analysis. It may be impossible for the compiler, for example, to know that the variables inBarrier0 and inBarrier1 actually point to the same memory addresses in both tasks.

Chapter 3 presents a variant of a barrier that does not use low-level operations for synchronization but high-level tasks with explicit happens-before ordering constraints. Because compilers are generally better at lowering the abstraction level than at extracting high-level models from low-level code, starting from a program with more tasks and explicit happens-before constraints makes it easier for the compiler to extract meaningful information about the program behavior.

## 2.3 Sources of task-order information

Over the last decade, much research and engineering effort has been put into designing languages and libraries that simplify concurrent programming. In general, the trend of modern parallelism solutions is shifting away from the unrestricted flexibility provided by processes and threads to more restricted programming models with stronger support for modeling task ordering.

Current parallel programming libraries and languages allow the programmer to specify task orderings with varying degrees of explicitness. For example, systems such as X10 [27] or OpenMP [93] syntactically enforce a fork/join style of programming where the forked subtasks are ordered with respect to the joining task. Other systems, such as Apple's Grand Central Dispatch [12], Intel's Threading Building Blocks [99], Microsoft's Task Parallel Library [68],

## 2.3. SOURCES OF TASK-ORDER INFORMATION 17

or Intervals [81] allow the programmer to explicitly define happens-before relations between task objects thus avoiding the limitations of lexically scoped parallelism.

Extracting task-order information from the program source can be more or less difficult for a compiler, depending on the parallel language or library that is being used. Figure 2.3 shows three examples written in three different languages using three different parallelism mechanisms to implement a simple fork/join pattern. Each program begins with a sequential phase /*A*/ before forking three parallel tasks /*B*/. The parallel tasks are then joined and the programs end with another sequential phase /*C*/.

**Java threads:** The first program in Panel 2.6(a) uses Java's built-in threads. After the sequential phase /*A*/, the method doForkJoin() creates three Thread objects in a loop and stores them in an array for later reference. The run() method of the threads are overridden to contain the code for the parallel phase /*B*/. After having created each thread object, the threads are actually spawned by calling start(). The main thread then waits for all threads to finish by calling join() on each thread stored in the thread array before it continues with the—again sequential—phase /*C*/.

Even though this Java program is relatively trivial, it demonstrates some of the difficulties a compiler may have when trying to extract task-order information. In order to reason about the ordered-ness of the parallel phases /*B*/ and the sequential phase /*C*/, the compiler must deduce that the call to join() is called on all the forked threads. This requires information about whether or not the array ts may be aliased or modified by another thread and whether or not the two **for** loops execute the same number of times. Such a detailed analysis quickly becomes too imprecise or even computationally infeasible when the corresponding fork/join logic is not syntactically located in the same method (as it is in this example) but spread across methods.

The unrestricted nature of threads compared with the low-level synchronization primitives makes it difficult for compilers to extract meaningful task-order information from Java programs using threads. Approaches such as [90, 28, 14] were successful mostly in those cases where the code that creates and joins threads is syntactically located in the same method.

**OpenMP fork/join:** The second Panel (b) of Figure 2.3 shows a C program using OpenMP [93]. OpenMP is a language extension that has the fork/join pattern built in. OpenMP therefore makes this example trivial to implement.

The function doForkJoin() starts with the sequential phase /*A*/. Through the **#pragma** annotation on the subsequent **for**-loop, the programmer indicates to the OpenMP compiler and runtime that the **for**-loop can be parallelized instead of executing the three loop iterations sequentially one after the other. The main thread of the program will implicitly wait after the **for**-loop until all the parallel /*B*/ tasks have finished. Then the main thread continues with the sequential phase /*C*/.

When a parallelism pattern is enforced syntactically, such as the fork/join in this example, it is often straight forward for the compiler to extract information about the task ordering. Various algorithms for computing execution-order information, such as [4], have been developed for systems where method-local syntactic reasoning is sufficient. Because in fork/join-style systems the parallelism constructs are syntactically restricted to a single method, they are often seen as less flexible than unrestricted models such as Java threads.

```
void doForkJoin() {


    /*A*/



















//fork
Thread[] ts = new Thread[3];
for(int i=0; i<3; i++) {
    ts[i] = new Thread() {
        public void run() {

            /*B*/

        }};
    ts[i].start();
}

//join
for(int i=0; i<3; i++)
    ts[i].join();

/*C*/



}
```
(a) Java threads

```
void doForkJoin() {


    /*A*/
















    









#pragma omp parallel for
for(int i=0; i<3; i++) {

    /*B*/

}





/*C*/



}
```
(b) OpenMP fork/join, C

```
struct ForkJoinTask: public task {
    task* execute() {

        /*A*/

        //create join task
        JoinTask& join =
            *new(allocate_continuation())
                JoinTask();
        //set ref_count to 3 children
        join.set_ref_count(3);

        //fork
        for(int i=0; i<3; i++) {
            ForkTask& t =
                *new(join.allocate_child())
                    ForkTask();
            spawn(t);
        }

        return NULL;
    }
};

struct ForkTask: public task {
    task* execute() {

        /*B*/

        return NULL;
    }
};

struct JoinTask: public task {
    task* execute() {

        /*C*/

        return NULL;
    }
};
```
(c) Intel Threading Building Blocks, C++

Figure 2.6: Comparison of fork/join constructs using different languages and parallelism mechanisms. After the sequential phase /*A*/, three parallel tasks /*B*/ are spawned and joined before the sequential phase /*C*/.

**Intel Threading Building Blocks:** The third Panel 2.6(c) shows the fork/join pattern implemented with Intel's Threading Building Blocks (TBB). We chose TBB as an example for a modern threading library that positions itself somewhere between unrestricted threads and syntactically restricted fork/join frameworks.

Libraries such as TBB allow the programmer to create and spawn tasks and explicitly specify task-ordering information, such as "task /*A*/ must finish before task /*B*/". The task ordering constraints are created in the program by either explicitly calling the libraries' API functions or implicitly by the way the libraries' data-structures and API is designed.

In addition to tasks and task-order management functionalities, many threading libraries provide syntactic shortcuts and helper functions that simplify common parallelism patterns. For example, TBB provides a built-in fork/join construct that would result in code very similar to the `OpenMP` version of the fork/join example from Figure 2.3. However, for illustrative purposes we present how tasks and their ordering relations can be directly managed in TBB.

The TBB example from Panel 2.6(c) defines three classes as subtypes of type `task`: `ForkJoinTask`, `ForkTask`, and `JoinTask`. `ForkJoinTask` plays the role of the main task and contains the `execute()` method that corresponds to the `doForkJoin()` of the other two versions. This method starts with the sequential /*A*/ phase. After that, the main task creates a *continuation* task of type `JoinTask` which will join the forked sub-tasks and execute the final sequential phase /*C*/. The `ForkJoinTask` then creates the three instances of `ForkTask` inside the **for**-loop and specifies them to be children of the `join` continuation task.

In TBB, when a parent task creates a continuation task, the parent task exits and does not block on its children. Instead, the continuation task takes the parent task's place in the scheduler. The children then subsequently run, and after they (or their continuations) finish, the continuation task starts running. This effectively creates a happens-before ordering between the children and the `join` task.

While many approaches have been developed to extract task-order information from Java programs using threads and from syntactically restricted fork/join frameworks, only little work has been done for exploiting the ordering information available in higher-level threading libraries such as TBB.

## 2.4 Summary

Lamport's model defines a partial ordering of program operations through happens-before and can-affect relations. This model has been designed specifically to reason about the correctness of multithreaded programs but it has also influenced areas other than formal proofs. One famous example is the Java Memory Model (JMM) that adapted Lamport's happens-before relations to form the semantic basis of the Java language, compiler, and runtime system.

The flexibility and wide applicability of Lamport's model comes mainly from the fact that operations are not required to be atomic but are modeled as sets of single events. Because operations are not single indivisible events, multiple lower-level operations can be combined into higher-level operations, abstracting away low-level detail. Therefore, the same model—operations plus happens-before and can-affect relations—can be used to analyze a system on different levels of abstraction.

We present *task schedules* as the highest level of abstraction for parallel programs. For a given program execution consisting of low-level operations and their relations, we generate a task schedule by merging all operations that execute in the same task and update the relations with other operations accordingly. This process stops when the schedule contains exactly one operation per task.

Typically, a compiler does not have the detailed information contained in runtime task schedules. Rather, the compiler must statically compute an abstract, conservative approximation of all possible runtime schedules by inspecting the program code. While the lack of explicit ordering information in unstructured thread-based languages makes it difficult to statically compute meaningful schedules, many modern parallel languages and libraries offer more opportunities to extract ordering information.

# 3
# A generic task model with ordering information

This chapter describes a model for fine-grained parallelism based on lightweight tasks with explicit happens-before relations. This model is general enough to express a wide variety of existing concurrency patterns: structured fork/join style parallelism, semi-structured tasks with ordering information, and unstructured threads.

## 3.1 Tasks with explicit scheduling constraints

The basic building block of the execution model is a *task*. A task is similar to a method in that it contains code that is executed in the context of a **this**-object (or the class, in the case of **static** methods/tasks). Unlike a method, however, one does not *call* a task, which would result in the immediate execution of the body, but instead *schedules* it for later execution. In the program, the currently executing task can be referenced using the keyword **now**.

As an example, consider a task T() that starts two long-running computations Compute1() and Compute2() and schedules a task Print() that will print the result after the computations have finished:

```
task T() {
  Task print = schedule this.Print();
  Task compute1 = schedule this.Compute1();
  Task compute2 = schedule this.Compute2();
  compute1→print;
  compute2→print;
}
```

A task schedule is represented as a graph of object.Task() pairs. The statement **schedule this**.Print(), for example, creates a new node in the schedule with the **this** object and the Print() task method and returns an object of type Task representing that node. Like any other object, Task objects can be kept in local variables, passed around as parameters, and stored in fields.

At runtime, a *scheduler* constantly chooses tasks that are eligible for execution and starts them. The order in which the scheduler is allowed to start the tasks is specified by the edges in the schedule graph. In the example, the statement compute1→print creates an explicit happens-before relation between the two referenced task objects and adds the happens-before edge **this**.Compute1()→**this**.Print() to the schedule. In the above program, the scheduler guarantees that both tasks Compute1() and Compute2() have finished execution before task Print() is started. The tasks Compute1() and Compute2(), however, are not ordered and may therefore be executed in parallel.

Whenever a new task is scheduled, the scheduler automatically adds an initial happens-before relation between the currently executing task and the newly created task node. In the example method T() those implicit edges have a similar effect as if the programmer were to explicitly add →-edges between **now** and the subtasks, as shown in the following modification of the previous example:

```
task T() {
  Task print = schedule this.Print();
  now→print; \\implicit

  Task compute1 = schedule this.Compute1();
  now→compute1; \\implicit

  Task compute2 = schedule this.Compute2();
  now→compute2; \\implicit

  compute1→print;
  compute2→print;
}
```

There is one important semantic difference between implicit creation edges and explicitly adding the edge between **now** and a subtask, however. As opposed to a manually added edge, an implicit edge prevents the immediate execution of the newly scheduled tasks and enables the current task to add additional constraints to the schedule before the task finishes. In the example above, if there were no implicit creation edges, the scheduler would be allowed to start the print task already before the statement now→print was executed.

There are multiple designs possible to address the problem of delaying the execution of a task until the initial →-constraints have been added. For example, we could require that a task must be explicitly started (e.g., by calling a start() method) after it has been scheduled and the →-relations have been added. Another possibility is to define a more *declarative* semantics for the →-statements where the →-statements are not executed one-by-one in a sequential fashion but where the compiler collects all **schedule** sites and their corresponding →-statements inside a method (regardless of their position in the source code) into a single atomic operation. The design decision of delaying sub-tasks until the parent task has finished has been made to keep the model as small and general as possible. Other behaviors can be achieved by program transformations. For example, the effect of and explicit Task.start() method can be modeled by a transformation similar to *continuation passing style*: at each call to start() the parent task is split into two tasks, one for the prelude and one for the remainder of the task [10].

## 3.2 Task objects as parameters: The *now happens-before later* pattern

A task method can take task objects as parameters. One common use for task parameters is to allow task methods to schedule subtasks relative to tasks that have been scheduled outside. In the next example, the task method Compute() schedules additional subtasks to perform the computation but all those subtasks must have finished before the Print() task is allowed to execute.

```
1 task T() {
2   Task print = schedule this.Print();
3   //pass reference to print task:
4   Task compute = schedule this.Compute(print);
5   compute→print;
6 }
7
8 task Compute(Task later) {
9   while(moreTasks()) {
10    Task subtask = schedule this.Subtask(later);
11    //schedule subtask before later
12    subtask→later;
13  }
14 }
```

When scheduling the Compute() task on line 4, task T() passes the print task object as a parameter to Compute(). Line 5 further schedules the print task to happen after compute. Because the execution of print is delayed at least until compute has been finished, the Compute () task can schedule additional subtasks and, on line 12, order them to happen before the passed print task object.

In Compute() the reference later is passed along even further to Subtask(), allowing Subtask() (and its subtasks, if there are any) to push the execution of the Print() task further and further into the future until the whole computation has finished. Once the subtasks terminate without inserting new tasks, the scheduler will be able to execute Print().

We call the pattern of passing a task that has been scheduled to happen after the current task **now** the *now happens-before later* pattern. This pattern allows the current task to arbitrarily delay already scheduled tasks by ordering subtasks to happen before. The *now happens-before later* pattern demonstrates the increased flexibility of the presented task model over lexically scoped fork/join models.

## 3.3 Example: Barrier synchronization

This section discusses an example from the sor benchmark. The original version is implemented using a barrier. However, as noted earlier in Chapter 2, barriers as low-level synchronization primitives are difficult to analyze statically. Therefore, this section additionally presents a re-modeled version of the original code where the barrier is replaced with explicit task synchronization that can be analyzed statically by an analysis such as the schedule analysis introduced in Chapter 4.

### 3.3.1 Example with threads and barriers

```
1  class Sor {
2    Barrier barrier = new Barrier(NumWorkers);
3    Worker[] workers = new Worker[NumWorkers];
4
5    void begin() {
6      for(int i=0; i<NumWorkers; i++) {
7        workers[i] = new Worker(this, i);
8        workers[i].start();
9      }
10     this.end();
11   }
12   void end() {
13     for(int i=0; i<NumWorkers; i++) {
14       try {
15         workers[i].join();
16       } catch(InterruptedException e) {}
17     }
18   }
19 }
20
21 class Worker extends Thread {
22   Sor sor; int id;
23
24   Worker(Sor sor, int id) {
25     this.sor = sor;
26     this.id = id;
27   }
28   void run() {
29     for(int count=0; count<NumRounds; count++) {
30       /* phase 1 ... */
31       this.sor.barrier.wait();
32       /* phase 2 ... */
33       this.sor.barrier.wait();
34     }
35   }
36 }
```

Figure 3.1: Simplified version of the `sor` benchmark using threads and barriers.

Figure 3.1 shows a simplified excerpt of the `sor` benchmark (successive over-relaxation over a 2D grid). In method `begin()`, `sor` first starts a number of worker threads on line 8 before the main thread waits for all workers to finish on line 15 in method `end()`.

Every worker successively refines the overall result by repeating the same computation a number of times. Each worker executes the same loop on line 29. As a data-parallel application,

## 3.3. EXAMPLE: BARRIER SYNCHRONIZATION

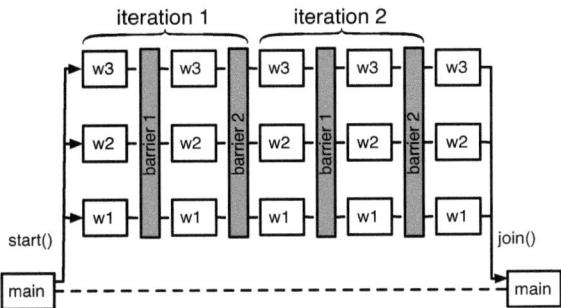

Figure 3.2: One main and three worker threads w1, w2, and w3 while executing the example from Figure 3.1. Dashed lines depict periods where a thread is blocked.

the workers generally work in parallel on separate parts of the input data (not shown in the example). Due to data-dependencies, however, all workers must synchronize twice in every iteration on lines 31 and 33 to separate the two computation phases on lines 30 and 32.

The execution behavior of this program is depicted in Figure 3.2. The basic pattern implemented by the Sor class is a fork and successive join of the worker threads. For the correct functioning of the program it is important that all workers execute the loop the same number of times and that on each iteration all workers call the same barriers in the same order. If one worker would exit the loop early, for example, the barrier will block the other workers resulting in a deadlock.

The implicit dependency on the number of loop iterations and the number of calls to barrier .wait() each worker executes makes this example hard to analyze statically. The problem is that it is non-trivial to reason about what phases of the different tasks may interleave and what phases are guaranteed to be ordered. For example, in the presence of aliasing it can be difficult to reason that all threads always synchronize on the same barrier object.

### 3.3.2 Example with explicit scheduling constraints

Figure 3.3 shows the Sor class, rewritten to use explicit scheduling constraints instead of threads and barriers. The fork/join pattern of the original code was transformed into a scheduling of the End() task on line 9 and passing the end task object as a parameter from iteration to iteration on line 10 (and then indirectly on line 18) until the computation has finished.

The biggest change to the original example in Figure 3.1 is that the original loop from line 29 was moved out of the workers and transformed into the recursive task Round() in the Sor class. Instead of letting every worker execute the loop separately, the Sor object works as an orchestrator, scheduling the execution of the two work phases for each worker in each iteration.

The task Round() implements one iteration. After testing on line 17 whether to continue, line 18 schedules the next iteration and orders it before the original End() task on line 19.

Line 21 schedules the Barrier() task. Barrier() is only used for ordering purposes and has no functional behavior. On lines 23 to 28 the Sor class then schedules the two phases for

```
1  class Sor {
2    Worker[] workers = new Worker[NumWorkers];
3    int NumRounds = 100;
4
5    task Begin() {
6      for(int i=0; i<NumWorkers; i++) {
7        this.workers[i] = new Worker(this, i);
8      }
9      Task end = schedule this.End();
10     Task round = schedule this.Round(0, end);
11     round → end;
12   }
13
14   task End() { /* nothing to do */ }
15
16   task Round(int count, Task later) {
17     if(count < NumRounds) {
18       Task nextRound = schedule this.Round(count++, later);
19       nextRound→later;
20
21       Task barrier = schedule this.Barrier();
22       for(int i=0; i<workers.length; i++) {
23         Task phase1 = schedule workers[i].Phase1();
24         Task phase2 = schedule workers[i].Phase2();
25
26         phase1→barrier;
27         barrier→phase2;
28         phase2→nextRound;
29       }
30     }
31   }
32
33   task Barrier() { /* nothing to do */ }
34 }
```

Figure 3.3: The sor benchmark from Figure 3.1 using explicit scheduling constraints.

each worker for this iteration and orders the Phase1() before the barrier and Phase2() after the barrier but before the next iteration. After the Round() task for one iteration has finished, the scheduler can continue to start executing all the Phase1() tasks of the workers.

For the Round() method, the analysis presented in this paper statically extracts the schedule shown in Figure 3.4. The unfilled circle stands for the logical **now** task that executes Round(). The double-headed arrows represent the happens-before edges that are implicitly added between the creating task **now** and the created tasks. The other edges indicate explicit happens-before relations resulting from the →-statements in Round(). Because the Phase1() and Phase2() tasks may be scheduled multiple times inside the loop, the corresponding nodes in the graph are marked as "multiple" as indicated by the asterisk and the gray boxes.

Given this extracted schedule, the analysis can conclude that the two phases, the barrier,

## 3.4. EXCEPTION HANDLING AND INTER-TASK EXCEPTION PROPAGATION

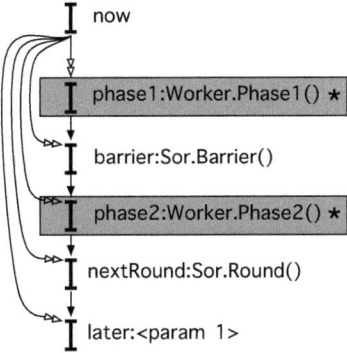

Figure 3.4: Schedule statically extracted from task Round() from Figure 3.3. Double-headed arrows indicate implicit creation edges, gray boxes indicate schedule sites inside loops.

the next iteration, and the later parameter are all ordered and therefore will never execute in parallel. The analysis can further deduce that there may be more than one Phase1() tasks that are not ordered with one another and that similarly, Phase2() may be scheduled multiple times without any internal ordering.

## 3.4 Exception handling and inter-task exception propagation

Java provides exceptions as a built-in mechanism for handling error conditions in a program. If an exception is thrown, the Java virtual machine (JVM) unwinds the stack of current method calls until an exception handler is found that is prepared to catch and handle the exception. If no exception handler is found on the current call stack, the JVM terminates the current program execution.

A exception mechanism that unwinds the call stack works well for sequential programs because the call stack correlates to the current state of program execution. Translating exceptions into a parallel context is not as straight forward, however, because each task has its own call stack and the behavioral dependencies between tasks are generally unknown. If during a parallel computation one task fails with an exception, it can be difficult to decide which task(s) should be responsible to catch and handle the exception and whether or not the siblings of the failing task should continue with their computation or not.

Handling exceptions and recovering from errors in a parallel context is highly dependent on the program and implemented algorithm. For this reason, the task model described in this chapter only defines a task local exception mechanism and leaves inter-task exception propagation over to the programmer.

As with sequential programs, exceptions are thrown using a **throw** statement and they can be caught using a **try/catch** statement. When a thrown exception is handled, the call stack of the current task is unwound until an exception handler is found. For uncaught exceptions the program execution—including all currently running and scheduled tasks—is forcefully terminated by the JVM.

With only local exception handling, the task model does not provide any built-in mechanism to propagate exception information from one task to another. Instead, this behavior must be manually implemented by the programmer. As an example, consider the following implementation of a fork/join pattern:

```
class ForkJoin {
  volatile Exception exception = null;
  task T() {
    Task f1 = schedule Fork();
    Task f2 = schedule Fork();
    Task join = schedule Join();
    f1→join;
    f2→join;
  }
  task Fork() {
    int i = 0;
    try {
      while(i++ < 100 && exception == null)
        doStep(i);
    } catch(Exception ex) {
      exception = ex;
    }
  }
  task Join() {
    if(exception != null) {
      //there was an error during computation
    } else {
      //no error
    }
  }
}
```

If in the fork-phase any call to `doStep(i)` on line 14 throws an exception, the exception is saved in the shared field `exception` on line 16. The test of the `exception` field on line 13 will cause all other `Fork()` tasks to interrupt their computation with the next iteration. The `exception` field is also used to propagate the exception information to the `Join` task, which uses it on line 20 to decide whether or not the fork-phase has successfully finished.

While being simple, this example illustrates the many different ways parallel exception handling can be implemented. This relatively large design space makes it difficult to come up with a single built-in mechanism and lead us to the decision to make the programmer responsible for inter-task exception propagation, if needed.

For instance, the above example only propagates a single exception to the `Join()` task. However, it can happen that the calls to `doStep(i)` on line 14 throw an exception in both tasks `f1` and `f2` in which case one exception is quietly discarded. Depending on the program, this behavior can be acceptable or not. Secondly, the `Fork()` tasks in the above program only check at the beginning of each iteration whether an exception has been thrown by the sibling. If calls to `doStep(i)` generally return quickly, the fork-phase is aborted relatively soon after the exception has been thrown. However, if `doStep(i)` blocks for a significant amount of time, the exception cannot abort the fork-phase in a timely manner.

As we will show in Chapter 4.2.1, providing only task-local exception handling and terminating program execution in the case of uncaught exceptions also simplifies the static analysis.

## 3.5 Explicit task ordering vs. lock-based synchronization

In systems that use processes or threads as their parallel computation primitives, the task execution order is the order in which threads or processes spawn other threads or processes. In those systems, the only mechanism a programmer can use to express finer-grained ordering intentions are synchronization primitives like joining, locks, or barriers.

Enforcing the programmers' intended execution order through synchronization primitives, however, can lead to unnatural code and has been shown to be prone to errors. A recent study by Lu et al. [73] found that around one third of the non-deadlock concurrency bugs were caused by violations of the order in which tasks must execute. As a result they advocate "language features to support 'order' semantics to further ease concurrent programming". A parallel programming language or library with explicit constructs for specifying task-ordering constraints can help programmers with reasoning about the program behavior. Explicit ordering constraints also help with avoiding order violations introduced through inappropriate use of synchronization primitives.

The apparent benefits of specifying task ordering constraints explicitly in the program code instead of using low-level synchronization primitives raise the question whether or not synchronization primitives such as locks are needed at all. In [13], the authors prove that it is impossible to build concurrent implementations of many algorithms and data-structures such as sets, queues, and mutual exclusion without low-level synchronization. Specifically, they prove that parallel programs cannot avoid the use of either *read-after-write* (RAW) or *atomic write-after-read* (AWAR) operations.

A RAW is defined as a write to shared variable A that is followed by a read to a different shared variable B without a write to B in between. Implementing RAW requires memory ordering instructions such as memory barriers and fences. An AWAR is an atomic operation that atomically reads and then writes to shared locations, which requires atomic primitives such as compare-and-swap.

Therefore, unfortunately low-level synchronization cannot be avoided in all algorithms. On the flip side, algorithm designers can improve the effectiveness of the optimizing compiler by preferring explicit task-ordering over low-level synchronization wherever possible. Rewriting the sor example from Section 3.3.1 into the version with explicit scheduling constraints from Section 3.3.2, for example, enables the compiler to gather more useful scheduling information that improves the precision of the analysis and therefore the quality of the optimizations.

## 3.6 Programming model or intermediate representation?

The task model is designed to be as minimal as possible while being expressive enough to model many of the features provided by current parallel libraries and languages in a straightforward way. The programming model introduced here is therefore not necessarily meant to be used directly by the programmer but instead functions as an intermediate language used for the compiler analyses.

Our experience with the case studies have shown, however, that it is possible and reasonable to use the task model in real-world programs even though a language with some syntactic support could help with simplifying the actual code.

## 3.7 Structural properties of schedules

At runtime, the task schedule is implicitly created through the execution of **schedule**-statements and →-statements. The scheduler keeps track of scheduled tasks and their happens-before relations and makes sure that at any given time only tasks that are eligible for execution are actually running.

The goal of the schedule analysis described in Chapter 4 is to compute a conservative abstraction of all concrete runtime schedules that the execution of a given program may produce. As a first step towards computing abstract schedules this section provides a deeper understanding of basic structural properties that all valid runtime schedules have in common.

Generally, it cannot be (statically) guaranteed that a program will not violate some structural properties when executed. It is, for example, possible for a program to create circular →-relations between tasks, which violates the *wellformed-ness* property described below and results in a deadlock. While a deadlock is a realistic outcome of a program, it is also a faulty behavior. Therefore, the compiler can assume that all correct executions result in a well-formed schedule.

### 3.7.1 Well-formed schedules

A well-formed schedule guarantees that the scheduler can always choose at least one task for execution (progress) and that every task is eventually executed (liveness). The progress and liveness conditions require that the schedule is a directed acyclic graph. A cycle in the schedule would result in a deadlock where two tasks block each other and prevent progress. Assuming that the execution of a task always terminates, an acyclic graph ensures that there is always at least one node that has only incoming edges from already executed tasks.

Besides being acyclic, a well-formed schedule also restricts the addition of new happens-before relations. Because tasks can be stored in fields, a task object may reference a task that has already been executed. Imagine that a program tries to order two tasks a and b by executing a→b. If task b has already finished, the scheduler has no chance of satisfying this edge. At the time when the edge a→b is added to the schedule, task b already lies in the past and the scheduler cannot retroactively execute anything before that.

To prevent such unresolvable scheduling conflicts, the scheduler allows an edge a→b to be added from within a task **now** only if there exists a direct or transitive edge **now**→b from **now** to the right hand side b. This edge ensures that task b is scheduled in the future of **now** and therefore is still unexecuted at the time of the edge creation. It is not necessary to require an edge **now**→a, however, because it is not a problem for the scheduler to obey the →-semantics if the source task of a happens-before edge has already been executed.

## 3.7.2 Creation trees

As described in Section 3.1, the scheduler implicitly adds an edge between the current task **now** and all the tasks it schedules. Those initial edges are called *creation edges*. In diagrams, we depict creation edges with double arrow heads. Because a task has exactly one creator, the creation edges form a *spanning tree* that is embedded into the schedule.

The creation tree is a fundamental structure inside a task schedule that exhibits two useful properties:

1. If one task $\mathcal{A}$ is the direct or indirect parent of another task $\mathcal{B}$ in the creation tree, it is guaranteed that $\mathcal{A}$ always executes before $\mathcal{B}$ because $\mathcal{A}$ creates $\mathcal{B}$.

2. If $\mathcal{A} \twoheadrightarrow \mathcal{B}$ is a creation edge, the existence of the child task $\mathcal{B}$ *implies* the existence of its parent $\mathcal{A}$, written $\mathcal{B} \Rightarrow \mathcal{A}$. This relationship is transitive, thus implying the existence of all parents up to the root of the creation tree (the initial task that started the program). The inverse, however, is not true; due to conditional tasks, one cannot deduce the existence of a child task simply from the existence of the parent.

## 3.7.3 Exclusive tasks

Conditional control flow can result in a conditional scheduling of tasks as shown in the following example:

```
1  Task a = schedule this.A();
2
3  Task b = null;
4  if(random()) {
5    b = schedule this.B1();
6  } else {
7    b = schedule this.B2();
8    Task c = schedule this.C();
9    b→c;
10 }
11
12 a→b;
```

The runtime schedule of this program depends on the outcome of the call to random() on line 4. At compile-time, the analysis generally cannot determine which branch will be executed at runtime and therefore, all possible executions must be taken into account.

If the **true** branch is taken, task B2() is scheduled on line 5 and bound to variable b. The →-statement on line 12 then orders tasks A() and B1() resulting in the schedule A()→B1().

If the **false** branch is taken on line 4, then variable b will be bound to the newly scheduled task B2() on line 7. In addition, task C() will be scheduled on line 8 and ordered after B2() on line 9. With the →-statement from line 12 this results in the runtime schedule A()→B2()→C().

Two tasks that are created in different branches of a conditional statement cannot co-exist in the same run of the program but they are *exclusive* of each other. In the above example, B1() is exclusive of both B2() and C().

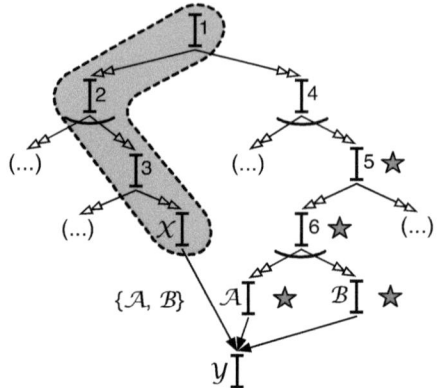

Figure 3.5: Marking tasks in the creation tree to test if $\mathcal{A} \to \mathcal{B}$ is genuine. The fence is circled by the dotted line, marks are shown as stars. Arcs denote exclusive tasks.

Because a static analysis must approximate runtime behavior, it may not always be possible to compute accurate information about whether two tasks are exclusive of each other. This can be especially difficult in the presence of loops and recursion. In some cases, however, because exclusive tasks cannot conflict with each other, they can simply be treated as if they were non-exclusive but ordered.

### 3.7.4 Genuine edges

The task model presented in this chapter does not explicitly restrict how happens-before relations are created. Therefore, it is possible to execute a statement a→b conditionally, even though the tasks bound to variables a and b may be have been scheduled unconditionally. Such a program is not necessarily erroneous, but it can lead to problems when in some executions two tasks are ordered when in other executions the same tasks are unordered.

We call edges that exists "in all relevant executions" *genuine edges*. A genuine edge $\mathcal{A} \to \mathcal{B}$ is an edge where the existence of the source task $\mathcal{A}$ implies that the edge exists, denoted $\mathcal{A} \Rightarrow \mathcal{A} \to \mathcal{B}$. This means that in all executions in which task $\mathcal{A}$ is scheduled, the edge has been created, too. Edges that are not genuine should be ignored by a static analysis, thus over-approximating the parallelism.

Given a (runtime) schedule, an algorithm to determine whether $\mathcal{A} \Rightarrow \mathcal{A} \to \mathcal{B}$ first finds all the tasks $creators(\mathcal{A} \to \mathcal{B})$ that unconditionally create the edge $\mathcal{A} \to \mathcal{B}$.

The problem $\mathcal{A} \Rightarrow \mathcal{A} \to \mathcal{B}$ can now be rephrased as a check whether the existence of $\mathcal{A}$ implies the existence of at least one task $\mathcal{C}$ that creates the edge: $\exists \mathcal{C}. \mathcal{A} \Rightarrow \mathcal{C} \land \mathcal{C} \in creators(\mathcal{A} \to \mathcal{B})$. This predicate can be approximated using the creation tree and its property that the existence of a child task implies the existence of its parent.

Figure 3.5 shows an example of a creation tree. We want to compute whether the edge $\mathcal{X} \to \mathcal{Y}$ is genuine. The algorithm starts by marking the *fence*. The fence is comprised of all the

3.8. RELATED WORK                                                                                     33

tasks from the edge source $\mathcal{X}$ up to the root of the creation tree. The existence of the fence tasks is implied by the existence of $\mathcal{X}$ because they are the parents in the creation tree.

The goal is now to check whether any task in the fence implies the existence of any task that creates the edge $\mathcal{X} \to \mathcal{Y}$. We do so by iteratively marking tasks, walking up the creation tree, until we either mark a task in the fence, in which case the edge is genuine, or no more tasks can be marked, in which case the edge is not genuine.

The label on edge $\mathcal{X} \to \mathcal{Y}$ indicates that the edge was created by both tasks $\mathcal{A}$ and $\mathcal{B}$. Therefore, the algorithm initially marks the tasks $\mathcal{A}$ and $\mathcal{B}$ and continues with task 6 as the parent of $\mathcal{A}$ and $\mathcal{B}$. Because by marking $\mathcal{A}$ and $\mathcal{B}$ all exclusive children of task 6 were marked, and thus all possible execution paths are covered, task 6 can be marked as well. The mark on 6 is sufficient to further mark task 5 because task 6 was created unconditionally.

In the example, task 4 cannot be marked because there is an exclusive sibling of task 5 that is unmarked. Therefore, there is a program execution that will create task $\mathcal{X}$ but not tasks $\mathcal{A}$ or $\mathcal{B}$ and thus not the edge $\mathcal{A} \to \mathcal{B}$. This concludes that $\mathcal{A} \to \mathcal{B}$ is not genuine.

If the program was modified to create task 5 unconditionally, the algorithm would eventually mark the fence in task 1, showing that $\mathcal{A} \to \mathcal{B}$ were genuine.

## 3.8 Related work

This section provides additional background material on related programming and execution models for parallel programs.

**Structured parallelism and task-based runtimes.** Models following a structured fork/join style are well understood and researched because their syntactic scoping greatly simplifies static analysis. The reduced flexibility of syntactically scoped parallelism, however, resulted in the development of various task-based runtime systems that are more suitable for real-world applications—but they are also harder to analyze. Structured parallelism as well as task-based runtimes have been discussed in detail in Section 2.3.

**Intermediate representations for explicitly parallel programs.** Srinivasan et al. [107] were among the first to develop a static single assignment form for explicitly parallel programs. They use a parallel Fortran extension that introduces a construct to syntactically declare parallel sections in a program. Lee et al. [65] propose a Concurrent SSA framework (CSSA) for explicitly parallel programs with cobegin/coend parallel sections. They introduce a π-assignment that summarizes the information of interleaving statements among threads. Similar to Φ-functions, the π-function distinguishes values of variables coming from different incoming control flow edges. Unlike a Φ-function, however, the π-function additionally takes incoming conflict edges into account to model possible thread interleavings. Lee et al. also introduce a concurrent control-flow graph, which contains information about conflicting statements in addition to control flow and synchronization information. Novillo et al. [91] extend the CSSA form with information about locks and mutual exclusion. The knowledge about locks increases the precision when computing conflicting statements by ignoring some reaching definitions that use the same lock. All of the above intermediate representations for explicitly parallel programs assume a very restricted fork/join style of parallelism that prevents many common patterns such as parallel regions inside loops or recursive creation of parallel threads.

**Intermediate representations for parallelizing compilers.** The Hierarchical Task Graph (HTG) presented in [95, 44] is an intermediate representation for parallel programs that encapsulates data and control dependence ordering as well as thread management and scheduling policies.

The construction of the HTC starts from the program's control-flow graph (CFG). It then computes a hierarchical graph where a loop and all statements immediately nested inside that loop are summarized into a single node on the next higher hierarchy level. The HTG is composed of three types of nodes:

**Simple node:** a node representing a task with no subtasks;

**Compound node:** a node representing a task that consists of other tasks;

**Loop node:** a node representing a task that is a loop whose iteration body is an HTG.

Similarly to Hierarchical Task Graphs, Kimble [15] is an intermediate representation where program constructs are organized in a hierarchy of directed graphs. The structure of a Kimble IR is described as a hierarchy of directed acyclic graphs (DAGs). A single DAG represents control and data dependence between program constructs in a single task. The individual task DAGs are put into a hierarchy through nesting relationships. Nesting relationships can form cycles in order to express recursive flows.

Kimble and Hierarchical Task Graphs are tools for parallelizing compilers that perform automatic extraction of parallelism from serial programs. Parallelism is introduced to a program by the compiler and not by the programmer as in our task model. It is also unclear how the construction of an IR that takes a single CFG as its input scales to real-world object-oriented programs.

The general structure and abstraction level of both IRs matches well with our task model and the schedule analysis presented in the next chapter. For example, the call-graph of a program that uses our task model can be transformed into a forest of call-graphs where task-methods are the roots for each (task-internal) call-graph[1]. By connecting the individual call-graphs with edges from each **schedule**-statement to the corresponding task call-graph and by exploding the call-graphs by inlining the corresponding control-flow graphs of each method, a structure very similar to the Kimble IR emerges. Because of the structural similarities between all of those approaches we think that many techniques and algorithms originally developed for HTG and Kimble may prove useful for future work on our task model.

**Process calculi and the actor model.** A process calculus defines an algebra for describing and analyzing the interaction, communication, and synchronization between concurrent processes. As algebras, process calculi permit formal reasoning about many of their non-trivial properties, such as behavioral equivalence through bisimulation [43].

---

[1]This transformation clones call-graph nodes such that the individual call-graphs are disjoint.

The join-calculus [42], π-calculus [84], and Communicating Sequential Processes (CSP) [50] are examples of process calculi for concurrent systems. CSP, for example, influenced the design of multiple programming languages such as *occam* [70], *JCSP* [92], and *Go* [63]. In a process calculus, a system is described as independent processes that interact through messages sent over named channels.

The actor model [5, 55] is closely related to process calculi. Actors in the actor model are long-lasting processes that possess an identity. Actors communicate by sending messages to each other. Each actor is driven by an internal messaging loop which repeatedly checks the actor's mailbox and handles new messages.

ERBIUM [85] is an intermediate representation based on a streaming execution model derived from Kahn Process Networks [54]. Like in the actor model, ERBIUM uses persistent processes that communicate and synchronize through multi-producer multi-consumer streams (buffers). As an intermediate representation, ERBIUM is explicitly parallel and supports dynamic creation and termination of concurrent processes.

The actor model and ERBIUM both favor persistent, longer-running processes communicating through point-to-point data streams. In comparison, our task model favors small short-lived tasks with explicit ordering that communicate through shared memory.

**The task graph pattern.** In [83], the authors describe a programming and design pattern for parallel programs, called the *task graph pattern*. The task graph pattern suggests to break down a complex problem into a set of atomic tasks with dependencies between them. Each task is a separate unit of work that may take dependencies on one or more antecedents. A task may only start when all the dependencies to its antecedents are satisfied. Task graphs are defined statically at design time or—in a variation of the pattern—defined programmatically prior to the execution of the graph. The task graph pattern with its restricted task-graph creation and ordering constraints describes a subset of our task model. It provides a collection of guidelines for how a complex problem can be broken down into a set of ordered tasks.

## 3.9 Summary

Optimizations for parallel programs are more effective the more detailed knowledge the compiler has about the ordering in which tasks can be executed. For a fully automatic compiler that does not rely on manual programmer intervention, this knowledge must come from analyzing the program code.

Java's unstructured threads, however, make it hard if not impossible to gather meaningful ordering information. The only mechanism a programmer can use to express ordering intentions are synchronization primitives like locks or barriers. Locks and barriers are represented as object instances and possible aliasing makes it hard for the compiler to recognize even relatively simple patterns such as fork/join. Besides the difficulties for the compiler analyses, unstructured threads with synchronization primitives have also been shown to be prone to error and difficult to use.

For this reason, many current parallel programming libraries and languages deliberately restrict the unbound flexibility of unstructured tasks to different degrees. Those restrictions often contain additional task-ordering information that remains unused in current compilers.

The task model presented in this chapter is based on lightweight tasks with explicit happens-before relations and is general enough to capture the ordering information contained in many parallel programming models. By making the ordering constraints explicit in the program code, compilers can extract useful scheduling information more easily. This chapter also identifies different structural properties of runtime task schedules that all valid program executions have in common.

# 4

# Schedule analysis in optimizing compilers

Compiler optimizations are program transformations that try to minimize some program attribute (e.g., runtime or memory footprint) or maximize a program attribute (e.g., register usage or memory throughput) in a favorable way. Compiler optimizations must be *safe* and *conservative*: the compiler must guarantee that an optimization does not turn a correct program into an incorrect one. In general, this means that an optimization must not change a program's outcome. More specifically, being safe and conservative implies that the program should not be able to observe directly whether or not the optimization has been applied. [87, pp. 319–328]

Many classical optimizations that fulfill this "unobservability" property in single-threaded programs become observable in a parallel setting, however. As an example, consider a load elimination optimization that replaces an access to main memory with a read of a compiler-generated temporary that can be allocated in faster storage such as registers or local memory. The compiler can rewrite, for example, two consecutive field loads such as:

```
this.a = this.f;
this.b = this.f;
```

Into code that loads the field only once:

```
int tmp = this.f;
this.a = tmp;
this.b = tmp;
```

In a single-threaded program, this transformation cannot be observed by the program. In a parallel program, however, a concurrent task may be able to observe whether the transformation has been applied or not. Imagine a task, that constantly updates the field **this.f** and then compares **this.a** and **this.b**. In the first version with two loads, there exists an interleaving where the update to **this.f** happens in between the two loads and the observer task sees different values for **this.a** and **this.b**. In the second example, however, the observer will always see that **this.a == this.b** because the value of **this.f** is actually only loaded once.

This scenario requires a very (un-)lucky interleaving of the tasks such that the observer is able to distinguish between the two program versions. However, even if it may happen rarely on a real system, the infrequence of such an event makes it just harder to detect, reproduce, and debug.

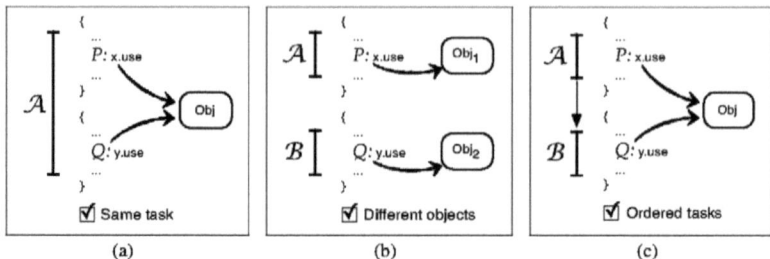

Figure 4.1: The three cases where two program points $P$ and $Q$ commute.

The core question a compiler has to answer when optimizing parallel programs is, if the transformation may be observable by any parallel task. For answering this question, the compiler must prove for a given program point $P$ (such as a single bytecode) that there is no other program point $Q$ that may interfere with $P$. This reduces the question of whether or not an optimization can be safely applied at program point $P$ to the question of whether two program points $P$ and $Q$ commute:

$$canTransform(P) \iff \forall Q \in Prog : commute(P,Q).$$

Two program points $P$ and $Q$ commute for any of the three cases depicted in Figure 4.1: $P$ and $Q$ commute if they are *always* executed by the same task, as shown in Panel (a), if they *always* access different memory, as shown in Panel (b), or if the tasks that execute $P$ and $Q$ are *always* ordered by happens-before relations, shown in Panel (c).

In practice, however, it is difficult to decide whether or not the above conditions *always* hold. Therefore, it is easier to rephrase the predicate $commute(P,Q)$ into the question whether two program points may interfere:

$$\neg mayInterfere(P,Q) \implies commute(P,Q).$$

The program points $P$ and $Q$ may interfere if they *may* access the same memory *and* if they *may* ever be executed by unordered tasks. In general, the set $\neg mayInterfere(P,Q)$ is smaller than the set $commute(P,Q)$ due to imprecisions in the compiler analyses. For safe and conservative analyses, however, $\neg mayInterfere(P,Q)$ is a subset of $commute(P,Q)$: $\neg mayInterfere(P,Q) \subseteq commute(P,Q)$, meaning that if $P$ and $Q$ are classified to not interfere, they are guaranteed to commute.

The more precisely $mayInterfere()$ can be computed, the more effective optimizations for parallel programs become. Figure 4.2 shows a rule GENERIC-OPT for a generic program optimization. GENERIC-OPT computes all pairs of program points $P$ and $Q$ with potential read-/write or write/write interference.

The result of the GENERIC-OPT rule is the relation $mayInterfere(P,Q)$ between pairs of program points $P$ and $Q$. For program points $P$ and $Q$ that are reachable by tasks $\mathcal{A}$ and $\mathcal{B}$

## 4.1. Terminology and notation

GENERIC-OPT
$$\frac{\begin{array}{l}(1a)\,P \text{ WRITES v1 in } \mathcal{A}\\ (1b)\,Q \text{ MAY ACCESS v2 in } \mathcal{B}\\ (2a)\,\text{v1 MAY POINT TO } Obj\\ (2b)\,\text{v2 MAY POINT TO } Obj\\ (3)\,Obj \text{ MAY ESCAPE } \mathcal{A} \text{ and } \mathcal{B}\\ (4)\,parallel(\mathcal{A},\mathcal{B})\end{array}}{mayInterfere(P,Q)}$$

Figure 4.2: A generic optimization.

respectively, clauses (1a) and (1b) select the variables v1 and v2 that $P$ and $Q$ access (where $P$ is the write operation and $Q$ is either a read or a write).

Clauses (2a) and (2b) consult a points-to set, computed by a points-to analysis, to check whether v1 and v2 may point to the same (analysis-time) object $Obj$. If v1 and v2 do not point to the same analysis-time object it is guaranteed that at runtime $P$ and $Q$ never access the same memory.

Clause (3) tests whether $Obj$ may escape tasks $\mathcal{A}$ and $\mathcal{B}$ as computed by an escape analysis. The escape information helps with disambiguating cases where—due to imprecision—the points-to analysis unnecessarily conflates distinct runtime objects into the same analysis-time object, introducing spurious aliasing. If the escape analysis can show that object $Obj$ is local to task $\mathcal{A}$ (that is, only task $\mathcal{A}$ can ever obtain a reference to $Obj$) then the single analysis-time object $Obj$ represents multiple disjoint runtime objects each local to tasks $\mathcal{A}$ or $\mathcal{B}$.

If any of the clauses (2a), (2b), or (3) is false, the program points $P$ and $Q$ are guaranteed to access disjoint memory and therefore commute as shown in Figure 4.1(b). If they are true, however, the we must assume that $P$ and $Q$ may access the same memory. In this case, $P$ and $Q$ can only be shown to commute if an analysis can prove that their memory accesses are ordered either by program order inside a single task or by happens-before relationships between tasks.

This chapter presents *schedule analysis* as one algorithm for computing task-order information from a program with tasks and explicit scheduling constraints. The result of the schedule analysis is the relation *parallel*$(\mathcal{A},\mathcal{B})$ used in clause (4). If $\mathcal{A}$ and $\mathcal{B}$ are not classified as (potentially) parallel by the schedule analysis then $\mathcal{A}$ and $\mathcal{B}$ are either the same task or they are always ordered by happens-before relationships, covering panels (a) and (c) of Figure 4.1.

## 4.1 Terminology and notation

**Points-to analysis and call graph construction:** Starting from a bytecode representation of the program, a *points-to analysis* computes points-to sets for each program variable. The result of the points-to analysis is a relation v1 MAY POINT TO $Obj$ relating program variables v1 to analysis-time objects $Obj$. Analysis-time objects are approximations of runtime objects. In the simplest case, an analysis-time object $Obj$ directly correlates to the statement $S$ of a single object creation site (such as a distinct **new** statement) inside a method m( ). In a more complex context-sensitive points-to analysis, the creation site is augmented with additional (finite) data that allows the analysis to disambiguate different contexts in which $S$ may be executed. For example, in a $n$-call-site-sensitive analysis a string of at most $n$ caller methods $[n_1(),\ldots,n_n(),m()]$ is used to augment $S$. A method-invocation path $p = [n_1(),\ldots,n_n(),m()]$ ending in m() containing $S$ helps with distinguishing all executions of $S$ via $p$ from other executions of $S$ that reach m() through a different path. In all cases, an analysis-time object $Obj$ represents an equivalence class of a (potentially infinite) number of runtime objects which the analysis cannot track in more detail.

The points-to analysis also performs on-the-fly *call graph* construction. Call graph construction uses the points-to information as well as type information to find the possible target methods for a call site. At the same time, the points-to analysis must know about possible target methods at a call site to correctly compute points-to information. While performing the points-to analysis, virtual call sites of the form v1.m() are resolved by looking at possible concrete object types $T$ of objects referenced by v1 and the concrete method implementations m$1(), m$2(), ... for m() defined by each $T$. The resolved virtual call site is then stored in the call graph. Each node in the call graph represents one concrete method implementation, possibly augmented with an additional context string for higher precision. A directed edge [c1, m$1()]→[c2, m$2()] is added between two nodes [c1, m$1()] and [c2, m$2()] if method m$1() executed in context c1 may call method m$2() with context c2[1].

The schedule analysis itself has exactly one dependence on a points-to analysis: to resolve task method implementations at virtual call sites. If a points-to analysis is not available or considered too expensive, a quicker type-based approximation of the call-graph can be used to compute the set of target tasks at each schedule site. Since none of the benchmarks evaluated in this dissertation requires virtual dispatch for task methods, the results of the schedule analysis would be the same if we used a type-based call graph instead of the points-to analysis. (However, the optimizations would still require points-to information.)

During the points-to analysis, **schedule**-statements are treated as normal method calls. In a flow sensitive points-to analysis, this treatment may lead to wrong results because a method call happens immediately while a scheduled task only executes later. Treating **schedule**-statements as simple method calls therefore is only valid for a *flow insensitive* points-to analysis. A flow insensitive analysis ignores the flow of control in the program and the program becomes a set of statements which can execute multiple times, in any possible order [53, 102]. While being less precise than their flow sensitive counterparts, flow insensitive points-to analyses are significantly more performant. Also, by transforming the program into SSA form (see Section 4.2.1), a limited form of control flow sensitivity is re-gained.

---

[1] For the $n$-call-site-sensitive analysis example and context c1 = $[n_1(),\ldots,n_n(),m\$1()]$, context c2 results from c1 by shifting the string to the left and appending m$2(): c2 = $[n_2(),\ldots,n_n(),m\$1(),m\$2()]$. This operation maintains the maximum context string length $n$.

## 4.1. TERMINOLOGY AND NOTATION   41

**Escape analysis:** A task *escape analysis* [94, 30] is commonly based on a points-to analysis and uses the points-to sets to decide whether a task $\mathcal{A}$ may leak references to objects created by $\mathcal{A}$. For each task object $\mathcal{A}$, the escape analysis starts with finding all nodes in the call graph that represent possible task entry methods of $\mathcal{A}$. From there, the analysis follows the edges in the call graph to find all methods $m()$ that may be invoked during the execution of $\mathcal{A}$. For each object $Obj$ created in method $m()$ reachable by $\mathcal{A}$, the escape analysis decides whether $Obj$ may escape $\mathcal{A}$.

An object $Obj$ is said to escape $\mathcal{A}$ if it is passed as a parameter to any of $\mathcal{A}$'s entry methods, if it may be stored in a static field, if it may be passed as a parameter to another task, or (recursively) if it is reachable by any object that escapes $\mathcal{A}$.

The schedule analysis itself does not make use of escape information. However, an escape analysis can improve optimizations by increasing the precision of the interference analysis.

**Task methods, objects, and variables:** *Task methods* are methods that function as the entry points of tasks. Task methods are written in a method-notation A( ), B( ), and T( ).

At runtime, *task objects* are normal objects that can be passed to and be returned from methods as well as stored in fields. As a result, a program is allowed to add happens-before relations to and from tasks that have been loaded from fields. The only restriction in the task model is the wellformed-ness requirement described in Section 3.7.1. To avoid complex must-alias analysis, however, our analysis focusses on analyzing the common case of happens-before edges that are created between local task variables. Happens-before edges involving task objects that were loaded from fields are ignored by the analysis, thus over-approximating the parallelism in the program. Over-approximating parallelism is generally the safe and conservative assumption.[2]

At analysis-time, runtime task objects are approximated by analysis-time objects tracked by the points-to analysis. We write analysis-time *task objects* in a calligraphic font $\mathcal{A}$, $\mathcal{B}$, and $\mathcal{T}$. In this chapter, the term 'task object' always refers to an analysis-time task object and not a runtime task object, unless explicitly stated otherwise. At runtime, a task object refers to exactly one task method as its entry point. Due to imprecisions in the points-to analysis, however, an analysis-time task object may refer to multiple task methods as possible entry points. Nevertheless, in the examples in this chapter we sometimes use task methods as well as task variables as representatives of the corresponding analysis-time task object if the meaning is clear from the context.

*Task variables* are program variables that point to task objects and are written as lower-case letters in a sans-serif font a, b, and t. We consider a task variable to be *local* to a task method T( ) if it is either defined at a schedule site inside T( ) or if is a formal parameter of T( ). Non-local task variables, especially task objects read from fields, cannot be accurately identified by the analysis and must generally be ignored as described above.

Because the analysis works on a static single assignment (SSA) representation of the input program, a task method T( ) contains at most one assignment to a task variable. Therefore, a local task variable that is not a parameter is equivalent to the *schedule site* (i.e., the **schedule** -statement) where it is defined. Depending on the context, we thus use the term schedule site interchangeably with the corresponding **schedule**-statement and the defined task variable; in

---

[2]None of the benchmarks evaluated in the case studies in chapters 5 and 6 required task objects to be stored in fields and could therefore be analyzed without restrictions.

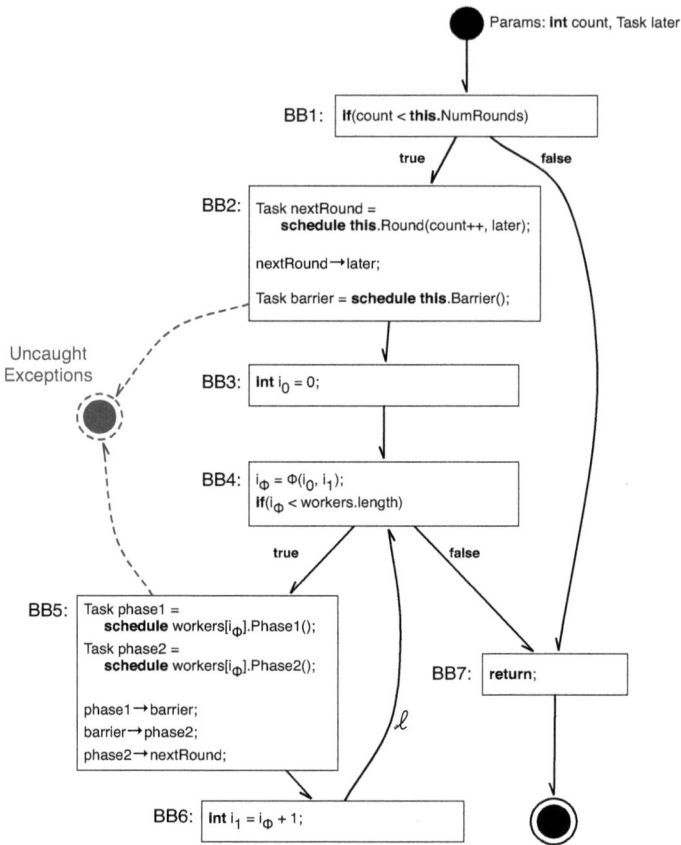

Figure 4.3: Control-flow graph for the Round() task method of the Sor class from Figure 3.3

all cases we mean *local task variable*, unless explicitly stated otherwise.

### 4.1.1 Running example: The sor benchmark

Throughout this chapter, we use the sor benchmark from Figure 3.3 as the running example to explain the individual steps of the schedule analysis. Figure 4.3 shows the control-flow graph (CFG) of the sor program after it has been transformed into SSA form.[3] The next Section 4.2.1 discusses SSA form in some more detail.

The subscripts on variable i denote the different versions of i that the SSA transformation introduces to accommodate for the multiple assignments to i: i is assigned 0 before the loop in

---

[3]We use "harpoon" arrows ⇀ for control-flow edges to distinguish them from happens-before edges →.

basic block *BB*3 and incremented by 1 after each loop iteration in basic block *BB*6.

Basic block *BB*4 is the head of the **for**-loop, represented by the path *BB*4 → *BB*5 → *BB*6 → *BB*4. Two control flows join at *BB*4, one coming from *BB*3 and the other coming from *BB*6 via the back-edge $\ell$. The $\Phi$ function $\Phi(\text{i}_0,\text{i}_1)$ assigns to $\text{i}_\Phi$ the version of i depending on where the control-flow came from.

## 4.2 The schedule analysis algorithm

The goal of the schedule analysis is to determine whether at runtime two tasks may be executed in parallel or whether they are always ordered by happens-before relations. Schedule analysis thus computes the relation *parallel*$(\mathcal{A},\mathcal{B})$ for pairs of tasks $\mathcal{A}$ and $\mathcal{B}$.

The key insight behind the schedule analysis algorithm presented in this chapter is to not compute what tasks are ordered with each other but the opposite: what tasks *may be unordered*. Consider as an example the following task methods T1() and T2():

```
task T1() {
  Task a = schedule A;
  Task b = schedule B;
  a→b;
}

task T2() {
  Task a = schedule A;
  Task b = schedule B;
}
```

When looking for ordered-ness, discovering the statement a→b in task method T1() may make the compiler record the fact that tasks $\mathcal{A}$ and $\mathcal{B}$ are ordered. With the given precision, the analysis further assumes that task method T2() also schedules (the same) tasks $\mathcal{A}$ and $\mathcal{B}$. However, because task method T2() leaves $\mathcal{A}$ and $\mathcal{B}$ unordered, the compiler now would have to remove the fact *ordered*$(\mathcal{A},\mathcal{B})$ from the set of known facts.

The property of "ordered-ness" is non-monotonic in the sense that finding more information may add facts as well as remove facts from the set of ordered tasks. Taking "unordered-ness" as a property, however, we can re-gain the monotonicity. If we deduce in task method T2() that the tasks $\mathcal{A}$ and $\mathcal{B}$ may be scheduled to be parallel, no **schedule**-statement and no happens-before relation that we discover later will invalidate this fact.

The result of the schedule analysis is computed in the five steps shown in Figure 4.4. After bringing the input program into a normalized form in the first step, the schedule analysis extracts for each task method a graph that represents →-relations between task variables (including task parameters). For maximizing the precision of the analysis, the graph extraction algorithm clones a schedule site for each loop context it may be executed in.

In the third step, the analysis computes for each pair of task variables of a task method a relation a *REL* b that summarizes the effects of all the corresponding clones of schedule sites in different loop contexts. This step also deals with conditional control flow where multiple task variables may reach the left and/or right-hand side of a single →-statement.

The fourth step computes for each task variable of the task method the set of (analysis-time)

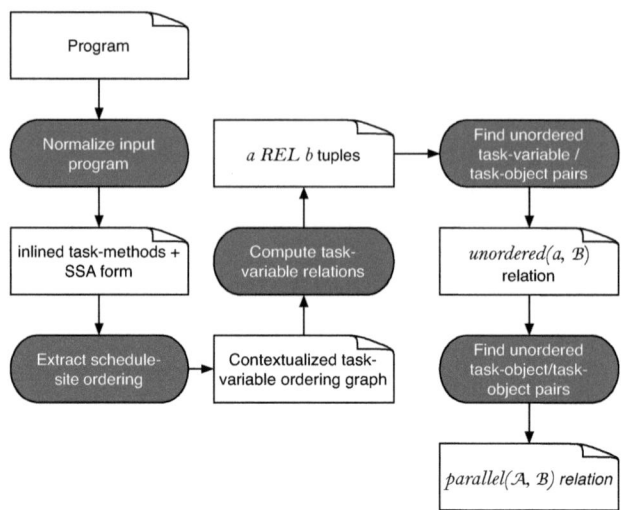

Figure 4.4: Steps of the schedule analysis and the intermediate products.

task objects that are unordered with that site. This step is an inter-task analysis that works not only on the code of the task method T() but also takes results computed about possible subtasks $S$ of T() into account. The important *now happens-before later* pattern introduced in Section 3.2, where a task variable is passed as a parameter to a subtask, is also handled in this step.

The fifth and final step is to compute the result $parallel(\mathcal{A},\mathcal{B})$ of the schedule analysis by combining the information about unordered task-variable/task-object pairs in relation $unordered(a,\mathcal{B})$ with the tasks and subtasks that may be represented by each task variable $a$.

The following sections describe each of the steps in more detail.

## 4.2.1 Step 1: Normalizing the input program

Before the schedule analysis extracts the scheduling information from the program code, the program is first transformed into a normalized version. In particular, the program is translated into a static single-assignment form (SSA) and non-task methods that contain **schedule**-statements or →-statements are inlined into all task methods that may execute them. After inlining, the schedule analysis can ignore non-task methods and concentrate on analyzing only the task methods.

As described in Section 3.4, uncaught exceptions in a task terminate the program execution. This allows the normalization step to prune the task-method control-flow graphs and remove all exceptional edges from inner nodes to the exit node.

The remainder of this section explains all three normalization steps in more detail.

## 4.2. THE SCHEDULE ANALYSIS ALGORITHM

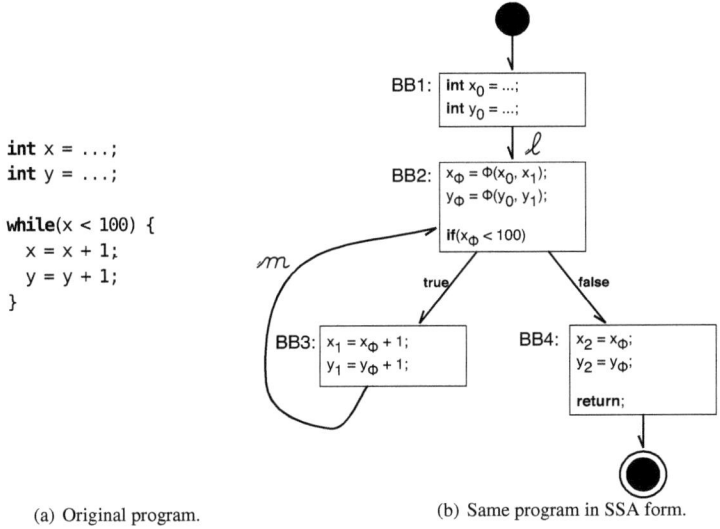

```
int x = ...;
int y = ...;

while(x < 100) {
    x = x + 1;
    y = y + 1;
}
```

(a) Original program.

(b) Same program in SSA form.

Figure 4.5: A small example in SSA form.

**SSA-form:** The schedule analysis assumes that the whole program code has been transformed into a static single-assignment form (SSA). A method is in SSA form if every variable that is assigned a value occurs as the target of only one assignment. If in the original method the variable is assigned multiple values, the corresponding method in SSA form contains multiple distinct copies ("versions") of the variable where each copy is assigned a value only once. This discipline of copying variables encodes information about definition and uses of variables in the name space of the variable: a use of a variable may use the value produced by a particular definition if and only if the definition and the use have exactly the same name for the variable in the SSA form. [87, pp. 252–258]

When transforming a program into SSA form, the compiler inserts Φ-functions at join points of the control-flow graph where multiple control-flow paths merge. Each Φ-function has as many argument positions as there are versions of the variable coming together at that node. Each argument position in the Φ-function further corresponds to a particular control-flow predecessor.

Figure 4.5(a) shows a small program consisting of a **while**-loop that iteratively updates two variables x and y. The corresponding control-flow graph and SSA form is depicted in Figure 4.5(b). Variable names include subscripts to create a distinct name for each definition. The original initializations of x and y are transformed into definitions of $x_0$ and $y_0$ in basic block BB1 and the updates inside the loop are transformed into definitions of variables $x_1$ and $y_1$ in basic block BB3.

Basic block BB2 is the head of the loop. In BB2, two control-flows are joined: the control flows from edge $\ell$ and edge $m$. In basic blocks where multiple distinct versions of a single variable must be merged, SSA inserts Φ functions. Φ functions are pseudo instructions that represent control-flow merge points and behave in an unusual way: A Φ function defines its left-hand side SSA variable with the value of its argument that corresponds to the edge along which control entered the block.

Two Φ-functions for variables x and y have been inserted into BB2. Therefore, the first parameters of the Φ-functions defining $x_\Phi$ and $y_\Phi$ correspond to the variables coming from edge $\ell$ ($x_0$ and $y_0$ respectively) and the second parameters correspond to the variables coming via edge $m$ ($x_1$ and $y_1$ respectively).

Edge $m$ is called a back-edge. A back-edge is defined as an edge from a node to one of its ancestors in a depth-first spanning tree starting from the entry node.

**Task-method inlining** The schedule analysis as presented in this dissertation assumes that **schedule**-statements and ↠-statements are only present in task methods. It is easy for the compiler to enforce this syntactically by simply disallowing **schedule**-statements and ↠-statements to occur in normal methods. This restriction, however, forces the programmer to manually re-engineer the program which can be cumbersome. Instead of the programmer manually changing the program, the compiler uses method inlining to ensure that all **schedule**-statements and ↠-statements are located in **task** methods.

The input to this normalization step is the call-graph of the program. In a call-graph, nodes represent methods and a directed edge between two nodes m() and n() exists if method m() may call method n().

Inlining is a mechanism that replaces all calls to a method n() inside a method m() with copies of the body of n(). Given two method nodes m() and n() with a call edge m()→n(), inlining method n() into method m() effectively increases the code size of m() (because it now also contains the code of n()) but it also removes the edge m()→n() from the call-graph.

A single virtual call site, where the exact method implementation depends on the runtime type of the receiver object, can result in multiple edges in the call-graph, one for each possible concrete method implementation. When inlining the virtual call, the virtual dispatch mechanism can be made explicit in the caller by choosing the correct implementation depending on the object type. For example, consider two classes A and B where B extends A and both classes have a concrete implementation of a method m(), called m$1() and m$2() respectively. Then, a virtual call of the form obj.m() can be expanded into a form without virtual calls:

```
if(obj instanceof B) {
  obj.m$2();
} else {
  obj.m$1();
}
```

Once all virtual call-sites have been expanded, the compiler starts inlining non-**task** methods that contain **schedule**-statements and/or ↠-statements into their callers. The inlining process stops when only task methods and methods unreachable in the call graph contain **schedule**-statements and ↠-statements. The expanded control-flow graphs of the task methods (with inlined non-task methods where necessary) are the input to the rest of the schedule analysis.

**Pruning of exception edges of uncaught exceptions** As described in Section 3.4, the exception handling mechanism of the task model specifies that the program execution is terminated whenever there is an uncaught exception in any of the running tasks. This behavior is more than

## 4.2. THE SCHEDULE ANALYSIS ALGORITHM

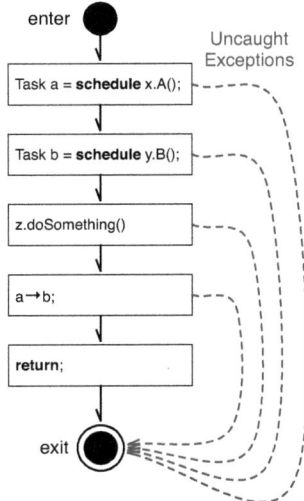

Figure 4.6: Control-flow graph with exception edges representing uncaught exceptions.

just a description of the runtime implementation; it is somewhat fundamental for the correctness of the schedule analysis and ensures that the schedule analysis can extract any meaningful information.

Imagine that uncaught exceptions were defined to only terminate the current task but not the whole program. Further, imagine the following simple task:

```
task T() {
  Task a = schedule x.A();
  Task b = schedule y.B();
  z.doSomething();
  a→b;
}
```

Every single line in the above example can throw exceptions, such as an OutOfMemoryError or a NullPointerException. If only the task $\mathcal{T}$ currently executing T() would be terminated on such an uncaught exception, the schedule analysis could not legally deduce that x.A()→y.B() because the statement a→b may never be executed in the case of an exception.[4]

The uncertainty that uncaught exceptions bring to the analysis comes from their corresponding edges in the control-flow graph. Figure 4.6 depicts the control-flow graph for the above example of task T(). The dashed edges represent exceptional control flow. When analyzing the exit node, the analysis merges all the facts that were computed for the nodes at the source of the incoming control-flow edges. Because it must do so conservatively, it can only rely on →-statements that were executed on all possible control flows. In the example, the analysis

---

[4]Another approach to terminating the whole program could be to automatically un-schedule child tasks when the parent is terminated with an uncaught exception.

therefore must conclude that a→b may not be executed and therefore cannot extract any meaningful information.

However, knowing that uncaught exceptions will terminate the program execution, the analysis can prune all exceptional control-flow edges that lead into the exit node. Exceptional control-flow for exceptions that are explicitly caught by the programmer, however, remain in the control-flow graph. If the body of task method T() would be wrapped in a **try/catch**-block, for example, the analysis would (correctly) conclude that tasks x.A() and y.B() may be scheduled but not ordered.

### 4.2.2 Step 2: Extracting the loop-contextualized task-variable ordering graph

The second step of analyzing a task method is to extract information about the effects of →-statements on the ordering of local tasks variables. The difficulty is to decide for each →-statement whether it orders the tasks conditionally or unconditionally and to compute the ordering effects of →-statements when tasks are scheduled inside loops. As an example, consider this simplified version of the sor example from Figure 3.3 with only one barrier and only the second phase phase2:

```
task Round() {
  Task barrier = schedule this.Barrier();
  Task phase2 = schedule this.phase2();
  Task nextRound = schedule this.Round();
  barrier→phase2;
  phase2→nextRound;
}
```

Because all three schedule sites execute unconditionally, we can conclude that the two happens-before edges have the transitive effect of ordering barrier and nextRound. This conclusion is not true, however, if any node on a transitive path may be scheduled conditionally, as in the following example:

```
task Round() {
  Task barrier = schedule this.Barrier();
  Task nextRound = schedule this.nextRound();
  while(random()) {
    Task phase2 = schedule this.Phase2();
    barrier→phase2;
    phase2→nextRound;
  }
}
```

Here, if random() is **false** already the first time, the schedule site at phase2 is never executed and the two happens-before edges are not created. Therefore, it is not guaranteed that barrier and nextRound are transitively ordered in all cases, and so the analysis must consider them to be potentially parallel. However, no matter how many Phase2() tasks are scheduled inside the loop, the analysis should conclude that all Phase2() tasks are ordered with respect to barrier and nextRound and that the Phase2() tasks are not ordered among themselves. If the

## 4.2. THE SCHEDULE ANALYSIS ALGORITHM

`while` loop is replaced with a `do/while` loop, the loop will be executed at least once and so the analysis may conclude that tasks `barrier` and `nextRound` are ordered transitively.

Tasks are commonly scheduled inside loops or recursive methods (which are translated into loops by the method inlining done during normalization). Therefore, it is important for the precision of the whole analysis to recognize scheduling patterns across loops. The goal of this step is to extract as much scheduling and ordering information from loops as possible.

This section describes a *data-flow analysis* that keeps track of the loop context in which schedule sites are executed. The result of this step is a graph where nodes are loop-context/task-variable pairs and edges represent genuine →-edges that are created by →-statements. The data-flow analysis is a standard fixed-point analysis on the control-flow graph (CFG) of the task method. The analysis is defined as a transfer function $Trans$ that, given the the entry state $State_{in}(n)$ of a control-flow block $n$, computes the exit state $State_{out}(n)$ for that block:

$$State_{out}(n) = Trans(State_{in}(n)).$$

The *State* values are propagated between control-flow graph nodes using the meet operator ⊓. The meet operator ⊓ combines the output states of all predecessors $pred(n)$ of $n$ into the input state $State_{in}(n)$ that is used by the transfer function:

$$State_{in}(n) = \bigsqcap_{m \in pred(n)} State_{out}(m).$$

The data-flow analysis ends once the states reach a fixed point and do not change any more.

After introducing the running example, the following sections formally define the *State* value, the meet operator ⊓, and the transfer function $Trans$.

**Running example**

Table 4.1 shows how the data-flow analysis progresses for the running example of the `sor` benchmark. For this simple example, the data-flow analysis only requires a single iteration. Table 4.1 shows each of the four data-flow-value components for the interesting basic blocks. Basic blocks that simply forward the flow-value without changes were omitted from the figure.

For the $TaskVars_{out}(n)$, Table 4.1 only shows the full loop-context/task-variable pair the first time the task variable is defined. After that, a unique integer ID is used to clarify the presentation. The same integer IDs are also used in $VarMap_{out}(n)$ and $HBEdges_{out}(n)$.

We re-visit the example from Table 4.1 frequently throughout this section and explain in detail how each data-flow-value component is computed. Section 4.2.2 presents a second example with a more complex task schedule where happens-before relationships are created between tasks that are scheduled in different loop iterations.

**The data-flow value $State(n)$**

The data-flow value $State(n)$ that flows in and out of each block $n$ is a complex value consisting of four parts:

| | entry | BB2 | BB4 | BB5 |
|---|---|---|---|---|
| **iteration 1** | | | | |
| $LoopCtxts_{out}(n)$ | $\{\varepsilon\}$ | $\{\varepsilon\}$ | $\{\varepsilon\},\{\varepsilon,\ell\}$ | $\{\varepsilon\},\{\varepsilon,\ell\}$ |
| $TaskVars_{out}(n)$ | $0:[\{\varepsilon\},\mathbf{now}]$ $1:[\{\varepsilon\},\mathtt{later}]$ | $0,1,$ $2:[\{\varepsilon\},\mathtt{nextRound}],$ $3:[\{\varepsilon\},\mathtt{barrier}]$ | $0,1,2,3$ $4:[\{\varepsilon,\ell\},\mathbf{now}],$ $5:[\{\varepsilon,\ell\},\mathtt{later}],$ $6:[\{\varepsilon,\ell\},\mathtt{nextRound}],$ $7:[\{\varepsilon,\ell\},\mathtt{barrier}]$ | $0,1,2,3,4,5,6,7,$ $8:[\{\varepsilon\},\mathtt{phase1}],$ $9:[\{\varepsilon\},\mathtt{phase2}],$ $10:[\{\varepsilon,\ell\},\mathtt{phase1}],$ $11:[\{\varepsilon,\ell\},\mathtt{phase2}]$ |
| $VarMap_{out}(n)$ | ∅ | ∅ | $4\mapsto\{0\},$ $5\mapsto\{1\},$ $6\mapsto\{2\},$ $7\mapsto\{3\}$ | $4\mapsto\{0\},$ $5\mapsto\{1\},$ $6\mapsto\{2\},$ $7\mapsto\{3\}$ |
| $HBEdges_{out}(n)$ | ∅ | (graph: 0→3, 0→2→1) | (graph: 0→3, 0→2→1) | (graph with nodes 0,8,9,3,2,1,10,11) |

Table 4.1: Extracting the loop-sensitive task-variable ordering graph from the sor example.

$$State(n) := \begin{cases} LoopCtxts(n) \\ TaskVars(n) \\ VarMap(n) \\ HBEdges(n) \end{cases}$$

$LoopCtxts(n)$ keeps track of the loop contexts in which block $n$ may be executed. A single loop context $lc$ is a set of back-edges $e \in BackEdges$ from the control-flow graph. The loop context $lc$ contains a back-edge $e$ if the edge may have been taken one or more times in the control flow that is represented by this loop context. A special element $\varepsilon$ (the 'empty' loop) is used in loop contexts to represent the first execution where no back-edge has been taken yet.

The $LoopCtxts(n)$-part of a state $State(n)$ is a set of loop contexts (which are sets of back-edges). The set of loop contexts $LoopCtxts(n)$ at a given block $n$ represents the possible paths through the control-flow graph that, starting from the *entry* node, can reach block $n$. As an example, consider a control-flow graph with two nested loops represented by back-edges $\ell$ and $\wp$. For a block $n$ that is outside both loops (that is, there is no looping path from $n$ to $n$ that contains either $\ell$ or $\wp$) the only possible loop context during analysis is $\{\varepsilon\}$ (assuming no other back-edges exist). For a block $m$ that is inside the two loops (that is, the CFG contains at least one path from $m$ to $m$ that contains $\ell$ and at least one path that contains $\wp$) the analysis will compute $LoopCtxts(m) = \{\{\varepsilon\},\{\varepsilon,\ell\},\{\varepsilon,\wp\},\{\varepsilon,\ell,\wp\}\}$. Those loop contexts represent the facts that $m$ can be reached directly without taking any back-edge: $\{\varepsilon\}$; that $m$ can be reached multiple times, first directly and then by looping around only $\ell$: $\{\varepsilon,\ell\}$; that $n$ can be reached multiple times, first directly and then by looping around only $\wp$: $\{\varepsilon,\wp\}$; and that $n$ can be reached multiple times, first directly and then arbitrarily looping around $\ell$ and $\wp$: $\{\varepsilon,\ell,\wp\}$.

$TaskVars(n)$ contains *loop-contextualized* copies of the SSA task variables, that is, SSA task variables that are additionally distinguished by a loop context. A loop-

## 4.2. THE SCHEDULE ANALYSIS ALGORITHM

contextualized task variable is represented as a loop-context/SSA-task-variable pair. In the previous example, assume that block $m$ inside the nested loops contains a schedule site that defines task variable $t_1$. Given the active loop contexts at $m$, $LoopCtxts(m) = \{\varepsilon\}, \{\varepsilon, \ell\}, \{\varepsilon, \wp\}, \{\varepsilon, \ell, \wp\}$, the analysis will consider the loop-contextualized task variables: $TaskVars(m) = \{[\{\varepsilon\}, t_1], [\{\varepsilon, \ell\}, t_1]\}, [\{\varepsilon, \wp\}, t_1]\}, [\{\varepsilon, \ell, \wp\}, t_1]\}$. Loop-contextualization effectively creates clones of task variables (and their corresponding schedule sites) representing all combinations of different loop iterations.

$VarMap(n)$ is a simple mapping from an element in $TaskVars(n)$ to a set of other elements of $TaskVars(n)$. $VarMap(n)$ keeps track of aliasing between loop-contextualized task variables resulting from Φ-functions and loop-invariant task variables.

$HBEdges(n)$ contains happens-before edges between elements of $TaskVars(n)$. By the way the rules of the data-flow analysis are designed, $HBEdges(n)$ only contains edges between elements of $TaskVars(n)$ for which no mapping exists in $VarMap(n)$. That is, $a \to b \in HBEdges(n) \implies a \notin Keys(VarMap(n)) \land b \notin Keys(VarMap(n))$.

**The result.** The result of this analysis step is the loop-contextualized task-variable ordering graph $G$. $G$ is given by the $TaskVars$ and $HBEdges$ components of the input state computed for the *exit* node of the CFG: $G = \{TaskVars_{in}(exit), HBEdges_{in}(exit)\}$. This graph is the only input to the subsequent schedule analysis steps; the other data-flow values computed in this step can be discarded.

**Initial states** $State_{in}(n)$ **and** $State_{out}(n)$. For all basic blocks $n$ of the CFG other than the *entry* node, we initialize each component of $State_{in}(n)$ and $State_{out}(n)$ to the empty set ∅.

The *entry* node, $State_{out}(entry)$ is defined as follows, where $TaskParam$ is a set of those SSA task variables that are input parameters to the current task method:

$$State_{out}(entry) := \begin{cases} LoopCtxts_{out}(entry) &= \{\{\varepsilon\}\} \\ TaskVars_{out}(entry) &= [\{\varepsilon\}, \mathbf{now}] \cup \{[\{\varepsilon\}, p] \mid p \in TaskParam\} \\ VarMap_{out}(entry) &= \varnothing \\ HBEdges_{out}(entry) &= \varnothing \end{cases}$$

The Round() task method from the sor example has one explicit task parameter later and the implicit task parameter **now**. The initial state $TaskVars_{out}(entry)$ in Table 4.1 therefore contains two elements for **now** and later, both in the empty loop context $\{\varepsilon\}$.

**The meet operator ⊓**

The meet operator ⊓ defines how the input state $State_{in}(n)$ for a block $n$ is computed. The meet operator merges the out states of all predecessor blocks of $n$ to compute $State_{in}(n) = \sqcap_{m \in pred(n)} State_{out}(m)$. Because of the complex nature of the *State* flow-value, the following paragraphs define ⊓ for each component of *State* individually.

**Computing** $LoopCtxts_{in}(n)$: Computing $LoopCtxts_{in}(n)$ is basically done by merging all loop contexts of the predecessor nodes. However, if $n$ is a loop head, we must also expand the incoming loop contexts with back-edges that may end in $n$. In addition, we can kill those loop contexts that contain back-edges that do not loop around $n$.

For a block $n$, we define the *ReachingLCs* to be the set of loop contexts that can reach $n$:

$$ReachingLCs(n) := \left( \bigcup_{m \in preds(n)} LoopCtxts_{out}(m) \right) \times \{x \rightarrow n \mid x \rightarrow n \in BackEdges\}.$$

The basis for this set is the set-union of all predecessor's *LoopCtxts*. Each loop context in this set is expanded by the back-edges $x \rightarrow n$ that end in the current node $n$. The expansion operator $LCs \times BEs$ expands each loop context in $LCs$ on the left-hand side by all possible combinations of back edges (that is, the power-set $\mathcal{P}$) from the right-hand side:

$$LCs \times BEs := \bigcup_{lc \in LCs} \left( \bigcup_{edges \in \mathcal{P}(BEs)} lc \cup edges \right).$$

Given an incoming loop context $\{\varepsilon\}$ and two back-edges $\ell$ and $\wp$ ending in $n$, the $\times$ operation yields the loop contexts: $\{\{\varepsilon\}, \{\varepsilon, \ell\}, \{\varepsilon, \wp\}, \{\varepsilon, \ell, \wp\}\}$.

At block $n$, the analysis kills all loop contexts from $ReachingLCs(n)$ that are not current at $n$. A loop context $lc$ is not current at $n$ if it contains a back-edge $x \rightarrow y$ that is not a loop edge for $n$. We say that $x \rightarrow y$ loops around $n$ if the control-flow graph contains at least one path from $n$ to $n$ that contains $x \rightarrow y$:

$$KillLCs(n) := \{lc \in LoopCtxts_{in}(n) \mid \exists x \rightarrow y \in lc \text{ such that } x \rightarrow y \text{ does not loop around } n\}.$$

By killing all loop contexts that do not actually loop around $n$, $LoopCtxts(n)$ contains only "active" loop contexts. Note, however, that killing elements from $LoopCtxts(n)$ does not affect the other components of $State(n)$. Particularly, no elements are removed from $TaskVars(n)$ by this operation.

Using the definitions for $ReachingLCs(n)$ and $KillLCs(n)$, the meet operator for $LoopCtxts_{in}(n)$ becomes:

$$LoopCtxts_{in}(n) := ReachingLCs(n) \setminus KillLCs(n).$$

In the sor example CFG from Figure 4.3 and from Table 4.1, computing $LoopCtxts_{in}(BB4)$ of the join-block $BB4$ results in the set of loop contexts $\{\{\varepsilon\}, \{\varepsilon, \ell\}\}$ by expanding the incoming loop context $\{\varepsilon\}$ from $BB2$ with the back edge $\ell$. Because basic block $BB5$ is inside the loop of $\ell$, no loop contexts are killed and therefore $LoopCtxts_{out}(BB4) = LoopCtxts_{in}(BB5) = \{\{\varepsilon\}, \{\varepsilon, \ell\}\}$. At the **return** block $BB7$ (not shown in Table 4.1), however, the loop context containing $\ell$ would be killed resulting in $LoopCtxts_{out}(BB7) = \{\{\varepsilon\}\}$.

## 4.2. THE SCHEDULE ANALYSIS ALGORITHM

**Computing $TaskVars_{in}(n)$ and $VarMap_{in}(n)$:** The basic operation when computing task variables flowing into basic block $n$ is to union all task variables that were defined by all predecessors. However, if $n$ is a loop-head, we must save task variables that are invariant to the loop across loop iterations. In SSA, loop invariant task variables are simply all task variables that were defined before block $n$.

To clarify this idea, consider a loop-contextualized task variable $[lc, \text{a}]$ that has been defined before block $n$ and $n$ is a loop-head for a back-edge $m \rightarrow n$. A use of the SSA-variable a inside the loop will always refer to the loop-invariant task variable $[lc, \text{a}]$, regardless of how often the control-flow includes the edge $m \rightarrow n$. The analysis models this behavior by creating a mapping $[lc \cup \{m \rightarrow n\}, \text{a}] \mapsto [lc, \text{a}]$ in $VarMap(n)$ that maps a inside the loop to the loop-invariant task variable from before the loop.

The task variables that are invariant to a loop starting at node $n$ (if any) are the task variables that flow into $n$ through non-back-edges:

$$InvariantTaskVars(n) := \bigcup_{m \in pred(n) \text{ where } m \rightarrow n \notin BackEdges} TaskVars_{out}(m).$$

The new task variables generated at node $n$ are then all the invariant task variables extended by each back-edge ending in $n$:

$$GenTaskVars(n) := \{[lc \cup \{m \rightarrow n\}, \text{a}] \mid [lc, \text{a}] \in InvariantTaskVars(n) \\ \wedge m \rightarrow n \in BackEdges\}.$$

Given $GenTaskVars(n)$, computing $TaskVars_{in}(n)$ is a simple set union that collects all the incoming task variables and adds the generated information:

$$TaskVars_{in}(n) := \left( \bigcup_{m \in pred(n)} TaskVars_{out}(m) \right) \cup GenTaskVars(n)$$

Computing the mappings $VarMap_{in}(n)$ is somewhat more complex because it pursues two goals: First, we must save loop invariant task variables from one loop iteration to the next by mapping the loop-contextualized task variable inside the loop to its corresponding loop invariant counterpart. Second, if a task variable is updated inside a loop and escapes the loop, we must capture the fact that the task variable after the loop will point to the value from the last iteration.

The first goal is computed by the function $GenVarMaps(n)$. For each loop-contextualized task variable that is invariant to the current loop, $GenVarMaps(n)$ contains a mapping from the version inside the loop to the loop invariant version:

$$GenVarMaps(n) := \{[lc \cup \{m \rightarrow n\}, \text{a}] \mapsto [lc, \text{a}] \mid [lc, \text{a}] \in InvariantTaskVars(n) \\ \wedge m \rightarrow n \in BackEdges\}.$$

The second goal is implemented by the two functions *KilledPhis(n)* and *EscapeLoop(n)*. In SSA-form, a variable can only escape a loop through a Φ-variable and every Φ variable generates at least one entry in *VarMaps(n)*. On exiting a loop $\ell$, we first kill all mappings of Φ variables associated with $\ell$ and then add new mappings for the remaining loop contexts (that do not contain $\ell$) to point to the last version created in the loop.

We define the function *KilledPhis(n)* to collect all Φ task-variables that were defined in a predecessor node $m \in preds(n)$, where $m$ is a loop head for an edge that does not loop around $n$:

$$KilledPhis(n) := \{a \mid \text{a is } \Phi \text{ variable defined in } m$$
$$\wedge m \in preds(n)$$
$$\wedge x \to m \in BackEdges$$
$$\wedge x \to m \text{ does not loop around } n\}.$$

For each killed task variable $a \in KilledPhis(n)$ and each remaining loop context $lc \in LoopCtxts_{in}(n)$, the function *EscapeLoop(n)* creates a mapping from $[lc, a]$ to the most specific task variable version from inside the loop:

$$EscapeLoop(n) := \{[lc, a] \mapsto spec \mid a \in KilledPhis(n)$$
$$\wedge lc \in LoopCtxts_{in}(n)$$
$$\wedge a \text{ is } \Phi \text{ defined in } m$$
$$\wedge spec \text{ is most specific version in } m\}.$$

The most specific version of a task variable is the version with the most specific (that is, longest) loop context of a task variable definition from inside the loop. If no most specific version can be found (e.g., for a loop that schedules tasks conditionally), the most specific version is the empty set. Given the functions *GenVarMaps(n)*, *KilledPhis(n)* and *EscapeLoop(n)*, the meet operator for *VarMap$_{in}$(n)* is defined as:

$$VarMap_{in}(n) := \left( \left( \left( \bigcup_{m \in preds(n)} VarMap_{out}(m) \right) \cup GenVarMaps(n) \right) \setminus KilledPhis(n) \right) \cup EscapeLoop(n)$$

In the running example from Figure 4.3 and Table Table 4.1, basic block *BB4* is a loop-head for the back-edge $\ell$. The existing task variables with IDs $0, 1, 2$, and $3$ are forwarded from *BB2* to *BB4* due to the set-union of the predecessors' task variables. At *BB4*, task variables $0, 1, 2$, and $3$ are also loop invariant. Therefore, *GenTaskVars(BB4)* extends those loop invariant variables with the loop edge $\ell$, resulting in the task variables with IDs $4, 5, 6$, and $7$, and *GenVarMaps(BB)* maps those new versions to their loop invariant counterparts.

In the second analysis iteration (not shown in Table 4.1), the task variables generated inside the loop at basic block *BB5* (IDs $8, 9, 10, 11$) would be merged back into *TaskVars$_{in}$(BB4)*.

## 4.2. THE SCHEDULE ANALYSIS ALGORITHM

However, because those task variables are not loop invariant, *GenTaskVars(BB4)* will not expand them in the second analysis iteration and no new task variables will be created.

This example does not contain $\Phi$ task variables and therefore no mappings are killed and re-mapped on the loop exit. Section 4.2.2 presents an example that demonstrates the handling of $\Phi$ task variables.

**Computing $HBEdges_{in}(n)$:** When multiple control flows meet at a join node in the CFG, the analysis must only consider happens-before edges that are genuine. If there is a flow through the CFG, for example, where two task variables are ordered and another flow where the same task variables are not ordered, the analysis must conservatively assume unordered-ness.

$KillHBEdges(n)$ computes the set of edges that are not genuine at node $n$. For all pairs $o, p$ of predecessor blocks of $n$, $KillHBEdges(n)$ checks that if $o$ and $p$ both "know" about two loop-contextualized task variables $[lc_1,\mathsf{a}]$ and $[lc_2,\mathsf{b}]$, they also agree on the existence of an happens-before edge $[lc_1,\mathsf{a}] \to [lc_2,\mathsf{b}]$. If block $o$ contains the edge $[lc_1,\mathsf{a}] \to [lc_2,\mathsf{b}]$ but block $p$ does not, the edge must be killed at $n$:

$$KillHBEdges(n) := \{[lc_1,\mathsf{a}] \to [lc_2,\mathsf{b}] \mid \exists o, p \in preds(n) \text{ such that}$$
$$[lc_1,\mathsf{a}],[lc_2,\mathsf{b}] \in TaskVars_{out}(o) \land [lc_1,\mathsf{a}],[lc_2,\mathsf{b}] \in TaskVars_{out}(p)$$
$$\land [lc_1,\mathsf{a}] \to [lc_2,\mathsf{b}] \in HBEdges_{out}(o) \land [lc_1,\mathsf{a}] \to [lc_2,\mathsf{b}] \notin HBEdges_{out}(p)\}$$

Given $KillHBEdges(n)$, the meet operator for $HBEdges_{in}(n)$ is simply the union of all $HBEdges_{out}(m)$ for all predecessors $m$ minus the happens-before edges that are killed at $n$:

$$HBEdges_{in}(n) := \left( \bigcup_{m \in pred(n)} HBEdges_{out}(m) \right) \setminus KillHBEdges(n)$$

In the example analysis shown in Table 4.1, no edges are killed at *BB4*. Even though (temporarily) the incoming control flows contain different happens-before edges, they only disagree on happens-before edges of disjoint sets of task variables.

Also no edges are killed at the **return** block *BB7*. $HBEdges_{out}(BB1)$ coming from $BB1 \to BB7$ does not contain any happens-before edges while ultimately $HBEdges_{out}(BB5)$ represents the whole resulting graph. Because *BB1* does not know about any of the task variables, however, the meet operation at *BB7* can keep all happens-before edges, concluding that if any of the task variables in $TaskVar_{out}(BB4)$ is created, the edges in $HBEdges_{out}(BB4)$ are created, too.

**Node transfer function**

The transfer function *Trans* of the data-flow analysis takes the input state $State_{in}(n)$ of a block $n$ and computes $State_{out}(n)$ depending on the body of $n$:

$$State_{out}(n) = Trans(State_{in}(n)).$$

For simplifying the presentation of the formulas, we assume that a basic block $n$ in the control-flow graph consists of at most one statement. It is straight forward to explode a complex basic block that consists of a list of statements (such as the basic blocks from the running example) into a chain of small basic blocks each of which contains at most one statement.

For all statements $s$ that are unrelated to task scheduling and task ordering, the transfer function is the identity function and leaves the state unchanged: $Trans_s := State_{out}(n) = State_{in}(n)$. This leaves four statements that have a non-trivial transfer function, namely **schedule**-statements, →-statements, assignment of task variables, and SSA-Φ-functions for task variables. The following paragraphs explain each of those four cases in detail.

**schedule statements:** The statement a = **schedule** A() at node $n$ defines the SSA-variable a. The corresponding transfer function $Trans_{\text{a = schedule A()}}$ adds a loop-contextualized task variable $[lc, \text{a}]$ for each loop context $lc \in LoopCtxts_{in}(n)$ the statement may be executed in. Formally, the set of loop-contextualized task variables defined by statement a = **schedule** A() is defined as:

$$DefinedTVs(n) := \bigcup_{lc \in LoopCtxts_{in}(n)} [lc, \text{a}].$$

When a loop-contextualized task variable $tv$ is defined, we remove all edges from the set $HBEdges_{in}(n)$ that have $tv$ as a source or target node. Killing those edges makes sure, that an edge created inside a loop does not get propagated to control-flow paths where the edge is not created when the data-flow analysis visits $n$ multiple times. For genuine edges, the edges will be re-created when the block with the corresponding →-statement is visited again. Given $DefinedTVs(n)$, $KillEdges(n)$ computes the edges that must be killed:

$$KillEdges(n) := \{x \to y \mid x \in DefinedTVs(n) \vee y \in DefinedTVs(n)\}.$$

With $DefinedTVs(n)$ and $KillEdges(n)$, the transfer function for the statement a = **schedule** A() at node $n$ is:

$$Trans_{\text{a = schedule A()}} := \begin{cases} LoopCtxts_{out}(n) &= LoopCtxts_{in}(n) \\ TaskVars_{out}(n) &= TaskVars_{in}(n) \cup DefinedTVs(n) \\ VarMap_{out}(n) &= VarMap_{in}(n) \\ HBEdges_{out}(n) &= HBEdges_{in}(n) \smallsetminus KillEdges(n) \end{cases}$$

In the running example from Table 4.1, if $BB5$ were visited a second time, the first two **schedule** statements in $BB5$ would kill the edges $8 \to 3$, $10 \to 3$, $3 \to 9$, $3 \to 11$, $9 \to 2$, and $11 \to 2$, effectively "re-setting" $HBEdges(BB5)$ to the state of $HBEdges(BB2)$. However, all those edges are immediately re-created by the two subsequent →-statements.

**→-statements:** A statement a→b at node $n$ defines edges in $HBEdges_{out}(n)$. In each loop context $lc \in LoopCtxts_{in}(n)$, a and b are represented by different loop-contextualized versions $[lc, \text{a}]$ and $[lc, \text{b}]$.

## 4.2. THE SCHEDULE ANALYSIS ALGORITHM

*VarMap(n)* contains mappings for loop-contextualized versions of loop invariant task variables as well as task variables defined by $\Phi$-functions. The function *Deref* "de-references" a task variable $[lc, \mathtt{a}]$ into a set of mapped task variables. If $VarMap_{in}(n)$ contains one or more mappings for $[lc, \mathtt{a}]$, *Deref* returns the set of the mapped loop-contextualized task variables. If no mappings are found, *Deref* returns a singleton set containing $[lc, \mathtt{a}]$:

$$Deref([lc, \mathtt{a}]) := \begin{cases} \bigcup_{[lc,\mathtt{a}] \mapsto tv \in VarMap_{in}(n)} tv & \text{if } [lc, \mathtt{a}] \in Keys(VarMap_{in}(n)), \\ \{[lc, \mathtt{a}]\} & \text{else.} \end{cases}$$

The edges defined by statement a→b are then the edges between the task variables of the left-hand side and right-hand side de-referenced in each loop context $lc$:

$$DefinedHBEdges(n) := \bigcup_{lc \in LoopCtxts_{in}(n)} Deref([lc, \mathtt{a}]) \overset{\cup}{\to} Deref([lc, \mathtt{b}]).$$

The operation $A \overset{\cup}{\to} B$ creates an edge for all combinations of task variables from the left-hand side and the right-hand side. Given the function $DefinedHBEdges(n)$, the transfer function for statement a→b at node $n$ is:

$$Trans_{\mathtt{a} \to \mathtt{b}} := \begin{cases} LoopCtxts_{out}(n) &= LoopCtxts_{in}(n) \\ TaskVars_{out}(n) &= TaskVars_{in}(n) \\ VarMap_{out}(n) &= VarMap_{in}(n) \\ HBEdges_{out}(n) &= HBEdges_{in}(n) \cup DefinedHBEdges(n) \end{cases}$$

In the example from Table 4.1 the row labeled $HBEdges_{out}(n)$ shows the evolution of $HBEdges(n)$ and the happens-before edges created by the →-statements in *BB2* and *BB5*. The edges created in *BB2* (and its only loop context $\{\varepsilon\}$) are simply propagated to *BB3*, *BB4*, and *BB5*.

The meet operation $\sqcap$ at *BB4* then adds another loop context $\{\varepsilon, \ell\}$ for the back-edge $\ell$ and creates mappings for the loop invariant task variables now, later, nextRound, and barrier.

Basic block *BB5* contains the three →-statements phase1→barrier, barrier→phase2, and phase2→nextRound. For loop context $\{\varepsilon\}$, $DefinedHBEdges(BB5)$ adds happens-before edges between the corresponding task variables, resulting in the edges 8→3, 3→9, 9→2.

For the second loop context $\{\varepsilon, \ell\}$, $Deref([\{\varepsilon, \ell\}, \mathtt{barrier}])$ finds a mapping in $VarMap_{in}(BB5)$ which it uses to de-reference $[\{\varepsilon, \ell\}, \mathtt{barrier}]$ to $[\{\varepsilon\}, \mathtt{barrier}]$ (ID3). Similarly, $[\{\varepsilon, \ell\}, \mathtt{nextRound}]$ is re-referenced to $[\{\varepsilon\}, \mathtt{nextRound}]$ (ID2). For the loop context $\{\varepsilon, \ell\}$, the three →-statements therefore result in the edges 10→3, 3→11, and 11→2.

The mapping of the loop invariant task variables from the inner iteration context $\{\varepsilon, \ell\}$ to the outer context $\{\varepsilon\}$ creates the "double diamond pattern" shown in the graph of basic block *BB5* in Table 4.1. This graph contains enough information for the subsequent steps to deduce that the Round() task method may schedule multiple unordered phase1 tasks (IDs 8 and 10) which are all ordered before a single barrier task (ID 3). Further, the barrier is ordered before potentially multiple phase2 tasks (IDs 9 and 11) which are ordered before a single nextRound (ID 2). Finally, nextRound is ordered before the task-parameter later (ID 1).

**Assignment statements involving task variables:** An assignment b = a between two SSA task variables a and b at node $n$ results in the definition of a loop-contextualized version of b for each loop context $lc \in LoopCtxts_{in}(n)$. In addition, for each loop context $lc$ we add a mapping from the corresponding version of b to the corresponding version of a to capture the semantics of the assignment:

$$Trans_{\texttt{a = b}} := \begin{cases} LoopCtxts_{out}(n) &= LoopCtxts_{in}(n) \\ TaskVars_{out}(n) &= TaskVars_{in}(n) \cup \{[lc,\texttt{b}] \mid lc \in LoopCtxts_{in}(n)\} \\ VarMap_{out}(n) &= VarMap_{in}(n) \cup \{[lc,\texttt{b}] \mapsto [lc,\texttt{a}] \mid lc \in LoopCtxts_{in}(n)\} \\ HBEdges_{out}(n) &= HBEdges_{in}(n) \end{cases}$$

**Φ-function statements involving task variables:** Whenever multiple SSA-copies of a single source-code variable reach a join node in the control-flow graph, an SSA-Φ-function defines a new copy of the variable and lists the reaching SSA copies in its arguments. In the Φ-function, the argument position corresponds to a particular control-flow predecessor. For a Φ-statement $\texttt{a}_\Phi = \Phi(\texttt{a}_1, \ldots, \texttt{a}_i)$ we define a function $edge(\texttt{a}_j)$ that, given an argument $\texttt{a}_j$ with $1 \leq j \leq i$, returns the corresponding control-flow edge $m \rightarrow n$ that the parameter represents. Using $edge(\texttt{a}_j)$, we can classify each parameter $\texttt{a}_j$ of a node $n$ by whether $edge(\texttt{a}_j)$ is a back edge or not.

In a given loop context $lc$, a parameter $\texttt{a}_j$ that does *not* correspond to a back edge only contributes to the final Φ variable if $lc$ does not represent a context where the loop at $n$ has been taken; that is, $lc$ must not contain any back edge $m \rightarrow n$ that ends in $n$. In this case, we call $lc$ to be *loop invariant* at node $n$. For a given loop context $lc$, a parameter $\texttt{a}_j$ that *does* correspond to a back edge contributes to the final Φ variable if $edge(\texttt{a}_i)$ is present in $lc$. In this case, we de-reference the value of $\texttt{a}_j$ in $lc$ (for the case where the loop has been taken) as well as in context $lc \smallsetminus edge(\texttt{a}_j)$ (for the case where the loop is entered for the first time). The auxiliary helper function $MapInLC(lc, \texttt{a}_j)$ computes the contribution of parameter $\texttt{a}_j$ in a given loop context $lc$ as a generated mapping for the Φ variable defined by statement $\texttt{a}_\Phi = \Phi(\texttt{a}_1, \ldots, \texttt{a}_i)$:

$$MapInLC(lc, \texttt{a}_j) := \begin{cases} [lc, \texttt{a}_\Phi] \mapsto Deref(lc, \texttt{a}_j) & \text{if } edge(\texttt{a}_j) \notin BackEdges \\ & \land lc \text{ is loop invariant at } n \\ [lc, \texttt{a}_\Phi] \mapsto Deref(lc, \texttt{a}_j) \cup Deref(lc \smallsetminus edge(\texttt{a}_j), \texttt{a}_j) & \text{if } edge(\texttt{a}_j) \in BackEdges \\ & \land edge(\texttt{a}_j) \in lc \\ \emptyset & \text{else.} \end{cases}$$

The variable mappings generated by statement $\texttt{a}_\Phi = \Phi(\texttt{a}_1, \ldots, \texttt{a}_i)$ is then given as the union of single mappings over all current loop contexts and all parameters $\texttt{a}_1, \ldots, \texttt{a}_i$:

$$GenPhiMaps(n) := \bigcup_{lc \in LoopCtxts_{in}(n)} \left( \bigcup_{\texttt{a}_j \in \texttt{a}_1, \ldots, \texttt{a}_i} MapInLC(lc, \texttt{a}_j) \right).$$

In addition to the mappings in $GenPhiMaps(n)$, the transfer function for Φ functions also adds the loop-contextualized Φ-copy of the defined Φ task variable to $TaskVars_{out}(n)$:

## 4.2. THE SCHEDULE ANALYSIS ALGORITHM

```
1  class ChainedSteps {
2
3    task Start(int numRounds, Task later) {
4      Task prev = now;
5
6      for(int i = 0; i < numRounds; i++) {
7        Task step = schedule this.Step(i);
8        Task print = schedule this.Print(step);
9
10       prev→step;
11       step→print;
12
13       prev = step;
14     }
15
16     prev→later;
17   }
18
19   private task Step(int num) {
20     now.result = //do computation;
21   }
22
23   private task Print(Task step) {
24     System.out.println(step.result);
25   }
26 }
```

Figure 4.7: Example with happens-before edges between tasks that were scheduled in different loop iterations. The diagram on the right depicts the schedule for the case numRounds = 3.

$$Trans_{a_\Phi = \Phi(a_1,...,a_i)} := \begin{cases} LoopCtxts_{out}(n) & = & LoopCtxts_{in}(n) \\ TaskVars_{out}(n) & = & TaskVars_{in}(n) \cup \{[lc, a_\Phi] \mid lc \in NewLCs(n)\} \\ VarMap_{out}(n) & = & VarMap_{in}(n) \cup GenPhiMaps(n) \\ HBEdges_{out}(n) & = & HBEdges_{in}(n). \end{cases}$$

The running sor example from Table 4.1 does not include a task Φ-variable but the next section presents an example that demonstrates how task Φ-variables are handled by the analysis.

**Example for handling task Φ-variables**

This section presents an example that demonstrates how the data-flow analysis extracts the loop-contextualized task-variable ordering graph from a task method that includes task Φ-variables.

Figure 4.7 shows the program source and the resulting runtime schedule. The Start() task method contains a loop that schedules multiple Step() tasks and orders them in a linear chain.

The chain is created by keeping track of the previous, stored in variable prev, and ordering the current step to happen after the previous step prev on line 10. Initially, prev is set to now on

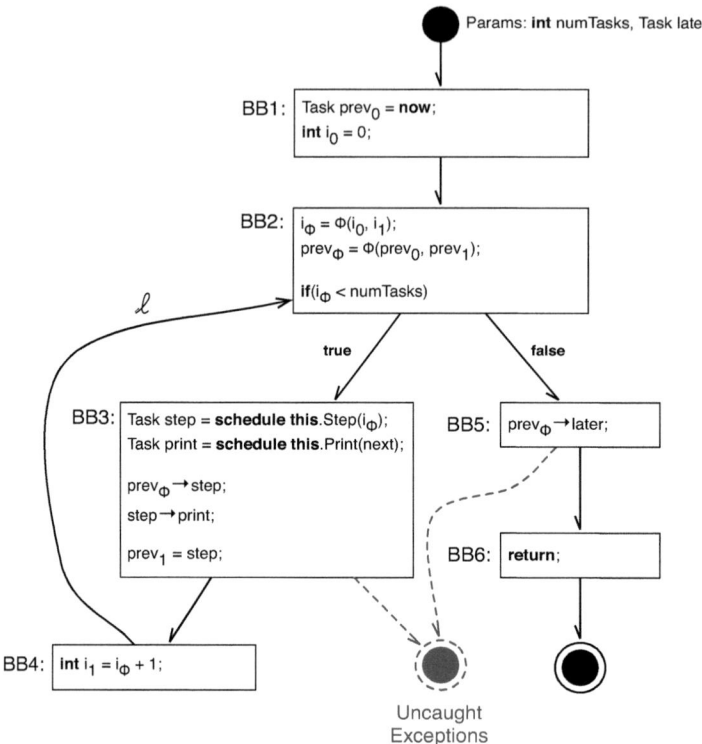

Figure 4.8: Control-flow graph for the Start() task method of the ChainedSteps class from Figure 4.7

line 4. At the end of each iteration, prev is updated on line 13 to reference the next step-task that was scheduled on line 7.

In addition to the chained Step() tasks, Start() also schedules one Print() task for each step on line 8. Because a print-task depends on the result of its corresponding step task (print prints the result of step on line 24), print is ordered after step on line stepHBPrint

The right side of Figure 4.7 shows the runtime schedule for the case where numRounds = 3. As expected, the Step() tasks together with the Start() task and later form an ordered chain. Each Print() task is ordered only with its one corresponding Step() task. The Print() tasks are unordered among themselves and they are unordered with respect to other Step() tasks.

The control-flow graph of the Start() method is shown in Figure 4.8. As in the sor example, the control-flow graph has only one back-edge $\ell$. However, the loop-head $BB2$ in this example contains a Φ-function for the task variable prev, representing the multiple assignments of prev on lines 4 and 13 in the static single-assignment form.

Table 4.2 presents the evolution of the data-flow value $State_{out}(n)$ for a selection of basic

## 4.2. THE SCHEDULE ANALYSIS ALGORITHM

blocks. The interesting part is the analysis of the task $\Phi$-variable $\text{prev}_\Phi$.

Due to the assignment $\text{prev}_0 = \text{now}$ in basic block $BB1$, $VarMap_{out}(BB1)$ maps $[\{\varepsilon\}, \text{prev}_0]$ (ID 2) to $[\{\varepsilon\}, \text{now}]$ (ID 0).

The loop head $BB2$ defines the task variable $\text{prev}_\Phi$ as either $\text{prev}_0$ (when coming from $BB1$) or $\text{prev}_1$ (when coming from $BB4$). In the first iteration, only $[\{\varepsilon\}, \text{prev}_0]$ (ID 2) is defined for the two variables $\text{prev}_0$ and $\text{prev}_1$ in the two current loop contexts $\{\varepsilon\}$ and $\{\varepsilon, \ell\}$. Therefore, the transfer function for $\text{prev}_\Phi = \Phi(\text{prev}_0, \text{prev}_1)$ creates for loop context $\{\varepsilon\}$ a mapping between $[\{\varepsilon\}, \text{prev}_\Phi]$ (ID 6) and $[\{\varepsilon\}, \text{now}]$ (ID 0) which was de-referenced from $[\{\varepsilon\}, \text{prev}_0]$ (ID 2). For the other loop context $\{\varepsilon, \ell\}$, variable $\text{prev}_\Phi$ is mapped to the empty set (ID 7).

The assignment $\text{prev}_1 = \text{step}$ in $BB3$ creates a mapping from $[\{\varepsilon\}, \text{prev}_1]$ (ID 10) to $[\{\varepsilon\}, \text{step}]$ (ID 8) for the $\{\varepsilon\}$ loop context; for $\{\varepsilon, \ell\}$, it creates a mapping $[\{\varepsilon, \ell\}, \text{prev}_1]$ (ID 13) to $[\{\varepsilon, \ell\}, \text{step}]$ (ID 11). After basic blocks $BB3$ and $BB4$ have been visited at least once, $\text{prev}_0$ and $\text{prev}_1$ are defined for both loop contexts. Therefore, when $BB2$ is visited in the second iteration, the transfer function for statement $\text{prev}_\Phi = \Phi(\text{prev}_0, \text{prev}_1)$ can finally generate mappings for $\text{prev}_\Phi$ in both current loop contexts $\{\varepsilon\}$ (ID 6) and $\{\varepsilon, \ell\}$ (ID 7). In loop context $\{\varepsilon\}$, only the first parameter $\text{prev}_0$ contributes because it corresponds to the non loop edge $BB1 \to BB2$. After de-referencing $[\{\varepsilon\}, \text{prev}_0]$ (ID 2) to ID 0, the mapping $6 \mapsto \{0\}$, which has already been generated in the first iteration, remains unchanged. In loop context $\{\varepsilon, \ell\}$, only parameter $\text{prev}_1$ (corresponding to edge $\ell$) contributes. Therefore, the second clause of $MapInLC(\{\varepsilon, \ell\}, \text{prev}_1)$ used in the transfer function for $\Phi$ statements generates a mapping from $[\{\varepsilon, \ell\}, \text{prev}_\Phi]$ (ID 7) to the two versions $[\{\varepsilon, \ell\}, \text{prev}_1]$ (ID 13) and $[\{\varepsilon, \ell\}, \text{prev}_1]$ (ID 10). After de-referencing those, we get the mapping $7 \mapsto \{8, 11\}$ in the second iteration at $BB2$.

After this, at $BB3$ the transfer function for statement $\text{prev}_\Phi \to \text{step}$ creates the two happens-before edges $8 \to 11$ and $11 \to 11$ because for loop context $\{\varepsilon, \ell\}$, $\text{prev}_\Phi$ de-references to the two task variables 8 and 11 and $\text{step}$ de-references to task variable 11. The edge $11 \to 11$ represents the fact that all $\text{step}$ tasks are ordered across loop iterations.

Basic block $BB5$ is the first block outside the loop. Therefore, the loop context $\{\varepsilon, \ell\}$ is killed, because edge $\ell$ does not loop around $BB5$. The killing of edge $\ell$ causes the meet operator $\sqcap$ to kill all mappings that contain task variable $\text{prev}_\Phi$, namely the mappings of ID 6 and ID 7. At the same time, the meet operator $\sqcap$ re-maps the task variable $\text{prev}_\Phi$ after the loop $\ell$ (that is, for loop context $\{\varepsilon\}$) to the most specific version from inside the loop, which is $[\{\varepsilon, \ell\}, \text{prev}_1]$ (ID 13). ID 13 in turn maps to $[\{\varepsilon, \ell\}, \text{step}]$ (ID 11) resulting in the generated mapping $6 \mapsto \{11\}$. The statement $\text{prev}_\Phi \to \text{later}$ in $BB5$ thus creates the edge $11 \to 1$ in $HBEdges_{out}(BB5)$.

The result of the data-flow analysis is the graph shown for block $BB5$ in Table 4.2. This graph contains enough information for the subsequent steps to deduce that all $\text{step}$ tasks are ordered (IDs 8 and 11) with respect to each other and with respect to $\text{later}$ (ID 1). Furthermore, the graph shows that there may exist multiple $\text{print}$ tasks (IDs 9 and 12) that are ordered with some of the $\text{step}$ tasks but unordered with respect to other step tasks and unordered with respect to each other. The information that some $\text{print}$ tasks are ordered with some $\text{step}$ tasks will be lost in the final result of the schedule analysis, however. Instead, the schedule analysis will conclude that all Step() tasks are ordered with each other and with later but that (some) Step() may be parallel with (some) Print() tasks.

|  | BB1 | BB2 | BB3 | BB5 |
|---|---|---|---|---|
| **iteration 1** | | | | |
| $LoopCtxts_{out}(n)$ | $\{\varepsilon\}$ | $\{\varepsilon\}, \{\varepsilon,\ell\}$ | $\{\varepsilon\}, \{\varepsilon,\ell\}$ | $\{\varepsilon\}$ |
| $TaskVars_{out}(n)$ | $0:[\{\varepsilon\}, \mathbf{now}]$ <br> $1:[\{\varepsilon\}, \mathtt{later}]$ <br> $2:[\{\varepsilon\}, \mathtt{prev_0}]$ | $0,1,2,$ <br> $3:[\{\varepsilon,\ell\}, \mathbf{now}]$ <br> $4:[\{\varepsilon,\ell\}, \mathtt{later}]$ <br> $5:[\{\varepsilon,\ell\}, \mathtt{prev_0}]$ <br> $6:[\{\varepsilon\}, \mathtt{prev_\Phi}]$ <br> $7:[\{\varepsilon,\ell\}, \mathtt{prev_\Phi}]$ | $0,1,2,3,4,5,6,7,$ <br> $8:[\{\varepsilon\}, \mathtt{step}]$ <br> $9:[\{\varepsilon\}, \mathtt{print}]$ <br> $10:[\{\varepsilon\}, \mathtt{prev_1}]$ <br> $11:[\{\varepsilon,\ell\}, \mathtt{step}],$ <br> $12:[\{\varepsilon,\ell\}, \mathtt{print}],$ <br> $13:[\{\varepsilon,\ell\}, \mathtt{prev_1}]$ | $0,1,2,3,4,5,6,7,8,9,10,$ <br> $11,12,13$ |
| $VarMap_{out}(n)$ | $2 \mapsto \{0\}$ | $2 \mapsto \{0\}, 3 \mapsto \{0\},$ <br> $4 \mapsto \{1\}, 5 \mapsto \{0\},$ <br> $6 \mapsto \{0\}, 7 \mapsto \varnothing$ | $2 \mapsto \{0\}, 3 \mapsto \{0\},$ <br> $4 \mapsto \{1\}, 5 \mapsto \{0\},$ <br> $6 \mapsto \{0\}, 7 \mapsto \varnothing, 10 \mapsto$ <br> $\{8\}, 13 \mapsto \{11\}$ | $2 \mapsto \{0\}, 3 \mapsto \{0\},$ <br> $4 \mapsto \{1\}, 5 \mapsto \{0\},$ <br> $6 \mapsto \varnothing, 10 \mapsto \{8\},$ <br> $13 \mapsto \{11\}$ |
| $HBEdges_{out}(n)$ | $\varnothing$ | $\varnothing$ | (graph) | $\varnothing$ |
| **iteration 2** | | | | |
| $LoopCtxts_{out}(n)$ | $\{\varepsilon\}$ | $\{\varepsilon\}, \{\varepsilon,\ell\}$ | $\{\varepsilon\}, \{\varepsilon,\ell\}$ | $\{\varepsilon\}$ |
| $TaskVars_{out}(n)$ | $0,1,2$ | $0,1,2,3,4,5,6,7,8,9,10$ <br> $11,12,13$ | $0,1,2,3,4,5,6,7,8,9,10$ <br> $11,12,13$ | $0,1,2,3,4,5,6,7,8,9,10$ <br> $11,12,13$ |
| $VarMap_{out}(n)$ | $2 \mapsto \{0\}$ | $2 \mapsto \{0\}, 3 \mapsto \{0\},$ <br> $4 \mapsto \{1\}, 5 \mapsto \{0\},$ <br> $6 \mapsto \{0\},$ <br> $7 \mapsto \{8,11\},$ <br> $10 \mapsto \{8\}, 13 \mapsto \{11\}$ | $2 \mapsto \{0\}, 3 \mapsto \{0\},$ <br> $4 \mapsto \{1\}, 5 \mapsto \{0\},$ <br> $6 \mapsto \{0\}, 7 \mapsto \{8,11\},$ <br> $10 \mapsto \{8\}, 13 \mapsto \{11\}$ | $2 \mapsto \{0\}, 3 \mapsto \{0\},$ <br> $4 \mapsto \{1\}, 5 \mapsto \{0\},$ <br> $6 \mapsto \{11\}, 10 \mapsto \{8\},$ <br> $13 \mapsto \{11\}$ |
| $HBEdges_{out}(n)$ | $\varnothing$ | (graph) | (graph) | (graph) |
| **iteration 3** | | | | |
| $LoopCtxts_{out}(n)$ | $\{\varepsilon\}$ | $\{\varepsilon\}, \{\varepsilon,\ell\}$ | $\{\varepsilon\}, \{\varepsilon,\ell\}$ | $\{\varepsilon\}$ |
| $TaskVars_{out}(n)$ | $0,1,2$ | $0,1,2,3,4,5,6,7,8,9,10,$ <br> $11,12,13$ | $0,1,2,3,4,5,6,7,8,9,10,$ <br> $11,12,13$ | $0,1,2,3,4,5,6,7,8,9,10,$ <br> $11,12,13$ |
| $VarMap_{out}(n)$ | $2 \mapsto \{0\}$ | $2 \mapsto \{0\}, 3 \mapsto \{0\},$ <br> $4 \mapsto \{1\}, 5 \mapsto \{0\},$ <br> $6 \mapsto \{0\},$ <br> $7 \mapsto \{8,11\},$ <br> $10 \mapsto \{8\}, 13 \mapsto \{11\}$ | $2 \mapsto \{0\}, 3 \mapsto \{0\},$ <br> $4 \mapsto \{1\}, 5 \mapsto \{0\},$ <br> $6 \mapsto \{0\}, 7 \mapsto \{8,11\},$ <br> $10 \mapsto \{8\}, 13 \mapsto \{11\}$ | $2 \mapsto \{0\}, 3 \mapsto \{0\},$ <br> $4 \mapsto \{1\}, 5 \mapsto \{0\},$ <br> $6 \mapsto \{11\}, 10 \mapsto \{8\},$ <br> $13 \mapsto \{11\}$ |
| $HBEdges_{out}(n)$ | $\varnothing$ | (graph) | (graph) | (graph) |

Table 4.2: Task-scheduling and task-ordering effect analysis of the `ChainedSteps` example.

### 4.2.3 Step 3: Computing relations between task variables

The loop-contextualized task-variable ordering graph computed in the previous step is the graph $G = \{TaskVars_{in}(exit), HBEdges_{in}(exit)\}$ that results at the *exit* node of the task-method's control-flow graph. Because this graph contains copies of local task variables for different loop contexts, the graph is very detailed. In general, this level of detail cannot be exploited by the rest of the compiler analyses such as the points-to analysis and the escape analysis, however, because those analyses work on the level of SSA-variables and do not have any notion of loop context. Therefore, the additional detail present in the loop-contextualized task-variable ordering graph cannot be exploited by the schedule analysis, because the precision of the schedule analysis is bound by the precision of the points-to information.

This step summarizes the loop-contextualized task-variable ordering graph into relations between non-loop-contextualized (SSA) task variables. This brings the schedule analysis onto the same level of detail as the rest of the compiler analyses and allows the compiler to integrate the results of the different analyses.

Computing relations between non-loop-contextualized task variables essentially "folds" all occurrences of a task variable into a single node. The function $Occ(\mathsf{a})$ computes the set of (loop-contextualized) occurrences of the SSA task variable a in $G$. A loop-contextualized task variable $[lc, \mathsf{b}]$ is an occurrence of a if both refer to the same SSA-variable (that is, a=b) and if $[lc, \mathsf{b}]$ is not used as the key in a variable mapping[5]:

$$Occ(\mathsf{a}) = \{[lc, \mathsf{b}] \in (TaskVars_{out}(exit) \smallsetminus Keys(VarMap_{out}(exit)))\text{ where }\mathsf{a} = \mathsf{b}\}$$

Folding all occurrences of a task variable into a single node of course also affects the happens-before edges in the graph. As an example, consider a simple graph $[lc_1, \mathsf{a}] \to [lc_1, \mathsf{b}] \to [lc_2, \mathsf{a}]$. While it is true that $[lc_1, \mathsf{a}]$ happens-before $[lc_1, \mathsf{b}]$, it is not true that a→b. Neither is it the case that b→a. Declaring a and b potentially parallel, however, is undesirable, too, because they in fact *are* strictly ordered, even though the direction is undefined.

Instead of a single directed →-relation between task variables, this step computes for each pair of (non-loop-contextualized) task variables one of four possible relations:

$$\mathsf{a}\text{ REL }\mathsf{b} ::= \begin{cases} \mathsf{a} \doteq \mathsf{b} & \text{if } \mathsf{a} = \mathsf{b} \wedge |Occ(\mathsf{a})| = |Occ(\mathsf{b})| = 1, \\ \mathsf{a} \dot{\to} \mathsf{b} & \text{if } \forall t \in Occ(\mathsf{a}), v \in Occ(\mathsf{b}): \quad t \stackrel{*}{\to} v, \\ \mathsf{a} \dot{\leftrightarrow} \mathsf{b} & \text{if } \neg(\mathsf{a} \dot{\to} \mathsf{b}) \wedge \forall t \in Occ(\mathsf{a}), v \in Occ(\mathsf{b}): \quad t \stackrel{*}{\to} v \vee v \stackrel{*}{\to} t, \\ \mathsf{a} \dot{\nleftrightarrow} \mathsf{b} & \text{if } \exists t \in Occ(\mathsf{a}), v \in Occ(\mathsf{b}): \quad t \stackrel{*}{\nrightarrow} v \wedge v \stackrel{*}{\nrightarrow} t. \end{cases}$$

The symbols $t$ and $v$ represent loop-contextualized task variables whereas a and b represent non-loop-contextualized task variables. $v$ is reachable from $t$, written as $t \stackrel{*}{\to} v$, if there is a genuine transitive ordering of $t$ and $v$ in $G$. A transitive ordering is genuine if a path from $t$ to $v$ exists in $G$ that only uses nodes $w$ where the existence of $t$ implies the existence of all intermediate nodes $w$.[6] If $t \stackrel{*}{\nrightarrow} v$ then $G$ does not contain a genuine path from $t$ to $v$.

---

[5]Loop-contextualized task variables that map to other loop-contextualized task variables are always dereferenced and therefore not part of the happens-before graph.

[6]see Section 3.7.4 for more information on genuine edges.

|           | now | later | nextRound | barrier | phase1 | phase2 |
|-----------|-----|-------|-----------|---------|--------|--------|
| now       | $\doteq$ | | | | | |
| later     | $\leftrightarrow$ | $\doteq$ | | | | |
| nextRound | $\leftarrow$ | $\rightarrow$ | $\doteq$ | | | |
| barrier   | $\leftarrow$ | $\leftrightarrow$ | $\leftrightarrow$ | $\doteq$ | | |
| phase1    | $\leftarrow$ | $\rightarrow$ | $\rightarrow$ | $\rightarrow$ | $\leftrightarrow$ | |
| phase2    | $\leftarrow$ | $\rightarrow$ | $\rightarrow$ | $\leftarrow$ | $\leftarrow$ | $\leftrightarrow$ |

Figure 4.9: The relation *REL* between the task variables computed from the loop-contextualized task-variable ordering graph for the running example from Table 4.1.

The singleton relation $\doteq$ is used only between a task variable and itself, never between two different task variables. $a \doteq a$ states that task variable a only occurs once in $G$. This implies that a is not a schedule site inside a loop. If $a \doteq a$ then at runtime variable a references only one task object. The relation $a \rightarrow b$ is true if *all* occurrences of a are ordered before *all* occurrences of b in the given task method. If all occurrences of a and b are ordered in $G$, but the directionality of the paths varies, then a and b are un-directionally ordered, written $a \leftrightarrow b$. In any other case, a and b are considered to be potentially parallel, written as $a \nleftrightarrow b$.

For the running example, this step computes the relations shown in Figure 4.9 given the loop-contextualized task-variable ordering graph $G$ shown at basic block *BB*5 in Table 4.1.

The task variables now, later, nextRound, and barrier are all singletons. The schedule sites defining task variables phase1 and phase2 on the other hand may be executed multiple times and therefore each occur twice in $G$ (as nodes 8 + 10 for phase1 and as nodes 9 + 11 for phase2). Because the occurrences are unordered, the analysis deduces *phase*1 $\nleftrightarrow$ *phase*1 and *phase*2 $\nleftrightarrow$ *phase*2.

With the exception of later, which is potentially unordered with now, the other tasks are all scheduled by now and are therefore ordered after now (the left column in Table 4.1).

All phase1 tasks (nodes 8 + 10) will be ordered before the singleton barrier (node 3) and (transitively) before all phase2 (nodes 9 + 11), nextRound (node 2), and later (node 1). barrier (node 3), however, may be parallel to nextRound (node 2) and later (node 1) because if the loop starting at basic block *BB*4 is not executed at all, there will be no transitive ordering of barrier via one or more phase2 tasks. In other words, there is no genuine path between the occurrence of barrier (node 3) and the occurrence of nextRound (node 2) in the example. The analysis therefore concludes barrier$\nleftrightarrow$nextRound (and consequently barrier$\nleftrightarrow$later).

### 4.2.4 Step 4: Computing unordered task-variable/task-object pairs

The fourth step is the computation of a relation *taskNotOrdered*(a,$\mathcal{B}$). The analysis computes this relation by comparing the relation *REL* for all pairs of task variables and recording task objects that may directly or indirectly be unordered with each task variable.

In addition to the relation a MAY SCHEDULE $\mathcal{A}$, which is the direct result of a points-to analysis, the computation of *taskNotOrdered*() uses a relation $\mathcal{C}$ MAY BE SUBTASK OF $\mathcal{A}$. The this relation is computed by a simple reachability analysis. Starting with all task methods A () that are possible entry points of task object $\mathcal{A}$, $\mathcal{C}$ MAY BE SUBTASK OF $\mathcal{A}$ collects all task

## 4.2. THE SCHEDULE ANALYSIS ALGORITHM

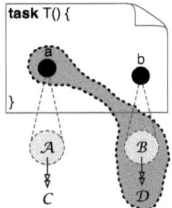
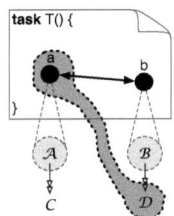

(a) UNORDEREDVARS: Variables a and b are unordered; a will be unordered with b's task $\mathcal{B}$ and all of $\mathcal{B}$'s subtasks $\mathcal{D}$. Likewise, b is unordered with $\mathcal{A}$ and $\mathcal{C}$ (not shown).

(b) ORDEREDVARS: a and b are ordered; a is ordered with task $\mathcal{B}$ but unordered with any of $\mathcal{B}$'s subtasks $\mathcal{D}$. Likewise, b is unordered with $\mathcal{A}$'s subtasks $\mathcal{C}$ (not shown).

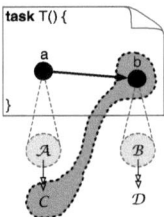
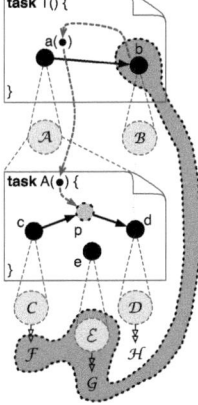

(c) HAPPENSAFTER-NOPARAM: a is ordered with $\mathcal{B}$ and (transitively) all of $\mathcal{B}$'s subtasks $\mathcal{D}$. In the other direction, b is ordered with $\mathcal{A}$ but it is not ordered with any of $\mathcal{A}$'s subtasks $\mathcal{C}$.

(d) HAPPENSAFTER-WITHPARAM: as before, b is ordered with $\mathcal{A}$. In addition, b is ordered with $\mathcal{C}$, $\mathcal{D}$ and $\mathcal{H}$ through parameter p. b is unordered with only some of $\mathcal{A}$'s sub-subtasks: $\mathcal{F}$, $\mathcal{E}$, and $\mathcal{G}$.

Figure 4.10: Illustrations for computing the *taskNotOrdered* relation.

objects $\mathcal{C}$ that may be created by any **schedule**-statement reachable from A() in the call graph.

Before we present the rules for computing *taskNotOrdered*() more formally, Figure 4.2.4 illustrates some of the cases for different task variable relations a *REL* b. Panel 4.10(a) shows the case where a ↮ b. Because the two task variables a and b are unordered, a is unordered with the task $\mathcal{B}$ represented by b as well as all of $\mathcal{B}$'s subtasks $\mathcal{D}$. Likewise, b is unordered with $\mathcal{A}$ and all of $\mathcal{A}$'s subtasks $\mathcal{C}$.

The case where a↔b is shown in Panel 4.10(b). Here, the tasks directly represented by a and b are ordered. However, because the direction of the happens-before edge is unknown it is not necessarily the case that a is transitively ordered (via creation edges) with $\mathcal{B}$'s subtasks

UNORDEREDVARS
$$\frac{\text{a} \leftrightarrow \text{b in T( )} \quad \text{b} \neq \textbf{now}}{\text{taskNotOrdered}(\text{a}, \mathcal{B} \cup \mathcal{D}) \textbf{ in } \mathsf{T}(\,)}$$

ORDEREDVARS
$$\frac{\text{a} \leftrightarrow \text{b in T( )} \quad \text{b MAY SCHEDULE } \mathcal{B} \text{ in T( )}}{\text{taskNotOrdered}(\text{a}, \mathcal{D}) \textbf{ in } \mathsf{T}(\,)}$$

HAPPENSAFTER–NOPARAM
$$\frac{\begin{array}{c}\text{a} \rightarrow \text{b in T( )} \quad \text{a} \neq \textbf{now} \\ \text{b IS NOT A PARAM TO a in T( )} \\ \text{a MAY SCHEDULE } \mathcal{A} \text{ in T( )} \quad \mathcal{C} \text{ MAY BE SUBTASK OF } \mathcal{A}\end{array}}{\text{taskNotOrdered}(\text{b}, \mathcal{C}) \textbf{ in } \mathsf{T}(\,)}$$

HAPPENSAFTER–WITHPARAM
$$\frac{\begin{array}{c}\text{a} \rightarrow \text{b in T( )} \quad \text{b IS ACTUAL PARAM } n \textbf{ to } \text{a in T( )} \\ \text{a MAY SCHEDULE } \mathcal{A} \textbf{ in } \mathsf{T}(\,) \quad \mathsf{A}(\,) \text{ IS ENTRY POINT OF } \mathcal{A} \\ p \text{ IS FORMAL PARAM } n \textbf{ of } \mathsf{A}(\,) \quad \text{taskNotOrdered}(p, \mathcal{C}) \textbf{ in } \mathsf{A}(\,)\end{array}}{\text{taskNotOrdered}(\text{b}, \mathcal{C}) \textbf{ in } \mathsf{T}(\,)}$$

Figure 4.11: Rules for computing unordered variable/task pairs

$\mathcal{D}$. Therefore, we must assume that a is potentially unordered with $\mathcal{B}$'s subtasks $\mathcal{D}$. Likewise, b may be unordered with any of $\mathcal{A}$'s subtasks C.

In Panel 4.10(c), the direction of the happens-before ordering between a and b is known. In this case, a is not only ordered with task $\mathcal{B}$ represented by b but also with all of $\mathcal{B}$'s subtasks $\mathcal{D}$. In the other direction, however, we must assume that b is unordered with $\mathcal{A}$'s subtasks C.

The last panel, Panel 4.10(d), handles the special case of the *now happens-before later* pattern introduced in Section 3.2. If task variable b is passed as a parameter to a and a→b then the set of tasks that are potentially unordered with b can be reduced from all of $\mathcal{A}$'s subtasks to only those tasks that are unordered with the parameter p in A.

The formal rules for computing the relation *taskNotOrdered* are shown in Figure 4.11.

The first rule UNORDEREDVARS applies to the case where a↔b. It selects for each task variable a in the task method T( ) all task variables b that are unordered with respect to a. It then concludes that all tasks $\mathcal{B}$ that may be scheduled by b as well as all subtasks $\mathcal{D}$ of $\mathcal{B}$ are unordered with the task variable a.

For pairs of ordered variables a↔b the second rule ORDEREDVARS marks all subtasks $\mathcal{D}$ of b's task $\mathcal{B}$ to be unordered with a.

The final two rules handle pairs of task variables where the direction of the ordering is known: a→b. For a given pair of schedule sites a and b, only one of the two subtask rules applies, depending on whether b is used as a parameter to a or not.

## 4.2. THE SCHEDULE ANALYSIS ALGORITHM

If task variable b is not passed as a parameter to a, rule HAPPENSAFTER-NOPARAM applies. HAPPENSAFTER-NOPARAM is similar to rule ORDEREDVARS and marks all tasks $\mathcal{C}$ that may be subtasks of any task $\mathcal{A}$ scheduled at a to be unordered with b.

The last rule HAPPENSAFTER-WITHPARAM specializes the case where b is passed as a parameter to a in order to reduce the set of tasks that are considered potentially parallel to b. Instead of simply taking all possible subtasks of $\mathcal{A}$, this rules selects only those subtasks of $\mathcal{A}$ that are unordered with respect to the corresponding parameter variable. This rule handles the *now happens-before later* pattern described in Chapter 3.

Given relation *REL* of the running example shown in Figure 4.9, applying the rules from Figure 4.11 results in the following conclusions:

- **now**, later, nextRound, and barrier are all singletons and do not add anything to *taskNotOrdered*().

- Variable phase1 is located inside a loop and phase1↔phase1. Therefore, rule UNORDEREDVARS applies and concludes that *taskNotOrdered*(phase1, Phase1()) (plus any tasks that Phase1() may directly or indirectly schedule).

- Similarly, ↔ lets us conclude that *taskNotOrdered*(phase2, Phase2()), *taskNotOrdered*(barrier, NextRound()), *taskNotOrdered*(nextRound, Barrier ()), and *taskNotOrdered*(later, Barrier()).

- For the parameter later, the relation MAY SCHEDULE returns the empty set. Therefore, rule UNORDEREDVARS does not add to *taskNotOrdered*() for barrier↔later and **now** ↔later.

- All other pairs of task variables are ordered by directed $\dot{\to}$-relations:

    - phase1 is ordered before barrier, phase2, nextRound, and later. Therefore, phase1 is ordered with respect to all their subtasks through the implicit creation edges. Neither HAPPENSAFTER rule applies.

    - The barrier variable is ordered after phase1. Because it is not used as a parameter to phase1, rule HAPPENSAFTER-NOPARAM applies and deduces that barrier is unordered with any subtask that may be created by Phase1().

    - Similar reasoning applies to the variable phase2, classifying it as potentially parallel with subtasks of Phase1() and Barrier().

    - The parameter later is passed along as a parameter to nextRound and ordered after nextRound and therefore the HappensAfter-WithParam rule applies. Assuming that in this example the tasks Barrier(), Phase1(), and Phase2() do not schedule any subtasks, this rule concludes that parameter later is ordered with all other tasks.

### 4.2.5 Step 5: Computing unordered task-object/task-object pairs

The final step is to compute what task objects may be unordered and therefore potentially parallel to each other. Figure 4.12 shows the two rules that are involved in this computation.

$$\frac{\begin{array}{c}\text{PARALLELTASKS–SCHEDULESITE}\\ \text{a MAY SCHEDULE } \mathcal{A} \text{ in } \mathsf{T(\,)}\\ taskNotOrdered(\mathsf{a},\mathcal{B}) \text{ in } \mathsf{T(\,)}\end{array}}{parallel(\mathcal{A},\mathcal{B})}$$

$$\frac{\begin{array}{c}\text{PARALLELTASKS–SIBLINGS}\\ \text{a} \neq \text{b in } \mathsf{T(\,)}\\ \text{a MAY SCHEDULE } \mathcal{A} \text{ in } \mathsf{T(\,)} \qquad \text{b MAY SCHEDULE } \mathcal{B} \text{ in } \mathsf{T(\,)}\\ \mathcal{C} \text{ MAY BE SUBTASK OF } \mathcal{A} \qquad \mathcal{D} \text{ MAY BE SUBTASK OF } \mathcal{B}\end{array}}{parallel(\mathcal{C},\mathcal{D})}$$

Figure 4.12: Computing parallel tasks

The first rule PARALLELTASKS-SCHEDULESITE states that if a schedule site a may schedule task $\mathcal{A}$, task $\mathcal{A}$ may be parallel to all tasks $\mathcal{B}$ that are not ordered with the variable a. This information comes from the relation *taskNotOrdered* computed in the previous step.

The second rule PARALLELTASKS-SIBLINGS relates all subtasks of the tasks scheduled in the same task method T(). Without parameter passing, even if the parent tasks are ordered there is no way to order their subtasks with respect to each other. For cases with parameter passing, however, this rule is overly conservative and introduces some imprecision. In an implementation, this rule can be further specialized to the case where a task variable that is ordered before a parameter can be considered transitively ordered with the children of the parameter.

For the running example, the first rule ParallelTasks-ScheduleSite concludes that in task method Round(), task Barrier() and NextRound() are potentially parallel. Further, it finds that Phase1() is parallel to itself, as is Phase2() parallel to itself. Because in this example the only task that creates subtasks is Round(), the second rule does not add any additional tasks to the *parallel*() relation.

## 4.3 Implementation

We have implemented the schedule analysis in two different prototypes. The first prototype is written mainly in Datalog and allows for rapid prototyping of new optimizations and analyses. However, the Datalog prototype does not contain a code generation module to actually write out optimized program code. This prototype therefore can only be used to report statistical data but does not allow us to evaluate improvements when the optimized program is executed.

The second prototype is a bytecode-to-bytecode translating optimizing compiler fully implemented in Java. Besides the schedule analysis and some basic optimizations, the Java prototype implements a code generation phase that allows us to evaluate runtime behavior of optimized programs.

This section gives a short overview of some of the implementation details for both prototypes.

### 4.3.1 Datalog implementation

The Datalog prototype is built on bddbddb as its Datalog backend. The source code of the Datalog prototype is listed in Appendix A. The pre-processor implementing the first normalization step uses the Wala framework [51] to transform the bytecode of the input program into static single assignment (SSA) form and extract the initial extensional database for Datalog. The results of the analysis are written into text files and can be manually inspected.

The Datalog points-to and escape analysis are extended forms of the analyses described by Whaley and Lam [115] where the original call-graph numbering context sensitivity has been replaced with a 1-task-object/1-receiver-object sensitivity. This means that the analysis distinguishes calls to a method not only based on the method name but also based on the method receiver and the task in which the call happens. As opposed to the original approach, which requires constructing a call-graph before the main analysis, our system computes the call-graph at the same time as it computes the points-to sets while still providing good context sensitivity.

bddbddb represents boolean relations using binary decision diagrams (BDDs). BDDs are a data structure that can efficiently represent large relations and provide efficient set operations. However, BDD algorithms are highly sensitive to the size of the decision trees, which is determined by the order on the used variables. In the worst case, a bad variable order can increase the size of the BDDs exponentially. Unfortunately, the problem of finding the best variable ordering is NP-complete. The variable ordering used in our experiments seems to work reasonably well but it is not known whether a significantly better ordering exists.

### 4.3.2 Java implementation

The Java prototype is implemented using Wala [51] for its analysis framework and Javassist [29] for code generation.

After initializing Wala with all Java class files, the compiler first runs various analyses (see below). During code generation, the prototype re-visits every class file and emits an optimized version, depending on what optimizations have been chosen. The optimized class files are written onto the file-system. Using the Java VM option -Xbootclasspath/p, the optimized class files are pre-pended to the class-path. Pre-pending to the class-path allows for replacing even classes from the standard Java library with their optimized counterparts.

The compiler runs the following analyses in the given order:

1. **Points-to analysis:** The Wala framework comes with a set of different configurable points-to analyses that provide different tradeoffs between analysis time, used memory, and precision. Points-to analyses can be configured with different strategies for their context-sensitivity. As in the Datalog prototype, call graph construction happens alongside the points-to analysis.

2. **Reachability analysis:** The reachability analysis takes the call graph and computes for each task-method node the set of normal-method nodes that may be directly or indirectly called by the task-method node.

3. **Schedule analysis:** The schedule analysis uses the points-to sets and the reachability information to compute the relation *parallel(TaskNode, TaskNode)*.

4. **Escape analysis:** The escape analysis first collects all objects that are reachable from static fields and all objects used as arguments to task methods and marks them as escaping. From this set, the escape analysis iteratively marks all objects as escaping that may be pointed-to by an escaping object. This is done until a fixed-point is reached.

5. **Parallel read/write sets analysis:** This analysis first collects for each task node $p$ in the call graph the set of objects that $p$ or any node in the call graph reachable from $p$ may read and/or write. It then uses this information to collects for each task node $n$ in the call graph the objects that are read and/or written by tasks $p$ that are parallel to $n$. The result of the escape analysis allows this step to reduce the number of parallel reads or writes for objects that do not escape $n$ or $p$.

6. **Bytecode read/write conflicts analysis:** This analysis takes the context-sensitive results of the parallel read/write sets analysis, where multiple call graph nodes may represent different invocations of a single method m(), and assembles a conservative context-insensitive view that can be used by the optimizations when working on an individual method m().

Concrete optimizations typically take the result of the read/write conflict analysis to check whether a given bytecode *b* in method m() may be involved in a read/read, read/write, write/read or write/write conflict with any other bytecode that may access the same object in a parallel task.

## 4.4 Related work

**Concurrency analysis with module interaction graphs.** Based on the work of Callahan, Kennedy, and Subhlok [24, 23], Duesterwald and Soffa [34] developed a data-race detection technique using a data-flow framework. The data-flow analysis works on a graphical representation of the program called a module interaction graph, and computes a partial execution order of program regions. In a first phase, the analysis computes for each region $r$ the sets $before(r)$ and $after(r)$ containing regions that are ordered to execute before any operation in region $r$ and the regions ordered after all operations in $r$ respectively. During this first phase, parallel units (that is, program units that may execute concurrently with itself) are ignored. The second phase of the algorithm consists of detecting parallel units by analyzing the previously determined order at activation sites and appropriately updating the ordering sets for parallel units. The approach presented by Duesterwald and Soffa assumes a synchronous intertask communication through entry call and accept commands as defined by the rendezvous concept of Ada'83 [64] but otherwise places no restrictions on the analyzed program, thus allowing unstructured parallelism and arbitrary recursion. Ada'83 defines task types as *limited types*, prohibiting assignment of task objects and task parameters with out mode. Task objects thus behave as constants [64, p.9-4] and reduce possible aliasing of task objects. Together with the rendezvous semantics of the intertask communication, restricted types make synchronization analysis in Ada'83 somewhat easier than a comparable analysis for Java.

**May happen in parallel analysis.** The result of a may happen in parallel (MHP) analysis are pairs of program statements that may be executed concurrently in a multi-threaded program. In the past, researchers have developed different approaches for computing MHP information.

## 4.4. RELATED WORK

Masticola and Ryder [80] describe an iterative algorithm for non-concurrency analysis that identifies sets of statements in a concurrent program that can never happen in parallel. They start out with an initial conservative assumption that all operations in one process may happen in parallel with any operation in another process. A small set of refinements are then applied in arbitrary order until a fixed point is reached.

Instead of focussing on statements that *can never* happen in parallel, Naumovich and Avrunin [89] describe a data-flow algorithm for computing pairs of statements that *may* happen in parallel. They show that their algorithm for computing MHP information subsumes at least two of the four refinement steps from Masticola and Ryder while reducing the complexity significantly. The improved precision and runtime is verified by a large set of Ada programs with a rendezvous model of concurrency.

The differences in the way communications between threads of control are realized in Ada and Java require different analysis approaches. Therefore, in [90] Naumovich, Avrunin, and Clarke adapt the approach from [89] and describe an algorithm for computing MHP information in threaded Java programs. Naumovich, Avrunin, and Clarke's approach relies on a simplified program structure where all methods need to be inlined and cloning is used to eliminate polymorphism and aliasing. Lin and Verbrugge [69] present a practical implementation of this algorithm that overcomes the limitations of whole-program inlining and exhaustive cloning. With those changes, Lin and Verbrugge can apply MHP to moderate size programs.

Barik [14] describes a different, scalable context and flow-sensitive MHP analysis for Java. In this work, Barik introduces a thread creation tree that distinguishes threads by their creation site. The thread creation tree captures start and join interactions among threads and allows the analysis to deduce some limited ordering information between threads.

In [4], Agarwal, Barik, and Sarkar adapt previous MHP analyses, which were designed for task- and thread-based parallelism found in Ada and Java, to the hither-level structured concurrency constructs provided by X10. Because of the restricted parallelism of X10, their approach can be based on simple path traversals in the program structure tree and does not require any points-to analysis for task objects. However, this MPH analysis is only applicable to languages that adopt the core concepts of places, async, finish, and atomic sections from the X10 programming model.

In general, the goals of MHP analysis and the schedule analysis presented in this dissertation are similar. However, instead of focussing on parallelism between individual statements or program operations, the schedule analysis focusses on parallelism (and ordering) between whole tasks. The information whether two statements $s$ and $t$ may be executed in parallel is then computed on demand by a simple reachability analysis that checks whether $s$ and $t$ can be reached by two parallel tasks $\mathcal{A}$ and $\mathcal{B}$. Focussing on tasks and task ordering instead of individual statements allows the analysis to scale even to large programs.

The schedule analysis itself does not take any information about low-level synchronization into account, which is a big part of all the discussed MHP algorithms. Without synchronization information, however, a compiler may miss important optimization opportunities for programs where happens-before ordering of tasks is not sufficient and locks must be used. Therefore, it may be beneficial to combine a schedule analysis with a MHP analysis. In this approach, the MHP analysis is used to compute low-level synchronization information only between potentially parallel tasks, as determined by the schedule analysis.

**Program dependence graphs and parallel program graphs.** Program dependence graphs (PDGs) [40] can be used to analyze the intrinsic parallelism in a sequential program. A PDG makes explicit both the data and control dependences for each operation in a program. However, PDGs are designed for sequential programs and cannot represent explicitly parallel programs. Sarkar [103] overcomes this limitation by introducing parallel program graphs (PPGs) as a general parallel program representation for analysis and optimization of programs with structured parallelism. PPGs are comprised of parallel control flow edges and synchronization edges. Ferrante et al. [39] introduce a similar data structure called parallel flow graphs (PFGs) and describe a data-flow analysis that can be used for optimizing programs with structured parallelism. All of the above graph-based analyses focus on structured parallelism with lexically scoped fork/join-style concurrency constructs.

**Barrier synchronization.** Concurrency analysis is a static analysis technique that determines whether two operations in a shared memory program may be executed in parallel by different tasks. For programming models that use low-level synchronization such as locks, concurrency analysis must account for the partial ordering of statements imposed by barriers. In [118] and [119], Zhang et al. present techniques for analyzing barrier synchronization in programs with unnamed and possibly textually unaligned barriers. Barriers structure the execution of parallel regions into a series of synchronized execution phases such that threads synchronize on barriers only at the beginning and at the end of each phase. Statements from different execution phases cannot execute concurrently and thus define ordering relationships among statements. Zhang et al. assume a fork/join-style concurrency model such as the model provided by OpenMP and cannot handle more flexible models such as threads or the task model presented in this dissertation. However, barrier synchronization may provide the basis for transforming an input program that uses barriers, such as the sor example from Figure 3.1, to a program that uses explicit →-statements, such as the transformed example from Figure 3.3.

**Delay set analysis.** Delay set analysis computes a delay set, i.e. a set of program edges $x{\rightarrow}y$ between memory accesses $x$ and $y$ such that $y$ must be delayed until $x$ has completed. If $x{\rightarrow}y$ is in the delay set then $x$ and $y$ may not be re-ordered under a sequentially consistent memory model because the effect of the re-ordering may be observed by a parallel task. Current delay-set analyses, such as the ones presented in [104] and [108], suffer from the unstructured nature of threads that results in imprecisions when analyzing thread interaction that is not local to a single method. Schedule analysis could be used to improve the precision of the delay set analysis. Most optimizations presented in this dissertation combine task-order information with points-to information to find possible program-point interferences. This combination is a simple but conservative approximation of the critical cycle detection of a delay-set analysis.

**Interval analysis and loop hierarchy analysis.** Section 4.2.2 presents a data-flow approach to extract the loop-contextualized task-variable ordering graph from a task method. The effect of loops on the task scheduling and task ordering and the loop nesting is tracked through the $LoopCtxts(n)$-part of the flow value. This technique is an imperative approach to the analysis of control flow containing nested loops. Another way to compute the same information could be to use a more declarative technique: Given a separate analysis that takes a task method and computes the structural nesting of loops, a declarative approach may allow for a more direct classification of →-statements. For example, knowing that schedule-site a is outside any loop and schedule-site b together with the statement a→b is inside a single loop $\ell$, we could directly deduce that $[\{\varepsilon\},\mathsf{a}] \to [\{\ell,\varepsilon\},\mathsf{b}]$. This fact can be expressed in a simple rule without the need for a full-fledged iterative data-flow analysis. A declarative approach—based on a separate loop analysis—may be beneficial because the evaluation in Chapter 5.3 showed a practical occurrence of a theoretical inefficiency in the presented data-flow analysis for the case where a task method contains many nested loops.

Interval analysis (and the related structural analysis) [87, pp.197–215] is a technique to divide up a control-flow graph into regions representing the nesting of control structures such as loops and conditionals. The result of an interval analysis is a *control tree* where leaves represent regions of the control-flow graph, intermediate nodes hold the classification of the control-structure, and edges represent the nesting of the control structures. Another possible data structure called *loop-level hierarchy*, which is similar to control trees but focusses on loops, is presented in [95].

## 4.5 Summary

This chapter introduces schedule analysis as one approach to gather task-order information from the program code without programmer intervention. The schedule analysis makes use of a standard points-to analysis and its associated call graph. The points-to analysis provides alias information information about possible task objects whereas the call graph defines possible execution paths for each task. An escape analysis can be added to improve the precision of later optimizations.

Given the result of the points-to analysis, the schedule analysis proceeds in two phases. First it extracts a loop-contextualized task-variable ordering graph from the code of each task method and uses this graph to compute an ordering relation for all pairs of task variables of the task method. In the second phase, the analysis computes the relation $parallel(\mathcal{A},\mathcal{B})$ for the whole program by looking for task objects that may be scheduled without direct or indirect ordering. The schedule analysis was specialized to handle the important *now happens-before later* pattern with higher precision.

# 5

# Case study 1: Sequentially consistent Java

From the beginning, Java was designed to be a safe and secure language that supports running untrusted code as part of trusted applications. As a multi-threaded language, Java therefore must prevent undefined behavior even for programs that are not correctly synchronized. The *Java Memory Model* [75] formally defines the basic semantics of shared variables and specifies what values a read of a shared memory location is allowed to return.

For correctly synchronized code, that is, programs without data races, the Java Memory Model guarantees *sequential consistency*. In a sequentially consistent system, all threads see write operations to the same memory location in the same order and the operations of each individual thread appear in the order specified by its program text. Because each thread must behave according to its program text, it is relatively easy for programmers to reason about sequentially consistent programs. However, many hardware and compiler optimizations commonly used in uniprocessors, such as register promotion, common subexpression elimination, and reordering, can potentially violate sequential consistency: the effects of an optimization in one thread may be observed by another thread and the program-text order can appear to be violated.

The Java Memory Model tries to minimize the possibly negative performance impact of strict memory models by relaxing the constraints on the order of shared memory accesses. This increases the opportunities for the compiler to apply well-known uniprocessor optimizations. However, a relaxed memory model not only makes it harder for programmers to reason about their applications; it also turned out to be extremely difficult to implement correctly [113].

This chapter presents an optimizing compiler for a Java version with a sequentially consistent memory model. The compiler exploits task-ordering information gathered from the program to compute whether two tasks are potentially executed in parallel or whether they are ordered by happens-before relations. This ordering information helps the compiler to decide for each program point whether a change in this point may be observed by a parallel task (and thus violate sequential consistency) or not. Because the compiler is a bytecode-to-bytecode translator, the programs can run on an unmodified standard Java Virtual Machine.

## 5.1 Sequential consistency

A memory consistency model defines the semantics of shared memory in a concurrent program by specifying the order in which memory operations are visible to other tasks. Under *sequential consistency*, all tasks must observe the same ordering of memory operations and the memory operations must be consistent with the order specified by the program.

A simple execution semantics for a sequentially consistent system is shown in Figure 5.1

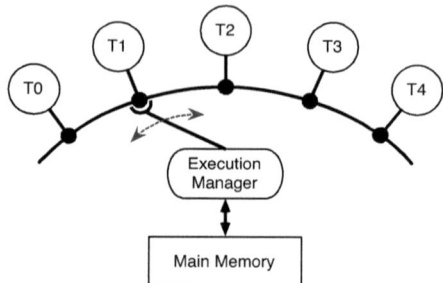

Figure 5.1: Execution semantics for sequentially consistent programs.

Initially: flag0 == flag1 == 0

| **Task 0** | **Task 1** |
|---|---|
| 1  flag0 = 1; | flag1 = 1; |
| 2  r0 = flag1; | r1 = flag0; |
| 3  **if**(r0 == 0) { | **if**(r1 == 0) { |
| 4      //critical section | //critical section |
| 5  } | } |

Figure 5.2: Dekker's mutual exclusion algorithm for two tasks. flag0 and flag1 are shared variables; r0 and r1 are thread-local registers.

and can be defined as follows: In each round, a central execution manager chooses one of the executing tasks. This chosen task performs the next single step in its execution specified by its program order where all reads and writes of shared objects are directly preformed on the main memory. This process of choosing a task and executing a single step is repeated until the program terminates.

This lock-step semantics results in a serialization of all accesses to shared memory where a read to a memory address is guaranteed to retrieve the value stored by the last write to the same address and where all tasks agree on the same serialization of the memory accesses.

As an example for how a relaxed memory model may result in surprising behavior, consider the implementation of Dekker's mutual exclusion algorithm [71, 33, 3] for two tasks shown in Figure 5.2. Dekker's algorithm is designed to allow at most one task to enter the critical section on line 4.

Initially, flags flag0 and flag1 are set to 0. A task signals its intention to enter the critical section by setting its corresponding flag (flag0 or flag1 respectively) on line 1. Before task 0 enters the critical section, it checks the other task's flag on lines 2 and 3 to see whether task 1 intends to enter the critical section, too. If flag1 is 0, task 1 has no intention to enter and it is save for task 0 to proceed.

The correctness condition for this algorithm states that when both tasks reach line 3, it is not possible that registers r0 and r1 are both 0. If both registers were 0, both tasks could enter the critical section at the same time.

5.1. SEQUENTIAL CONSISTENCY

| Execution 1 | | Execution 2 | | Execution 3 | |
|---|---|---|---|---|---|
| //Thread 0 | Thread 1 | //Thread 0 | Thread 1 | //Thread 0 | Thread 1 |
| flag0 = 1; | | | flag1 = 1; | flag0 = 1; | |
| r0 = flag1; | | | r1 = flag0; | | flag1 = 1; |
| | flag1 = 1; | flag0 = 1; | | r0 = flag1; | |
| | r1 = flag0; | r0 = flag1; | | | r1 = flag0; |
| //r0 $=$ 0 | | //r0 $=$ 1 | | \\r0 $=$ 1 | |
| //r1 $=$ 1 | | //r1 $=$ 0 | | \\r1 $=$ 1 | |

Figure 5.3: Some executions of Dekker's algorithm from Figure 5.2

Even in this small example, many possible interleavings exist of how the two tasks can execute their individual steps. Figure 5.3 presents three such possible interleavings and the final results of the non-shared registers r0 and r1. Although many other execution histories are possible, Dekker's algorithm assures that r0 and r1 can never both be 0 at the end of the execution, which would violate the correctness condition stated above.[1]

Intuitively, correctness can be proven by reasoning about the program code: any execution must start with assigning 1 to either flag0 or flag1 on line 1. Therefore, at least one later read of the flags on line 2 will see the 1 and it is not possible that r0 == r1 == 0.

However, this proof is valid only if the compiler and runtime system enforce a strong memory model such as sequential consistency. In a relaxed memory model such as the Java Memory Model, for example, the compiler may choose to reorder the two independent memory accesses on lines 1 and 2 (setting the task's own flag to 1 and reading the value of the sibling task's flag). Scheduling the read on line 2 early can be beneficial because issuing loads early tends to hide the load latency [2]. In addition, modern processors improve their performance through mechanisms such as caches and store buffers, which can effectively reorder the instructions issued by a task without the compiler being involved. When the instructions on lines 1 and 2 are reordered by the compiler or the hardware, the outcome r0 == r1 == 0 is possible, unexpectedly resulting in an incorrect program where both tasks may enter the critical section concurrently.

In general, instruction reordering by the compiler or the hardware breaks the sequential consistent semantics of the program. Without further information, optimizations in a sequentially consistent system must conservatively assume that the order of memory accesses must not be relaxed. While some standard optimizations, such as constant propagation or dead code elimination, can be allowed in a sequentially consistent system, many other optimizations must be weakened or cannot be used at all if sequential consistency should be preserved [78]. If task-schedule information is available, however, the compiler can identify parts of the program that at runtime will not conflict with any parallel task. Those parts can be optimized as if they were executed in a single-threaded context without violating sequential consistency.

---

[1] In Execution 3 of Figure 5.3 both r0 and r1 are 1 and the program deadlocks. Dekker's algorithm in the presented form is therefore not a practical implementation but merely an illustrative example.

Initially: X == Y == 0

**Original Code**

| Task 0 | | Task 1 |
|---|---|---|
| 1  r0 = X; | | r2 = Y; |
| 2  r1 = X; | | X = r2; |
| 3  **if**(r0 == r1) | | |
| 4     Y = 1; | | |

**After Compiler Transformation**

| Task 0 | | Task 1 |
|---|---|---|
| 1  Y = 1; | | r2 = Y; |
| 2  r0 = X; | | X = r2; |
| 3  r1 = r0; | | |
| 4  **if**(**true**); | | |

**Is r0 == r1 == r2 == 1 allowed?**

Figure 5.4: Redundant read elimination is permitted by the JMM but violates sequential consistency (example adapted from [2]).

## 5.2 An optimizing compiler for sequentially consistent Java

This section presents the implementation of an optimizing compiler for a sequentially consistent version of Java. The compiler combines a schedule analysis with a pointer analysis to find those parts in the code that can be optimized under the rules of the more relaxed Java Memory Model (JMM) while preserving sequential consistency semantics.

The JMM is a memory model with relaxed ordering constraints that is weaker than sequential consistency. The main goal of the JMM designers was to provide a model that unambiguously specifies the semantics of multithreaded Java programs while at the same time allowing many of the standard compiler optimizations [75]. The JMM guarantees sequential consistency only for correctly synchronized programs, that is, programs that are data-race free. For programs with data-races, however, the JMM sacrifices the benefits of sequential consistency in favor of more compiler optimizations—and therefore better performance.

Figure 5.4 illustrates the optimization opportunities the JMM provides over sequential consistency. Under sequential consistency, the outcome r0 == r1 == r2 == 1 would be prohibited because it violates causality: In order to set r2 == 1 the write Y = 1 on line 4 by task 0 must have happened before task 1 reads Y into r2 on line 1. However, this implies that the value of X is still the initial 0 because X is only written by task 1 on the next line 2. Therefore, the earlier reads of X into r0 and r1 must have returned 0.

For this example, the JMM allows the compiler to apply common optimizations such as redundant read elimination. This is, because neither X nor Y are flagged as **volatile** and the program does not contain any other synchronization. When performing a redundant read elimination optimization, the compiler eliminates the second read of X on line 2 by replacing r1 = X

## 5.2. AN OPTIMIZING COMPILER FOR SEQUENTIALLY CONSISTENT JAVA

with r1 = r0, as shown in the lower half of Figure 5.4. This allows the compiler to deduce that on line 3, r0 == r1 is always **true**. In a subsequent step, the compiler may therefore replace the tautology **if**(r0 == r1) on line 3 with a simple **if**(**true**). Because the write to Y on line 4 is now unconditional and because writing Y is independent from the read of X, the compiler can finally move the write to Y all the way up before the read of X. This results in the transformed version shown in the lower half of Figure 5.4.

In the transformed program, the outcome r0 == r1 == r2 == 1 is justifiable: task 0 first sets Y = 1 before task 1 loads this value into r2 and propagates it to X from where task 0 reads it into r0 and r1. This outcome appears to require a self-justifying speculative write of Y but it must be allowed if compilers are to perform the common redundant read elimination optimization.

Because in this example, the redundant load elimination together with the subsequent code transformations violates sequential consistency, an optimizing compiler for a sequentially consistent version of Java must not perform this optimization but keep the original program. However, the compiler can safely eliminate redundant reads that are either executed in a single-threaded setting or that do not access memory that may be accessed by any parallel task in parallel without violating sequential consistency.

### 5.2.1 Transforming Java into sequentially consistent Java

In the example from Figure 5.4 a classic redundant load elimination optimization classifies the two reads of X on lines 1 and 2 as being redundant because they access the same memory address and the memory address is not changed between the two reads. In a multi-threaded setting, however, this is only true if no other task writes to X in between the two reads.

A sequentially consistent language and runtime system must not only prevent reordering of reads and writes to shared memory; it must also guarantee that every single read of a shared memory address, even redundant ones, actually return the correct up-to-date value from main memory.

For a sequentially consistent input language, sequential consistency can be achieved on the hardware level through inserting memory fences. However the Java language, does not by default guarantee sequential consistency for programs with data races. A compiler can transform an arbitrary Java program into a sequentially consistent Java program by exploiting the JMM semantics for **volatile** memory accesses.

A Java program that does not use any arrays can be made trivially sequentially consistent by simply declaring every field of every class to be **volatile**. The JMM specifies that *"[...] a read to a volatile variable v returns the value of the write to v that is ordered last before the read by the synchronization order"* [75]. Because reads and writes to **volatile** variables are defined as *synchronization actions*, the memory accesses of a program with only **volatile** fields will be globally ordered, resulting in a sequentially consistent program.

There are two problems with this approach, however. First, by marking whole fields as **volatile** the opportunities for compiler optimizations are greatly reduced. If one part of the program accesses a field concurrently but other parts access the field in a single-threaded context, or if all accesses to this field are correctly synchronized by locks, marking the whole field as **volatile** unnecessarily constrains the non-concurrent accesses. The second problem is that

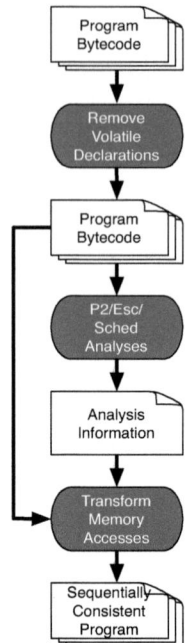

Figure 5.5: Phases of the optimizing compiler for sequentially consistent Java.

in Java defining an array to be **volatile** only affects the *reference to* the array but does not give any guarantees for accessing *elements inside* the array.

Therefore, instead of marking *memory locations* (fields) to be **volatile**, as in standard Java, the presented sequentially consistent version of Java makes the individual *memory access operations* volatile. It does so by rewriting all memory access bytecodes—reads/writes to object fields as well as reads/writes of array elements—into calls to sun.misc.Unsafe.getXYZVolatile() and sun.misc.Unsafe.putXYZVolatile()[2]. The volatile getters and setters in the class Unsafe represent compiler intrinsics that guarantee that the memory accesses follow the Java **volatile** semantics thus creating happens-before relations between concurrent reads and writes.

### 5.2.2 Optimizing away volatile memory accesses

Naïvely rewriting all memory accesses into their volatile counterparts is an overly conservative transformation resulting in unnecessary additional overhead. The goal of the optimization is to reduce the number of memory access bytecodes that must be rewritten. This not only removes the overhead directly associated with the required memory fences but also increases the optimization opportunities for the just-in-time compiler when the program is executed by allowing advanced optimizations such as redundant load elimination or instruction reordering.

---

[2]XYZ is a placeholder for the various basic Java types such as int, float, or Object.

## 5.3. EVALUATION

$$\frac{\begin{array}{l}\text{CONFLICTING}\\ \textit{v1 } \text{MAY POINT TO } \textit{Obj}\\ \textit{v2 } \text{MAY POINT TO } \textit{Obj}\\ \textit{Obj } \text{MAY ESCAPE } \mathcal{A} \text{ and } \mathcal{B}\\ \textit{parallel}(\mathcal{A},\mathcal{B})\end{array}}{\textit{conflicting}(v1,\mathcal{A},v2,\mathcal{B})}$$

$$\frac{\begin{array}{l}\text{RW--CONFLICT}\\ BC_R \text{ MAY READ } \textit{v1.f} \text{ in } \mathcal{A}\\ BC_W \text{ MAY WRITE } \textit{v2.f} \text{ in } \mathcal{B}\\ \textit{conflicting}(v1,\mathcal{A},v2,\mathcal{B})\end{array}}{\textit{readNeedsVolatile}(BC_R)}$$

$$\frac{\begin{array}{l}\text{WR-WW--CONFLICT}\\ BC_W \text{ MAY WRITE } \textit{v1.f} \text{ in } \mathcal{A}\\ BC_X \text{ MAY ACCESS } \textit{v2.f} \text{ in } \mathcal{B}\\ \textit{conflicting}(v1,\mathcal{A},v2,\mathcal{B})\end{array}}{\textit{writeNeedsVolatile}(BC_W)}$$

Figure 5.6: Computing required `volatile` memory accesses for sequentially consistent Java. Variable $f$ ranges over all fields. For array accesses, $f$ is a synthetic field `elements` representing the contents of the array.

The compiler for our sequentially consistent version of Java is realized as a bytecode-to-bytecode translator. The three main phases of the compiler are depicted in Figure 5.5. In the first phase, the compiler removes all programmer-provided `volatile` annotations on fields in the original program. Because the compiled program will be sequentially consistent, it is not necessary to manually declare a field to be `volatile`.[3] The compiler then performs the points-to analysis, escape analysis, and schedule analysis that are needed by the optimization. In the third phase, the compiler transforms all conflicting bytecodes that read or write fields and access array elements to be `volatile`.

The third phase uses the rules depicted in Figure 5.6 to decide whether a bytecode may conflict with another program point. The RW–CONFLICT and WR-WW–CONFLICT rules are variations of the GENERIC-OPT optimization rule from Chapter 4 specialized for the exact semantics required by sequential consistency.

Because parallel reads are allowed under sequential consistency, the RW–CONFLICT rule only adds those read bytecodes $BC_R$ to the *readNeedsVolatile* relation that may conflict with a concurrent write of the same field in the same object. The rule WR-WW–CONFLICT on the other hand adds all write bytecodes $BC_W$ to the *writeNeedsVolatile* relation that may conflict with any concurrent read or write bytecode $BC_X$ accessing the same field $f$ in the same object $Obj$.

## 5.3 Evaluation

We evaluate the performance and effectiveness of the schedule analysis for the sequentially consistent Java compiler. We use several multi-threaded benchmark programs taken from three different benchmark suites to measure the cost and precision of the schedule analysis and compare the runtime overhead of an unoptimized sequentially consistent version and the optimized versions.

---

[3] As described in Section 7.5, `volatile` annotations on a field may be used to check the programmer's awareness that the field is actually shared. In a sequentially consistent Java, however, `volatile` declarations do not have any semantic effect.

### 5.3.1 Setup of the experiment

All experiments were run on a machine equipped with a Intel Core 2 Duo 2.8GHz and 4Gb of RAM. The compiler implementation is single threaded, however, and therefore only one core is used during the compilation.

The first six benchmarks are taken from [111]. sor (successive over-relaxation over a 2D grid), and tsp (traveling salesman problem) are data- and task-parallel applications with data access patterns of scientific codes; threads are synchronized in a fork/join style based on barriers instead of locks. hedc is a warehouse for scientific astrophysics data that implements a meta crawler for searching multiple Internet archives in parallel. The individual queries are handled by reusable worker threads. The programs mol(dyn), ray(tracer), monte(carlo) are multi-threaded numeric applications taken from the Java Grande benchmarks [106].

The last five benchmarks are part of the Lonestar 2.0 benchmark suite, a collection of widely-used real-world sequential applications that exhibit irregular behavior [57]. The benchmarks are parallelized using the Galois runtime system [58]. The Galois runtime provides a framework for parallelizing irregular algorithms that are organized around object-oriented pointer-based data structures such as graphs and trees.

Barnes-Hut (barnes) simulates the gravitational forces acting on a galactic cluster. The Boruvka's algorithm (boruv) computes a minimal spanning tree of an edge-weighted undirected graph. clust is an implementation of a well-known data-mining algorithm called Agglomerative Clustering. Delaunay triangulation d-tri and Delaunay mesh refinement d-ref compute triangulations of sets of points such that each triangle satisfies certain quality constraints.

For most cases, adapting the benchmarks to the task model was straight forward and almost purely syntactical. Only the tsp benchmark required some more refactoring of the original algorithm because the original code was not written in a way that fits the task model very well.

### 5.3.2 Benchmark characteristics and analysis performance

Table 5.1 gives an overview of the size of the individual benchmarks as well as the performance of the schedule analysis. The reported numbers of application classes for the Lonestar benchmarks include the classes of the Galois runtime system.

For most cases, the schedule analysis takes only a small percentage of the overall compilation time, between 1% and 11%, with the moldyn benchmark being a notable exception.

The data-flow approach from Section 4.2.2 for extracting the loop-contextualized task-variable ordering graph from a given task method is sensitive to the number and nesting of back-edges in the control-flow graph. moldyn is implemented in a way such that almost all task objects are scheduled inside a single method. This method contains multiple nested loops, in each of which task objects are scheduled and happens-before relations are created, which causes the data-flow computation to converge only slowly. Therefore, about 98% of the time spent during schedule analysis is used for extracting the information from the bytecode and only about 2% is spent for actually analyzing the schedule. This behavior seems to be a pathological case that is related to the way this particular benchmark has been implemented; however, it also shows that further investigation in a more performant schedule extraction with better worst-case behavior is required.

## 5.3. EVALUATION

|  | sor | tsp | hedc | mold | monte | ray | barn | boruv | clust | d-ref | d-tri |
|---|---|---|---|---|---|---|---|---|---|---|---|
| *benchmark size* | | | | | | | | | | | |
| application classes | 4 | 9 | 59 | 13 | 19 | 18 | 355 | 381 | 367 | 364 | 366 |
| library classes | 40 | 42 | 68 | 40 | 44 | 25 | 82 | 85 | 78 | 82 | 69 |
| methods in call-graph | 202 | 258 | 826 | 251 | 445 | 225 | 3,670 | 3,792 | 3,769 | 3,736 | 3,700 |
| task methods | 9 | 2 | 14 | 11 | 3 | 6 | 5 | 3 | 3 | 2 | 3 |
| *analysis performance* | | | | | | | | | | | |
| compilation time | 2.8s | 2.1s | 6.2s | 120.2s | 3.6s | 3.5s | 17.9s | 16.9s | 17.5s | 15.5s | 18.0s |
| schedule analysis time | 0.3s | 0.1s | 0.5s | 115.8s | 0.1s | 0.2s | 0.8s | 0.3s | 0.2s | 0.2s | 0.3s |
| in % | 11% | 7% | 7% | 96% | 3% | 6% | 4% | 2% | 1% | 1% | 2% |

Table 5.1: Complexity and performance of the analysis.

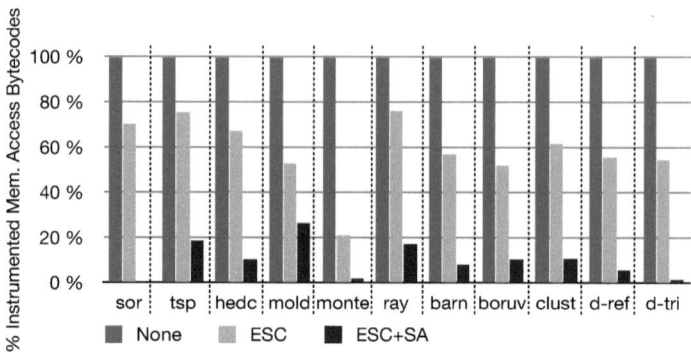

Figure 5.7: Relative number of instrumented field and array accesses.

### 5.3.3 Precision of the analysis

For evaluating the effects of each individual analysis on the overall result, we have compiled the benchmarks in three different configurations:

- In the None configuration, the compiler has no advanced analysis information and must instrument all field and array accesses in order to guarantee sequential consistency.

- The second configuration ESC uses an escape analysis plus a points-to analysis to decide whether two memory accesses executed by different tasks may require memory barriers.

- The third configuration ESC+SA adds scheduling information to the points-to analysis and escape analysis to distinguish between accesses that are ordered and accesses that may happen in parallel.

Figure 5.7 reports the precision of the different configurations in terms of the relative number of memory accesses that were instrumented. For the None configuration, 100% of the memory access bytecodes must be instrumented, because the compiler must conservatively insert memory barriers for each access.

If the compiler has escape information available (the ESC configuration), it can reduce the number of bytecodes that must be instrumented to about 60%.

For all benchmarks, adding the schedule analysis (the ESC+SA configuration) the number of instrumentations needed can be further significantly reduced. A large number of the instrumentations that are removed are located in single-threaded code that is executed during setup and tear-down of the applications and therefore have only relatively little effect on the overall runtime. However, in many cases the schedule analysis is able to identify and remove instrumentations in hot paths of the programs which can have a significant impact on the runtime overhead as presented in the next section.

In all benchmarks, the initial data structures are set up during the start phase and then passed to the subtasks. The subtasks perform their computation before a single-threaded teardown

5.3. EVALUATION 85

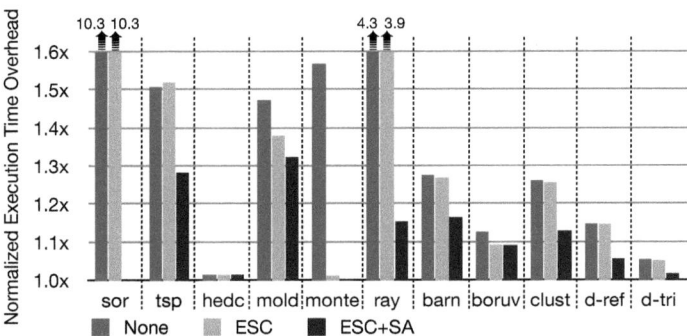

Figure 5.8: Runtime overhead of unoptimized and optimized sequential consistency compared to Java's relaxed memory model.

phase verifies the results and reports to the user. The escape analysis flags all objects that are passed to and from the parallel tasks as 'escaping'. Therefore, the compiler configuration that only uses escape information falsely identifies many memory accesses as conflicting. With scheduling information, however, the compiler can often find that shared objects are only written during the setup phase and only read in parallel.

### 5.3.4 Runtime overhead of sequentially consistent Java

Figure 5.8 shows the overhead of the benchmarks compiled with the None, ESC, and ESC+SA configurations. The baseline of this comparison is the runtime of the original version that uses the relaxed Java Memory Model.

For four out of the eleven benchmarks the fully-optimized sequentially consistent Java is within 2% of the original version whereas the configurations with no optimizations or only escape analysis show overheads between 10% and 50%. In the seven remaining cases the overhead of the fully optimized version was under 32% with an overall average overhead of 11%.

The sor and ray benchmarks show an exceptionally bad behavior for the sequentially consistent versions. The reason for this is that the authors of those benchmarks chose to never use any local variables but always access fields directly. However, instrumenting accesses inside hot loops hurt the performance especially. If the parallel tasks work on their own copies of the data the schedule analysis with the escape analysis can deduce that there are only few conflicting memory accesses and thus restore the performance of the original program.

The performance of hedc is mainly constrained by input/output operations which hides the overhead of sequential consistency even in the unoptimized version.

When looking at the runtime overhead it can be seen that the improvements for the Lonestar benchmarks are significantly smaller (about 5%-10% over the none configuration) than the improvements seen in the other benchmarks. This is, because most of the used Galois methods cannot be optimized. However, there are—often significant—sequential phases other than the setup/teardown phases that can be optimized. In barn, for example, each time step ends with a sequential Advance() task that advances all bodies by directly accessing each body's fields. The optimization removes the fences around all those field accesses (6 field reads + 6 field writes for each body in each time step) which accounts for most of the improvement seen in the barn benchmark.

## 5.4 Related work

There are two general directions of research to improve the performance of sequential consistency. Systems with hardware support and pure software implementations.

**Hardware based.** BulkSC [25] is a hardware implementation that enforces sequential consistency through an arbiter that determines whether groups of memory operations can be committed. Ahn et al. [6] presents BulkCompiler, a hardware-compiler interface that works with group-committing hardware to provide a whole-system high-performance sequentially consistent platform. [71] describe hardware supported conditional memory fences that decide dynamically if there is a need to stall at each fence. The conditional fence mechanism relies on compiler inserted fence instructions to achieve sequential consistency but requires an additional small hardware buffer.

**Software based.** Delay-set analysis, first presented by Shasha and Snir [104], computes a minimal set of delays that guarantees sequential consistency. Those delays are enforced by inserting memory fences. By exploiting the ordering constraints of the hardware consistency model and the property of fence and synchronization operations, Lee and Padua [66] were able to optimize the number of fence instructions that the compiler must insert. In the Pensieve project, Fang et al. [36] developed various additional fence insertion and optimization algorithms. In [108] Sura et al. combine multiple analyses, namely escape, thread structure, and delay-set analysis, into a single compiler for sequentially consistent Java. Their thread structure analysis tries to identify simple cases where tasks are arranged in trivial fork/join patterns inside a single method.

In [67], Lee and Midkiff present a two-phase offline/online interprocedural and inter-task escape analysis. By performing an offline pre-analysis followed by a dynamic online analysis that integrates offline results with dynamic information, the whole-program escape analysis becomes performant enough to be done at runtime by the just-in-time compiler (JIT). This precise online whole-program escape analysis enables the JIT compiler to compile Java programs on the fly under a sequentially consistent memory model. While our sequentially consistent version of Java must be compiled offline, the approach presented by Lee and Midkiff does not have task-order information available and therefore may be less precise than it could be. If an online schedule analysis were available, both analyses could be combined in a single JIT, however, resulting in an online version of the sequentially consistent Java presented in this chapter.

The above software based implementations target programs with traditional Java threads. The unstructured nature of threads, however, makes it difficult to gather good information about the relative order in which threads execute. In contrast, the schedule analysis presented in this paper can analyze task ordering across method boundaries as well as recursive task creation.

## 5.4. RELATED WORK

Many of the supporting analyses (especially delay-set analysis) presented in the related work, however, can be combined with schedule analysis to improve the overall analysis precision.

**Software based with hardware support.** In [78], Marino et al. present their observation that a large class of traditional compiler optimizations that are crucial for performance either already preserve sequential consistency or can be modified to preserve sequential consistency while retaining much of their effectiveness. The overhead of their compiler mainly comes from its inability to aggressively perform a certain class of optimizations that perform eager loading. They propose to expose a hardware speculation mechanism to the compiler that can efficiently detect whether a particular variable has changed its value since last read. Marino et al. conclude that before resorting to relaxing the memory model other ways for improving the performance of sequential-consistency-preserving compilers should be explored.

**Dynamic memory model exceptions.** A memory model exception is an exception that is thrown if the runtime detects possible data races. If a program executes without throwing this exception then it is guaranteed that the execution was sequentially consistent. If a program does throw a memory model exception then it is guaranteed that the execution had a data race. Treating concurrency errors as exceptions with fail-stop behavior is simple for programmers to understand while providing precise semantics and supporting many common compiler optimizations.

In [77], Marino et al. present a memory model that guarantees that if sequential consistency is violated in an execution of a program, then the execution eventually terminates with a memory model exception. This approach uses a combination between compiler and hardware mechanisms to detect sequential consistency violations between single-entry, multiple-exit portions of the program called *regions*. Lucia et al. [74] propose a similar hardware-supported exception mechanism but ensure atomicity of synchronization-free regions, which is a stronger property than sequential consistency.

Memory model exceptions are inherently a dynamic mechanism to give racy programs a precise semantics without the complexity of relaxed memory models. Task-order information may be used by the compiler, however, to statically identify and remove unnecessary data race checks.

**Nested synchronization.** The optimizing compiler presented in this chapter only uses the schedule analysis data in conjunction with the points-to and escape analysis information. However, there are other possible opportunities for optimizations.

The presented compiler, for example, does not take Java synchronization into account. If the compiler can deduce, for example, that *all* accesses to an object are always guarded by the *same* lock it could make those accesses non-volatile without violating sequential consistency. Such an optimization would require an analysis of the synchronization statements in the program with an approach such as [7] or [118, 119].

## 5.5 Summary

Sequential consistency provides stronger and more useful guarantees to the programmer than the more relaxed Java Memory Model. Giving stronger guarantees, however, also prevents many useful compiler and hardware optimizations that may otherwise violate the sequential consistency semantics.

The compiler presented in this chapter transforms a Java program into a sequentially consistent Java program by forcing accesses to fields and array elements to follow the Java `volatile` semantics. The compiler optimizes the program by rewriting only those accesses that may actually result in read-write or write-write conflicts. The experimental data shows that adding a schedule analysis to the compiler significantly improves the performance of the compiled program. As a result, the overhead of sequential consistency is reduced from 136% in the unoptimized version to 11% on average as compared to a hand-optimized version.

# 6
# Case study 2: Dynamic fractional permissions

With the rise of multithreaded programming, the number of problems related to concurrency is constantly growing [73]. One prevalent type of bugs found in concurrent systems are *data races*. A data race occurs when two concurrent access to the same memory location are not ordered by happens-before relations and at least one of the accesses is a write. In practice, there are three different approaches to design data-race free programs:

**Language-enforced data-race freedom:** Some languages guarantee data-race freedom through their type systems [81, 20]. From a high-level, the programmer provides program annotations that describe how data is shared and accessed by concurrent tasks. The language's type system uses the annotations to prove that accesses to shared memory are ordered or fails otherwise. In recent years, much research also went into transactional memory [86, 48, 1]. Transactional memory allows programmers to specify code regions that should be atomic; an accompanying runtime system implemented in hard- and/or software protects the accessed memory from concurrent accesses thus preventing data races.

**Static verification and model checking:** Static verification and model checking of concurrent programs are approaches that—conceptually—exhaustively explore the whole state space of the program to rule out potential data races [88, 96]. The major challenge of model checking techniques is the state space explosion: the number of states increases exponentially with the number of possible task interleavings. Numerous approaches exist for reducing the state space that must be effectively explored for guaranteeing data-race freedom.

**Dynamic detection:** Systems for dynamic data-race detection aim at finding data-races when they happen during program execution. This can be done online, that is, during program execution, or offline, by analyzing a pre-recorded program trace. In general, dynamic detection cannot guarantee the absence of data-races for *all possible* executions; rather, it focusses on data-races in the *observed* execution traces. Dynamic data-race detection systems further fall into two general categories: *Precise* and *imprecise* systems [41]. While precise race detectors never report false positives, they can impose a significant runtime overhead due to the additional bookkeeping they require. Imprecise race detectors increase the performance by giving up precision but—as a result—may report false alarms on data-race free programs.

This chapter introduces a dynamic variant of *fractional permissions* [20] in which the programmer explicitly manages task-access permissions for objects. In this system, each object is associated with an access control list (ACL) that contains all the tasks that are allowed to access the object.

A task is allowed to *write* an object if it's the *only* task in the object's ACL and therefore has full permission. In order for a task to *read* the object, however, it is enough if the task is one of several tasks in the object's ACL.

Each task in an object's ACL conceptually owns a fraction of the full access permission corresponding to the total number of tasks in the ACL. The system can detect data-races by checking the current task's access permissions on every read and write operation. By imposing restrictions on when and how tasks are allowed to modify an object's ACL, the system further forces the programmer to follow a structured access-right management regime and prevents privilege escalation where a task $\mathcal{A}$ with low privileges grants another task $\mathcal{B}$ higher access privileges.

There are two factors that result in a relatively large overhead for a naïve implementation of the dynamic fractional permissions system. First, the memory for storing the ACLs for each object have a negative impact on the memory footprint, memory allocation, cache behavior, and garbage collection. And second, checking whether a task has the correct access rights slows down every single field-read and -write operation.

Because of the imposed runtime overhead, dynamic fractional permissions are impractical for real-world application without optimizations. This chapter presents an optimizing compiler that significantly reduces the runtime overhead by not allocating ACLs for objects that are not shared as well as removing access checks on read and write operations that are not conflicting.

Section 6.1 describes the dynamic fractional permission system and its implementation. The example presented in Section 6.2 illustrates how dynamic fractional permissions can be used to dynamically enforce a data access policy in a `MapReduce()`. The compiler optimizations are presented in Section 6.3 and evaluated in Section 6.4.

## 6.1 Dynamic fractional permissions

This section describes the three components of the dynamic fractional permission system: access control lists (ACLs), permissions, and permission management operations.

### 6.1.1 Access control lists and permissions

At runtime, each object o is associated with an access control list (ACL). We define a function $ACL(o)$ to return the ACL of object o. The ACL is the set of all task objects that share the full access permission for the object. The fraction $Frac(o, \mathcal{A})$ of the full permission that a task $\mathcal{A}$ has for an object o directly correlates to the number of tasks that are in o's ACL. $Frac(o, \mathcal{A})$ is defined as:

## 6.1. DYNAMIC FRACTIONAL PERMISSIONS

$$Frac(o, \mathcal{A}) := \begin{cases} \frac{1}{|ACL(o)|} & \text{if } \mathcal{A} \in ACL(o) \\ 0 & \text{else} \end{cases}$$

If $\mathcal{A}$ is in o's ACL, it shares the permission equally with all other tasks in o's ACL. If $\mathcal{A}$ is not in o's ACL, however, $\mathcal{A}$'s fraction of o's access permission is 0.

The system distinguishes the following three types of permissions, depending on the fraction size:

**Write Permission:** A task $\mathcal{A}$ has write permission (or 'full' permission) for object o if it is the only task in o's ACL. We define the expression isWritable(o,$\mathcal{A}$) to be **true** if $Frac(o,\mathcal{A}) = 1$. Because $\mathcal{A}$ has the full permission, no other task can gain access rights for o. Therefore $\mathcal{A}$ can safely write the fields of o without risking data-races. Certain permission management operations require the performing task to have full permission on the object.

**Read Permission:** A task $\mathcal{A}$ has read permission (or 'partial' permission) to access object o if $\mathcal{A}$ is an element in the ACL. We define the expression isReadable(o,$\mathcal{A}$) to be **true** if $Frac(o,\mathcal{A}) < 1$. A read permission for object o, as the name implies, allows a task $\mathcal{A}$ to read the fields of o but not write them. A task $\mathcal{A}$ with read permission can grant read permission on o to another task $\mathcal{B}$ by adding $\mathcal{B}$ to o's ACL. This reduces the absolute value of the permission fraction that the tasks in o's ACL own. However, adding $\mathcal{B}$ does not change the access rights a third task $C$ may have on o.

**No Permission:** A task $\mathcal{A}$ has no permission for object o if it is not an element in o's ACL. We define the expression noAccess(o,$\mathcal{A}$) to be **true** if $Frac(o,\mathcal{A}) = 0$. It is legal for $\mathcal{A}$ to own a reference to o but $\mathcal{A}$ is not allowed to read or write o's fields nor can $\mathcal{A}$ change o's ACL in any way.

To enforce the dynamic data-race detection, the compiler automatically inserts assertions before all field accesses that check the current task's read and write permissions. If the check fails the program is aborted and an error message is shown, containing the offending program point, the required permission, and the actual ACL. The detailed information in the error message together with the early program termination helps the programmer to pinpoint the data-race.

### 6.1.2 Permission management operations

The dynamic fractional permissions system provides a set of operations that allow a task $\mathcal{A}$ to manage the permissions for an object o. Depending on the operation $\mathcal{A}$ wants to perform it must either have the full permission for o or a fractional permission. This section informally describes the management operations and their semantics.

**Split Permission:** The most common operation for managing permissions for an object o is to split the permission and share it between the current task $\mathcal{A}$ and a second task $\mathcal{B}$. In order to split the permission, the issuing task $\mathcal{A}$ **must** have at least read permission for o; that is, isReadable(o,$\mathcal{A}$). Otherwise, the program is aborted with an appropriate error message. In terms of o's ACL, the operation o.splitPermission($\mathcal{B}$) checks whether isReadable(o, **now**) and, if **true**, simply adds $\mathcal{B}$ to the ACL.[1]

**Yield permission:** A task $\mathcal{A}$ can transfer (yield) its permission for an object o to another task $\mathcal{B}$. After the yield, task $\mathcal{B}$ has the same permission (none, read, or write) on o as $\mathcal{A}$ had before the yield. In any case, after the yield, the issuing task $\mathcal{A}$ has no permission on o. In terms of o's ACL, the operation o.yieldPermission($\mathcal{B}$) executed by task $\mathcal{A}$ replaces the occurrence of task $\mathcal{A}$ (if any) in o's ACL with $\mathcal{B}$.

A task can yield its permission *explicitly* in the code by executing the yield() operation. A task can, however, also yield (or 'give back') its fraction of the permission *implicitly*. When a task $\mathcal{A}$ finishes, the runtime system removes $\mathcal{A}$ from all ACLs it is a member of. This automatically increases the absolute values of the permission fractions of the affected objects. For an object that only had two tasks $\mathcal{A}$ and $\mathcal{B}$ in its ACL, removing $\mathcal{A}$ from the ACL promotes task $\mathcal{B}$'s permission to a full permission. Objects where $\mathcal{A}$ was the only task in their ACL become permanently inaccessible (garbage) when $\mathcal{A}$ is removed.

As an example where implicitly yielding permissions is helpful, consider the ACL [W1, W2, W3, Join] for an object o. This ACL contains three worker tasks W1, W2, and W3 as well as a single Join task. While the workers are executing, they can concurrently read o because they all have read permission. Over time, the worker tasks will finish one after the other and each worker will be removed from the ACL. In the end, the Join task is the only task in the ACL. Join has collected the full permission and therefore has full access to o.

**Link and unlink permission:** By linking the permission of one object slave to another object master, slave will share master's ACL. Linking allows the programmer to express *ownership* relations where the permission for slave are always the same as the permission for master. When the permissions are linked, only master's ACL has to be managed explicitly. For a task $\mathcal{A}$ to execute the expression slave.linkToPermission(master) it must have full permission on the slave object; $\mathcal{A}$'s permission on master is not important, however. After the two permissions have been linked, $\mathcal{A}$ has the same permission for slave as it had for accessing master. In terms of slave's ACL, linking the permissions replaces slave's ACL with master's ACL and keeps them synchronized whenever updates happen to either slave's ACL or master's ACL

Two linked objects can be unlinked again by executing slave.unlinkPermission(master). For unlinking, the executing task $\mathcal{A}$ must have the full permission on the slave (and therefore the master, since they are linked). After the unlink operation, both objects master and slave have their own individual ACLs again, each of which only contains $\mathcal{T}$.

**Shared and immutable permission:** The dynamic fractional permissions system supports two special types of objects: immutable objects and shared objects. Marking an object as shared or immutable is permanent and cannot be undone. Immutability and sharing is implemented as two special types of ACLs.

---

[1]The term *split* stems from the notion of *fractional* permissions. The whole permission of size 1 is split between the $n$ elements in the ACL such that each element has $\frac{1}{n}$th of the permission.

The *immutable* ACL grants read access to every task, but no write access. When a task $\mathcal{A}$ issues the operation o.immutablePermission(), the system checks that $\mathcal{A}$ has read permission. If so, it replaces o's ACS with the immutable ACL.

The *shared* ACL grants read and write access to every task. By marking an object to be shared, the programmer asserts to the system that he is aware of the concurrent use of the object and manages concurrent accesses manually (e.g., through locks or atomic sections). For a shared objects, the system cannot detect data-races. Calling the operation o.sharedPermission() requires the issuing task $\mathcal{A}$ to have full permission for o. If this is the case, the system replaces o's current ACL with the immutable ACL.

## 6.2 Example: MapReduce with dynamic data-race detection

MapReduce is a programming model for processing large data sets [32]. A MapReduce program consists of a Map() function that takes a key/value pair as input and produces some intermediate data, and a Reduce() function that merges the intermediate data of multiple Map() tasks into either the final result or the key/value inputs for the next Map()-Reduce() phase.

In MapReduce, the high-level data access patterns are straight forward: The data structure containing the key/value inputs are read concurrently by each Map() task but it is only written when it is created by the preceding Reduce() task (or the initial task); the data structure that collects the intermediate results from the Map() tasks is written concurrently by the Map() tasks but read only by the subsequent Reduce() task.

In a concrete implementation of a MapReduce computation, a more detailed access policy must be worked out to prevent data-races. For example, what tasks are allowed to read/write the intermediate objects produced by the Map() tasks? Can one Map()-task access the intermediate result of another Map() task? What tasks need read/write access to the results after the MapReduce has finished? Especially larger applications are prone to introduce inconsistencies in the access policies, resulting in potential data races.

With the dynamic fractional permission system, the programmer is forced to explicitly manage the permissions a given task has on a given object. When executing the program, dynamic checks will detect reliably if the access permissions are managed inconsistently and report errors accordingly.

Figure 6.1 shows one possible implementation of a single MapReduce step using dynamic fractional permissions for specifying the data access policies. The program consists of three tasks: MapReduce() on line 3, the Map() task on line 22, and the Reduce() task on line 33.

The only public MapReduce() task is the entry point to the MapReduce computation. Following the *now happens-before later* pattern described in Chapter 3, MapReduce() expects as its first parameters a task later that will continue once the MapReduce phase is over. The second parameter input is an ArrayList of Strings that comprises the input in this example.

The data access policy for this example requires, that the MapReduce() task has full write access to the input list. This means, that the current **now** task is the only task in input's ACL. For reasons of simplicity, MapReduce() further requires that the **this** object is globally shared so that the Reduce() task can later simply publish the result by writing the public result field

```
1  public class MapReduce {
2    public volatile Result result;
3    public task MapReduce(Task later, ArrayList<String> input) {
4      assert isShared(this) && isWritable(input, now);
5      //the map tasks will access data concurrently
6      Vector<Data> data = new Vector<Data>();
7      data.sharedPermission();
8  
9      Task reduce = schedule Reduce(later, input, data);
10     reduce→later;
11     //grant read access to the reduce task
12     input.splitPermission(reduce);
13 
14     for(int i = 0; i < input.size(); i++) {
15       Task map = schedule Map(input, data, i);
16       //grant each map task read access to 'input'
17       input.splitPermission(map);
18       map→reduce;
19     }
20   }
21 
22   private task Map(ArrayList<String> input, Vector<Data> data, int index) {
23     assert isReadable(input, now) && isWritable(data, now);
24     //perform complex map operation using the input
25     String s = input.get(index);
26     Data mapped = new ComplexData(s);
27     //make the mapped Data follow the same regime as 'input'
28     mapped.linkToPermission(input);
29     data.add(mapped);
30     //implicitly remove 'now' from input's ACL
31   }
32 
33   private task Reduce(Task later, ArrayList<String> input, Vector<Data> data) {
34     //all Map tasks gave back their permissions for 'input'; therefore 'now' has write access
35     assert isWritable(input, now) && isReadable(data, now) && isWritable(this, now);
36 
37     //clear input array and compute the result from the data
38     input.removeAll();
39     Result r = new Result(data);
40     //make the result immutable and publish it
41     r.immutablePermission();
42     this.result = r;
43     //give write permission for 'input' to 'later'
44     input.yieldPermission(later);
45   }
46 }
```

Figure 6.1: Implementation of the MapReduce pattern using dynamic fractional permissions for data-race detection.

## 6.3. OPTIMIZING DYNAMIC FRACTIONAL PERMISSIONS

declared on line 2. This access policy is dynamically enforced by the assertion on line 4.[2]

On line 6, the MapReduce() task creates a new Vector object into which the concurrent Map() tasks will write their intermediate results. To indicate that this Vector will be accessed in parallel, the programmer must explicitly set the permission on the data object to be shared on line 7.

Starting from line 9, the MapReduce() task schedules a single Reduce() task, orders it before the passed later task (line 10), schedules a Map() task for each element in the input vector (line 15), and orders all Map() tasks to happen before the Reduce() task (line 18). On lines 12 and 17, the MapReduce() task splits its write permission for the input list and shares it with the Map() tasks and the Reduce() task. After the MapReduce() task has finished it is automatically removed from input's ACL leaving the Map() tasks as well as the single Reduce() task.

The scheduler can now start the Map() tasks. Line 23 asserts that each Map() task has read permission for the input list and write permission for the (shared) data vector. The Map() tasks read from the input list on line 25 and use it in the subsequent lines to compute some complex result object mapped which it then stores in the shared data vector on line 29.

The data access policy in this example is that the intermediate data produced by the Map() tasks should follow exactly the permissions of the input list. By linking the ACL for the mapped data object to the ACL of the input list on line 28, Map() tasks may read the results of siblings that have finished their computation.

Whenever a Map() task finishes, it is automatically removed from the ACL of the input list. When finally the Reduce() task is started, it is the last task remaining in input's ACL and thus has full write permissions on the input list as well as all the individual Data objects stored in the shared data vector (because their ACLs are linked to input). The Map() tasks have effectively yielded their permissions to the Reduce() task and the fractional permissions have been re-combined into a full permission. The assertion on line 35 verifies the permissions required by Reduce().

In this example, the Reduce() task clears the input array on line 38 so that it can be reused again. On line 39 Reduce() computes the result by combining the intermediate data into a Result object r. r is then made it immutable on line 41 and published to the world on line 42.

Because the input list is supposed to be reused, the Reduce() task must hand over its full permission to the later task by explicitly yielding its permission on line 44. This is necessary, because in the beginning later cannot be in input's ACL or otherwise MapReduce() would not have write permission. Therefore, implicitly yielding the permission to later is not possible in this case.

## 6.3 Optimizing dynamic fractional permissions

The overhead of dynamic fractional permissions comes from two sources: 1) Overhead of permission management operations and 2) overhead from the automatically inserted read/write permission checks.

Permissions only have to be managed for objects that are potentially accessed in parallel. For task-local objects or for objects that are only accessed from tasks ordered by happens-before

---

[2] The assertions are inserted automatically by the compiler, not the programmer.

relationships, the management operations—including the creation of the initial ACL for at **new** statements—are unnecessary and can be removed.

Similarly, read and write checks only have to be performed on objects that may be accessed in parallel. Furthermore, redundant read and write checks can be grouped by moving them as early as possible and removing duplicates. Imagine, for example, a task T1() that repeatedly accesses an object Obj through a variable v1 without intermediate splits or yields of its permission:

```
task T1() {
    v1 = /*some object*/;
    tmp1 = v1.f;
    v1.f = 42;
    tmp2 = v1.g;
}
```

A naïve insertion of permission checks would result in the following transformed code:

```
task T1() {
    v1 = /*some object*/;
    assert isReadable(v1, now);
    tmp1 = v1.f;
    assert isWritable(v1, now);
    v1.f = 42;
    assert isReadable(v1, now);
    tmp2 = v1.g;
}
```

Clearly, such redundant read and write checks on v1 are unnecessary because no other task can take away the given permission of T1(). By moving the checks as early as possible and then choosing the strongest permission check (here isWritable()), the example can be transformed into the optimized form with only a single permission check:

```
task T1() {
    v1 = /*some object*/;
    assert isWritable(v1, now);
    tmp1 = v1.f;
    v1.f = 42;
    tmp2 = v1.g;
}
```

### 6.3.1 Handling Permission Operations

A permission operation such as v1.yieldPermission(v2) may change the type of permission the current task **now** has on v1. Therefore, subsequent accesses to v1 require the compiler to insert permission checks again. Consider the following example, which is similar to the example from the previous section:

```
1 task T1() {
2     v1 = /*some object*/;
3     t1 = /*some task, may be ==now!*/;
```

## 6.3. OPTIMIZING DYNAMIC FRACTIONAL PERMISSIONS

```
 4    assert isWritable(v1, now);
 5    tmp1 = v1.f;
 6    v1.f = 42;
 7    v1.yieldPermission(t1);
 8    //Need to check permission on v1 again!
 9    assert isReadable(v1, now);
10    tmp2 = v1.g;
11  }
```

Note that the assertion on line 8 does not necessarily fail for the case where t1 == now. Therefore, because v1 is accessed after the permissions of now on v1 may have been changed on line 7, the check on line 3 is not sufficient and the compiler must insert the read check on line 8.

To capture the effects of read and write checks in the control-flow graph, the compiler rewrites a permission operation such as v1.addPermission(t1) to define a new SSA variable: v2 = v1.addPermission(t1). All subsequent uses of v1 in the original control-flow graph are replaced by v2, inserting Φ-nodes when needed. Through this transformation (treating a permission operation as a definition of a new SSA variable), permission checks can be done "as early as possible", meaning grouped directly after the SSA variable definition. Applying this transformation to the example results in the following code:

```
task T1() {
  v1 = /*some object*/;
  t1 = /*some task, may be ==now!*/;
  assert isWritable(v1, now);
  tmp1 = v1.f;
  v1.f = 42;
  v2 = v1.yieldPermission(t1);
  //v1.yieldPermission() defined v2; v1 is invalid from now on
  assert isReadable(v2, now);
  tmp2 = v2.g;
}
```

### 6.3.2 Auxiliary Rules

The optimizations for removing unnecessary permission operations and for finding optimized locations to insert permission checks make use of the helper functions shown in Figure 6.2.

The computation of variables that need a read check starts with rule NEEDSREADCHECK–LOCAL which selects all variables $v1$ that may point to objects that may be accessed in parallel by some other task. Rule NEEDSREADCHECK–PHI then propagates this information backwards across Φ nodes inside the surrounding method to mark all SSA variables that may reach the reading bytecode. NEEDSREADCHECK–GLOBAL globally propagates the access information to all variables that flow into parameters that may be read inside a method.

The rules for NEEDSWRITECHECK are functionally equivalent to the NEEDSREADCHECK but start from read and write bytecodes respectively.

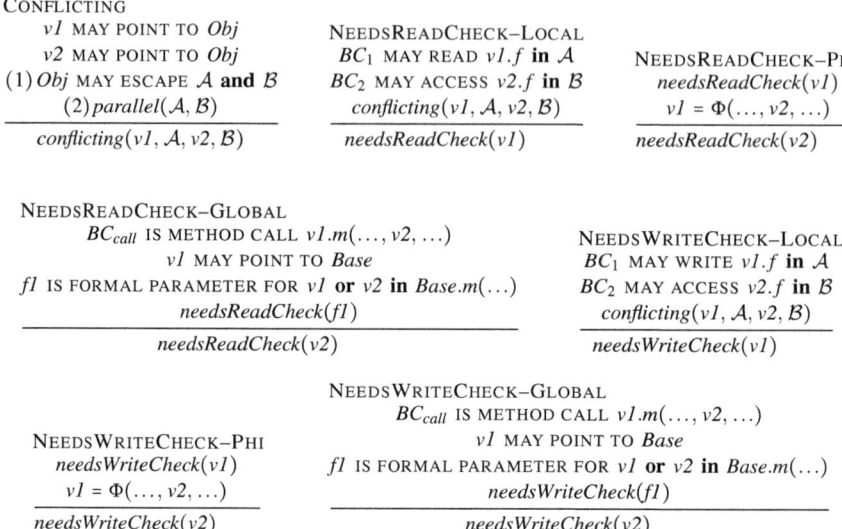

Figure 6.2: Auxiliary functions used for optimizing dynamic fractional permissions. The NEEDSREADCHECK and NEEDSWRITECHECK rules start with marking local variables that may be accessed concurrently and propagate this information inter-procedurally.

### 6.3.3 Optimizations

Figure 6.3 shows the optimizations for finding unnecessary permission management operations and for deciding on the locations, where read and write checks must be inserted.

UNNECESSARYOBJECTACL selects bytecodes $BC_{new}$ corresponding to **new**-statements that create objects $Obj$ that are never accessed in parallel (and therefore no read or write check is ever performed on $Obj$). For those $BC_{new}$, the permission system does not need to create an initial access control list, because no permission check is ever done for the corresponding object.

Similarly, UNNECESSARYPERMISSIONOPERATION chooses all bytecodes $BC_1$ corresponding to permission management operations that are performed on objects that never appear in permission checks.

INSERTREADCHECK then selects the earliest bytecode $BC_1$ that defines a SSA variable $v1$ without being a $\Phi$ node or a formal method parameter. The compiler will insert a read check at this definition of $v1$ if $v1$ requires a read check but no write check. Otherwise, INSERTWRITECHECK will make the compiler insert a write check.

$$
\begin{array}{c}
\text{UNNECESSARYOBJECTACL} \\
BC_{new} \text{ is } v1 = \textbf{new } \texttt{C()} \text{ CREATING } Obj \\
v2 \text{ MAY POINT TO } Obj \\
\textbf{not } needsReadCheck(v2) \\
\textbf{not } needsWriteCheck(v2) \\
\hline
unnecessaryObjectACL(BC_{new})
\end{array}
\qquad
\begin{array}{c}
\text{UNNECESSARYPERMISSIONOPERATION} \\
BC_1 \text{ is } v1.\{yield \,|\, add\} Permission(v3) \\
v1 \text{ MAY POINT TO } Obj \\
v2 \text{ MAY POINT TO } Obj \\
\textbf{not } needsReadCheck(v2) \\
\textbf{not } needsWriteCheck(v2) \\
\hline
unnecessaryPermissionOperation(BC_1)
\end{array}
$$

$$
\begin{array}{c}
\text{INSERTREADCHECK} \\
BC_1 \text{ DEFINES } v1 \,(v1 \text{ IS NOT A } \Phi \textbf{ or A } formal) \\
\textbf{not } needsWriteCheck(v1) \\
needsReadCheck(v1) \\
\hline
insertReadCheck(BC_1)
\end{array}
\qquad
\begin{array}{c}
\text{INSERTWRITECHECK} \\
BC_1 \text{ DEFINES } v1 \,(v1 \text{ IS NOT A } \Phi \textbf{ or A } formal) \\
needsWriteCheck(v1) \\
\hline
insertWriteCheck(BC_1)
\end{array}
$$

Figure 6.3: Rules used by the compiler to remove unnecessary permission operations and to decide where read and write checks must be inserted.

## 6.4 Evaluation

This chapter presents the performance evaluation of the dynamic fractional permission system. We compare four different optimization configurations with the original versions of the benchmarks that do not use a permission system.

### 6.4.1 Setup of the experiment

As discussed in Chapter 5, all experiments were run on a machine equipped with a Intel Core 2 Duo 2.8GHz and 4Gb of RAM. The compiler implementation is single threaded, however, and therefore only one core is used during the compilation.

The benchmarks are taken from the ERCO project [111] and were chosen because of their object-oriented parallelism where objects are used for inter-task communication as opposed to the shared matrices of numeric applications such as the Java Grande benchmarks [106]. sor (successive over-relaxation over a 2D grid), and tsp (traveling salesman problem) are data- and task-parallel applications with data access patterns of scientific codes; threads are synchronized in a fork/join style based on barriers instead of locks. hedc is a warehouse for scientific astrophysics data that implements a meta crawler for searching multiple Internet archives in parallel. The individual queries are handled by reusable worker threads. philo is a simulation of the dining philosophers problem. elevator is a real-time discrete event simulator where elevators are modeled as individual tasks that poll directives from a central control board. Communication through the control board is synchronized through locks.

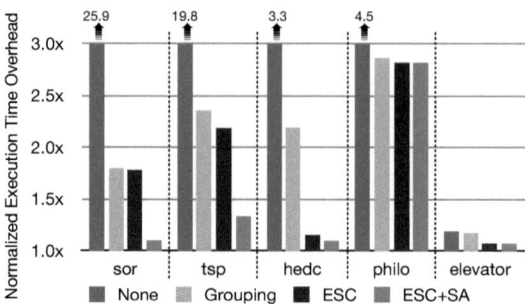

Figure 6.4: Runtime overhead of different optimization levels for dynamic fractional permissions compared to the original version without a dynamic fractional permission system.

## 6.4.2 Runtime overhead of dynamic fractional permissions

The effects of the individual optimization parts were evaluated by compiling the benchmarks in four different configurations:

- In the None configuration, the compiler has no advanced analysis information and must insert read and write checks on every memory access.

- In the Grouping configuration, redundant permission checks are avoided by inserting permission checks only after variable definitions or at the points where an object's ACL may be changed by splitPermission() or yieldPermission operations. While being a global optimization, this configuration does neither use escape nor schedule analysis information. This is achieved by removing clauses (1) and (2) of the CONFLICTING rule in Figure 6.2.

- The third configuration ESC uses an escape analysis plus a points-to analysis to decide whether two memory accesses executed by different tasks may conflict (clause (1) but not clause (2) of Figure 6.2).

- The third configuration ESC+SA adds scheduling information to the points-to analysis and escape analysis to distinguish between accesses that are ordered and accesses that may happen in parallel.

Figure 6.4 shows the runtime overhead of the benchmarks compiled with the None, Grouping, ESC, and ESC+SA configurations. The baseline of this comparison is the runtime of the original version without the dynamic fractional permission system.

For three of the five benchmarks, the fully optimized version (ESC+SA) is within 10% of the original version. The average performance overhead over all benchmarks is 48% which can be attributed to the poor performance of the philo benchmark. (Without philo, the average overhead is 15%.)

In the philo benchmark, most objects are shared and accessed concurrently and the compiler cannot remove expensive permission checks. This overhead could be reduced significantly by making the compiler aware of `immutablePermission()` and `sharedPermission()` operations. The compiler does not need to insert read (read/write) permission checks if it knows that an object has been flagged as immutable (shared). The current implementation of the optimizations does not know about immutable and shared permissions, however, and therefore does insert unnecessary read and write checks in the `philo` benchmark.

## 6.5 Related work

**Fractional permissions**  Boyland's work on fractional permissions [20] introduces a permission system where a single write permission of value 1 can be split into infinitely many read permissions with values < 1. Permission fractions can be distributed to subtasks and later reclaimed. If the system can prove that a task has the original write permission or that it has successfully reclaimed all fractions of the read permissions, the task can write the data. Because fractional permissions guarantee that only one task at a time can have the full write permission, data races are impossible. Terauchi [109, 110] and Boyland [21] later presented further improvements for inferring fractional permissions. As opposed to the dynamic fractional permissions presented in this chapter, the previous work on fractional permissions focus on static techniques to prove data-race freedom and therefore may statically reject programs that are otherwise safe.

**SP-bags**  The basic idea behind SP-bags, introduced by Feng and Leiserson's [38] and further refined by Raman et al. [97], is to attach two bags, $S$ and $P$, to each task. Each bag contains task IDs of descendent tasks that logically precede the task or that operate in parallel respectively. Each memory location is instrumented to contain two additional fields, a reader task ID and a writer task ID. Every time a shared memory location is accessed by a task, the algorithm uses the $S$ and $P$ bags to check whether the current task can interfere with the task that is recorded in the reader and/or writer fields. SP-bags share some similarities with the dynamic fractional permissions but instead of the tasks managing their own bags, dynamic fractional permissions use access control lists on objects. It is an open question, however, whether one approach is more flexible than the other or whether they are equally expressive.

**Dynamic data-race detection.**  Dynamic data-race detectors basically fall into two categories: precise detection, such as the RaceTrack [117] and FastTrack [41] detectors, where every memory operation is checked for data races; and detectors based on sampling, such as LiteRace [76] and Pacer [18]. With sampling, not every memory access is checked but periodic samples are scanned for potential data races. Sampling therefore deliberately introduces some imprecision for the benefit of increased performance. Dynamic fractional permissions do check every memory access and therefore fall under the category of precise detection. However, while the above data-race checkers do not impose any restrictions on the programmer, dynamic fractional permissions do enforce explicit permission management.

## 6.6 Summary

In the original work, fractional permissions are a mechanism to *statically* prevent data races. Permissions are linear capabilities that can be passed from one task to another. By splitting a permission into fractions, a task can grant multiple other tasks concurrent read access. Because writing data requires the full permission—and by definition at most one task can have the full permission—, fractional permissions prevent read/write conflicts. Only when all read fractions have been returned from the subtasks and the full permission is restored, a task is allowed to write again. Fractional permissions use a type- and effect-system to statically check a program.

This chapter introduces a dynamic variant of fractional permissions where the programmer manually manages the splitting and recovering of permissions. The manual management forces the programmer to come up with a rigid data management scheme and replaces the common ad-hoc approaches of current languages.

Permissions are maintained and checked at runtime. In the worst case, every read and write access to an object requires checking the permission of the current task, which introduces a significant runtime overhead. The optimization described in this chapter makes use of schedule analysis to remove permission checks whenever possible.

# 7

# Other applications in optimization and verification

This chapter outlines additional uses of compiler optimization and verification techniques that are enabled by or benefit from task-schedule information.

**Setup of the experiments.** The optimizations presented in this chapter have been implemented as prototypes. However, for time reasons we have not conducted systematic performance evaluations but only report anecdotal evidence. Unless explicitly stated, the experimental data presented in this chapter has been collected using the Datalog prototype described in Section 4.3.

All bddbddb-based experiments were performed on a typical developer machine equipped with a Intel Core 2 Duo 2.8GHz and 4Gb of RAM. The bddbddb implementation, however, is single threaded and therefore only one core is in use during the analysis. bddbddb has been configured to use its built-in pure Java implementation for BDDs.

The set of benchmarks is a subset of the benchmarks introduced in Chapter 5. For evaluating the effects of each individual compiler analysis on the overall result—points-to analysis, escape analysis, and schedule analysis—, we use four different configurations:

**points-to:** In the first configuration, we only use the points-to information to find program points that may access the same objects.

**points-to + schedule:** The second configuration uses the escape analysis in addition to the points-to information to reduce the number of objects that may potentially be accessed in parallel.

**points-to + schedule** The third configuration adds scheduling information to the points-to analysis but does not use escape information.

**points-to + escape + schedule:** The fourth configuration combines all three analyses for maximum precision. All optimization rules presented in this dissertation use this configuration as they contain clauses using all three analyses.

## 7.1 Synchronization removal

Like many imperative and object-oriented languages, Java provides a synchronization mechanism based on locks. Whenever a method or block may access data structures that are shared between multiple threads, the programmer must guard the critical section with a lock. Locks are an integral part of the Java language and made available to the programmer through the `synchronized` keyword.

When a Java thread `t1` wants to enter a `synchronized` section, it must first attempt to acquire the associated lock. If the lock is held by another thread `t2`, `t1` is blocked. When `t2` releases the lock, one or more waiting threads (including `t1`) are woken up, each of which tries to acquire the lock again. If `t1` successfully acquires the lock, it is allowed to enter the `synchronized` section; if another thread acquires the lock before `t1`, `t1` must continue waiting.

Synchronized sections implement the *mutual exclusion* property: only one thread at a time is allowed inside the section guarded by the same lock. In Java, every object is automatically associated with its own distinct `monitor` that provides the lock functionality.[1] Two code sections are mutually exclusive if and only if they synchronize on the same runtime object.

### 7.1.1 Unnecessary synchronization

Generally, a thread-safe library such as the Java standard library cannot know the context it is used in. To simplify their usage, general purpose libraries often conservatively assume a multi-threaded environment and guard all critical sections that potentially access shared data with `synchronized` sections. Therefore, in many programs a large number of locking operations may safely be removed because two parallel tasks never contend for the same lock.

If in a given application a thread-safe library is used in a purely single-threaded setting (even though the rest of the application may be multi-threaded) it may execute many unnecessary lock `acquire()` and `release()` operations. Many studies have shown that unnecessary synchronization operations can introduce a significant performance overhead, finding that typical single-threaded Java programs spend between 10%-50% of their execution time with synchronization operations [101, 8, 114].

### 7.1.2 Removing unnecessary synchronization

At the core of the synchronization removal optimization is the problem of classifying `synchronized` blocks into *required* and *unnecessary*. A `synchronized` section is required if two parallel tasks `t1` and `t2` may try to synchronize on the same object.

On the Java source code level, a `synchronized` block is syntactically given by matching curly braces. On the bytecode level, the synchronization is translated into a single `monitorenter` and one or more `monitorexit` bytecode instructions. Each `monitorenter` and `monitorexit` instruction references a variable that at runtime points to the object that will be used as the lock. The Java virtual machine specification requires `monitorenter` and `monitorexits` to be well balanced, meaning that every `monitorenter` is eventually followed by

---

[1] In addition to locking, monitors offer a `wait`/`notify` mechanism that can be used for inter-process signaling.

## 7.1. SYNCHRONIZATION REMOVAL

$$\frac{\begin{array}{l}\text{SYNC-REMOVAL}\\BC_1 \text{ IS MONITORENTER, MAY EXECUTE IN } \mathcal{A}\\BC_2 \text{ IS MONITORENTER, MAY EXECUTE IN } \mathcal{B}\\BC_1 \text{ SYNCHRONIZES ON } v1\\BC_2 \text{ SYNCHRONIZES ON } v2\\v1 \text{ MAY POINT TO } Obj\\v2 \text{ MAY POINT TO } Obj\\Obj \text{ MAY ESCAPE } \mathcal{A} \text{ \textbf{and} } \mathcal{B}\\parallel(\mathcal{A}, \mathcal{B})\end{array}}{requiredMonitorenter(BC_1)}$$

Figure 7.1: Computing required `monitorenter` bytecodes for synchronization removal. The *parallel*() relation is computed by the schedule analysis.

a corresponding `monitorexit` on the same object [72]. [2]

We can therefore translate the question whether a **synchronized** block is required or not into the question whether the corresponding `monitorenter` conflicts with another `monitorenter` instruction that may lock on the same object in parallel.

Figure 7.1 shows the rule for the synchronization removal optimization. For each `monitorenter` bytecode $BC_1$, the compiler checks whether *requiredMonitorenter*($BC_1$) holds true. $BC_1$ is required, if there is another `monitorenter` bytecode $BC_2$ that at runtime may synchronize on the same object $Obj$ in parallel. If $BC_1$ is not required, the compiler can remove the **synchronized** section by removing the `monitorenter` together with the corresponding `monitorexit` bytecodes.[3]

### 7.1.3 Experimental data

The result of the synchronization removal is shown in Figure 7.2. Most of the presented benchmarks are hand-optimized to make use of data-parallelism and work mainly on unsynchronized arrays, data objects, and scalar values. Synchronization is often avoided in favor of separating the computation into multiple ordered phases. From all benchmarks, only `hedc` actively uses **synchronized** methods in the application source code in a way that is more complex than just collecting the results in a synchronized `Vector` object.

Despite the benchmark authors trying to avoid synchronization as much as possible, all benchmarks directly or indirectly call library methods that are **synchronized**. Typical cases are calls to synchronized `StringBuffer.append()` to concatenate strings. Other synchronization

---
[2]To reduce bytecode size and allow for certain optimizations, **synchronized** methods are not translated into `monitorenter(this)` and `monitorexit(this)`; instead, the method is flagged as **synchronized** in the class file and the Java virtual machine specification requires the calling bytecode to acquire and release the lock. For simplicity, in this section we treat a method **synchronized void** foo(){ ... body ...} as the syntactically equivalent **void** foo(){ **synchronized**(this){ ... body ... }}

[3]Matching corresponding `monitorenter` and `monitorexit` bytecodes requires additional analysis of the method control flow and may be impossible in the presence of aliasing.

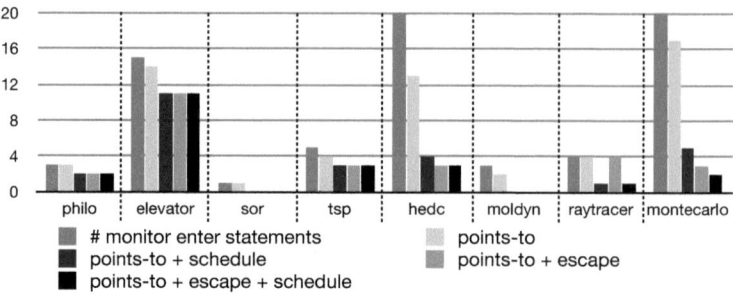

Figure 7.2: Number of monitor enter statements that are required.

statements are in library methods such as `Throwable.printStackTrace()` and are necessary because tasks may throw exceptions and print their stack traces concurrently.

For all benchmarks, the synchronization removal optimization was able to reduce the number of `monitorenter` bytecodes. In the first six benchmarks, adding the schedule analysis to the points-to and escape analysis did not improve the result. Probably, this is because the number of `monitorenter` bytecodes is already close to the minimal required amount in those hand-optimized benchmarks. For the `raytracer` and `montecarlo` benchmarks, however, the schedule analysis increased the precision significantly over the escape analysis.

In summary, the synchronization removal optimization was able to remove between 33% and 100% with an average of 68.84% of the **synchronized** blocks in the benchmarks.

### 7.1.4 Related work

**Escape-based synchronization removal.** There has been a fair amount of work on using escape analysis for synchronization removal. The system described by Bogda [17] statically detects thread-local objects through an inter-procedural, flow- and context-insensitive, constraint-based whole-program analysis. Their analysis proceeds in two steps. First they determine when a reference escapes the stack and second when a reference in the heap escapes local objects. Wang and Sun [114] describe a context-sensitive escape analysis that is based on a more traditional data-flow analysis. Their analysis consists of multiple phases that compute method summaries and then propagates call-context information as well as escape information along call graph nodes. Whaley and Rinard [116] and Choi et al. [31] use similar graph-based program abstractions for performing escape analysis. Whaley and Rinard's points-to escape graphs as well as the connection graphs introduced by Choi et al. can be summarized independently of the calling context, allowing for an efficient compositional analysis.

Purely escape-based techniques preserve synchronization on objects that are visible to multiple tasks. Whenever an object escapes at least one task, escape-based techniques conservatively assume that the object must be synchronized, regardless of whether multiple tasks may actually try to synchronize on the same object in parallel or not. The synchronization optimization presented in this section also uses an escape analysis, but it adds information about whether an object may be synchronized by more than one task during the object's lifetime.

**Equivalence-based synchronization removal.** The analysis described by Ruf [101] can eliminate synchronization operations even on objects that escape their allocating task if it can show that only one task accesses the escaping object. A dynamic synchronization operation in task $\mathcal{A}$ on an object $Obj$ can be eliminated whenever no other task $\mathcal{B}$ attempts to synchronize $Obj$ during the execution of the guarded code. In a first phase, Ruf identifies thread allocation sites and computes the set of methods the thread potentially executes and whether the allocation site may be executed more than once. By combining the information about threads with points-to information, the analysis can decide for each `synchronized`-block and method whether potentially multiple threads may synchronize on the same object. The synchronization removal optimization presented in this section follows the exact same idea. However, instead of using the relatively imprecise thread information, where any two threads are potentially parallel, our optimization is based on a schedule analysis that incorporates task-order information.

Aldrich et al. [7, 8] describe a collection of analyses fro eliminating unnecessary synchronization for thread-local objects, nested monitors, and synchronization on reentrant locks. The synchronization removal optimization presented in this section does not recognize nested or reentrant locks. However, the techniques presented by Aldrich et al. could be used to also handle those cases and improve the result of the optimization.

## 7.2 Optimizing strong atomicity in software transactional memory

Software Transactional memory (STM) is an alternative to synchronization that avoids many of the problems associated with locks. A STM system replaces existing synchronization mechanisms with atomic statements of the form `atomic{s}`, where s is a statement or a list of statements. The STM runtime guarantees that s is executed with transactional semantics, meaning s is executed *as though* there was no interleaving computation. When the transaction inside an `atomic` region completes, it either *commits*, making the changes visible to other processes, or it *aborts*, causing the transaction to be rolled back, undoing all memory operations. After an abort, the atomic region is re-executed until it successfully commits.

In contrast to traditional database transactions, STM systems must handle the case where the same memory location is accessed concurrently both inside and outside a transaction. The semantics of an STM systems can be categorized into *strong* and *weak* semantics, depending on how accesses to memory outside an `atomic` section are handled.

**Weak atomicity semantics:** A transactional system is said to have weak atomicity semantics if it provides the no-interleaving guarantee only among `atomic` sections but no guarantee is made on non-transactional memory accesses [79]. Under weak atomicity semantics, reads and writes outside transactions are allowed to be interleaved with transactions. Similar to the problem of data-races in lock-based systems, it is the programmers' responsibility to ensure that there are no conflicting memory accesses between transactional and non-transactional code. Being less rigorous in its guarantees, weak semantics allows for a more efficient implementation but it sacrifices ordering and isolation guarantees. Some implementation approaches for weak STM systems, such as eager versioning and lazy conflict detection, can lead to incorrect execution of programs that are correctly synchronized under locks [105].

```
                  Initially: x is even
            Task 0                  Task 1
        1   atomic {
        2      x++;                  r = x;
        3      x++;
        4   }
```

**Can r be odd?**

Figure 7.3: Weak versus strong atomicity (example from [105]): Under weak atomicity, task 1 can observe an odd value in r. Under strong atomicity, r is always even.

**Strong atomicity semantics:** With strong atomicity semantics, memory accesses outside an **atomic** section are treated as if they were single-operation **atomic** transactions. Without special hardware support and/or compiler optimization, strong atomicity is generally considered too performance limiting because it requires all reads and writes outside transactions to be synchronized with memory operations inside transactions. Even with strong atomicity semantics, data-races are possible between conflicting memory accesses outside transactions.

Weak atomicity semantics suffers from unpredictable and implementation specific behavior but it promises performance benefits. The stricter guarantees of strong atomicity on the other hand provide superior formal semantics but need compile-time and/or runtime optimizations for satisfiable performance. Figure 7.3 illustrates how strong atomicity provides more guarantees than weak atomicity. Task 0 maintains the invariant that x is even. However, under weak atomicity it is possible for task 1 to observe an odd value if it reads x between the two increments of task 0. Under strong atomicity, the read of x in task 1 is an implicit single-operation transaction and therefore invariant x is even is observed by both tasks.

### 7.2.1 Reducing strong atomicity overhead

The overhead of strong atomicity comes from the fact that memory operations outside an **atomic** section must be treated as implicit single-operation transactions. An implementation— especially if no hardware support is available—must therefore replace a simple memory read or write with a more complex protocol that implements the transactional semantics, such as calls to **static** helper methods. However, without additional knowledge the STM system must conservatively assume that all memory accesses outside **atomic** sections must be instrumented.

One obvious compiler optimization is therefore to only replace those read and write bytecodes that actually may conflict with **atomic** sections at runtime. Figure 7.4 presents such an optimization based on the schedule analysis. The compiler will check for each read bytecode $R$ and write bytecode $W$ whether they must be replaced with a single-operation transaction.

In both rules, the first clause checks that this transformation is only applied to bytecodes that may actually be executed outside a transaction. This check is a simple reachability predicate that, starting from a given task $\mathcal{A}$, contains all read respectively write bytecodes that can be reached without crossing an equal number of **atomic** section enter and exit statements.

Similarly, the second clauses in both rules look for potentially conflicting bytecodes that

## 7.2. Optimizing Strong Atomicity in Software Transactional Memory

$$\frac{\begin{array}{l}\text{REQIRES-READ-TRANSACTION}\\ BC_R \text{ IS READ OUTSIDE TRANSACTION, MAY EXECUTE IN } \mathcal{A}\\ BC_W \text{ IS WRITE INSIDE TRANSACTION, MAY EXECUTE IN } \mathcal{B}\\ \quad BC_R \text{ READS } v1.f\\ \quad BC_W \text{ WRITES } v2.f\\ \quad v1 \text{ MAY POINT TO } Obj\\ \quad v2 \text{ MAY POINT TO } Obj\\ \quad Obj \text{ MAY ESCAPE } \mathcal{A} \text{ and } \mathcal{B}\\ \quad parallel(\mathcal{A}, \mathcal{B})\end{array}}{requiresReadTx(BC_R)}$$

$$\frac{\begin{array}{l}\text{REQIRES-WRITE-TRANSACTION}\\ BC_W \text{ IS WRITE OUTSIDE TRANSACTION, MAY EXECUTE IN } \mathcal{A}\\ BC_X \text{ IS READ OR WRITE INSIDE TRANSACTION, MAY EXECUTE IN } \mathcal{B}\\ \quad BC_W \text{ READS } v1.f\\ \quad BC_X \text{ READS OR WRITES } v2.f\\ \quad v1 \text{ MAY POINT TO } Obj\\ \quad v2 \text{ MAY POINT TO } Obj\\ \quad Obj \text{ MAY ESCAPE } \mathcal{A} \text{ and } \mathcal{B}\\ \quad parallel(\mathcal{A}, \mathcal{B})\end{array}}{requiresWriteTx(BC_W)}$$

Figure 7.4: Rules deciding for each read bytecode $R$ and write bytecode $W$ whether they must follow transactional semantics in order to guarantee strong atomicity.

may be executed inside a transaction. Because a read may only conflict with a write, it is enough to check only for conflicting write bytecodes in the REQUIRES-READ-TRANSACTION rule. In the REQUIRES-WRITE-TRANSACTION rule, a write outside a transaction conflicts with both reads and writes.

The remaining clauses then test if the access outside the transaction and the access inside the transaction may actually access the same memory from parallel tasks.

### 7.2.2 Related work

Hindman and Grossman [49] present a system that achieves strong atomicity via a source-to-source translation and does not require special hardware or virtual machine support. Because of the prohibitively high overhead of the basic translation, Hindman and Grossman also briefly describe a set of compile-time analyses to remove barriers from non-transactional code while preserving strong atomicity. Complementary to standard escape and points-to analyses they particularly outline an analysis that exploits the fact that strong atomicity does not constrain two memory accesses that occur outside an **atomic** block. They can remove a barrier if the analysis shows that the accessed object could never be accessed within any transaction.

The main difference between the optimization described by Hindman and Grossman and the optimization presented in this section is the use of a schedule analysis. Adding the schedule analysis results in the additional clause *parallel*($\mathcal{A}, \mathcal{B}$) in each of the optimization rules. If in the worst case the schedule analysis cannot compute any task-order information (and therefore conservatively classifies all tasks as *parallel*) our analysis is essentially equivalent to Hindman and Grossman. If the schedule analysis can compute relevant ordering information, however, our analysis is more precise allowing the optimizer to remove more read- and/or write barriers.

## 7.3 Synchronization variant selection

When designing a library, the designers must decide what parts of the library should be thread-safe by default and what parts remain unsynchronized. Often, this decision is difficult to make for the general case, because the library designers do not know the context in which their library will be used. If the library is written without thread-safety, it's the library users' responsibility to correctly synchronize. Unsafe libraries increase the burden on the user and make the library more difficult to use, possibly resulting in a competitive disadvantage over similar libraries. Correctly synchronized libraries, however, may introduce extra performance overhead when used in a single-threaded context.

If the compiler were able to perfectly choose between synchronized and unsynchronized variants of classes and methods, the best of both worlds could be achieved: ease of use for the programmer because the compiler handles synchronization and high performance because unnecessary synchronization is avoided. This section describes an optimization that selects synchronization variants for some compiler-known classes and methods.

### 7.3.1 Code duplication in Java libraries

The tension between providing thread-safe versus thread-unsafe implementations often leads to code duplication. For example, take the evolution of the Java standard library (JDK) over the last decade. In the early versions of the JDK, utility classes such as `java.util.Vector` and `java.lang.StringBuffer` tended to be fully synchronized and therefore safe to use in multi-threaded environments. Providing thread-safety by default increased the ease of use for those classes. However, the lack of alternatives also meant that single-threaded code and thread-local objects suffered from a performance penalty.

In later versions of the JDK, multiple "drop-in-replacements" for thread-safe classes have been introduced. Those replacement classes provide equal (or at least very similar) interfaces to their thread safe counterparts but without synchronization. For example, `java.util.ArrayList` is an unsafe version of `java.util.Vector`[4] whereas `java.lang.StringBuilder` can replace `java.lang.StringBuffer` if synchronization is not needed.

In general, it is the programmers' responsibility to use the thread safe versions where needed and revert to the unsafe versions where the correct synchronization is guaranteed by the library client code. Only in very view cases can the Java compiler help with this decision. For example, in a string concatenation expression such as `String s = "abc" + foo() + "def"`, early Java

---

[4] `java.util.ArrayList` is not an exact copy of `java.util.Vector` (modulo synchronization) but it shows some slight differences in behavior, too. For example, when increasing the capacity, a `Vector` defaults to doubling the size of its array, while the `ArrayList` increases its array size by 50 percent. Therefore, in some rare cases a simple drop-in replacement may change the observable outcome of a program.

| USE-SAFE-CLASS-VARIANT | USE-SAFE-METHOD-VARIANT |
|---|---|
| $BC_{new}$ IS **new** STATEMENT CREATING $Obj$ | $BC_{call}$ IS METHOD CALL $v1.m(\ldots)$ |
| $\mathcal{A}$ MAY ACCESS $Obj$ | $BC_{call}$ MAY EXECUTE IN $\mathcal{A}$ |
| $\mathcal{B}$ MAY ACCESS $Obj$ | $v1$ MAY POINT TO $Base$ |
| $Obj$ MAY ESCAPE $\mathcal{A}$ **and** $\mathcal{B}$ | $Base.m(\ldots)$ MAY ACCESS $Obj$ |
| $parallel(\mathcal{A}, \mathcal{B})$ | $\mathcal{B}$ MAY ACCESS $Obj$ |
| | $Obj$ MAY ESCAPE $\mathcal{A}$ **and** $\mathcal{B}$ |
| | $parallel(\mathcal{A}, \mathcal{B})$ |
| $useSafeClassVariant(BC_{new})$ | $useSafeMethodVariant(BC_{call})$ |

Figure 7.5: Safe variant selection optimization with class-level and method-level granularity.

compilers replaced the + concatenations with calls to StringBuffer.append() rewriting the expression to:

```
String s = new StringBuffer("abc").append(foo()).append("def").toString();
```

Starting with version 1.5, however, the Java compiler performs a local escape analysis to decide whether the StringBuffer can safely be replaced by a more performant (albeit unsynchronized) StringBuilder.

The current strategy of many general purpose libraries, such as the JDK, is to provide thread safe and unsafe alternatives for some or all of their classes. This not only results in code duplication and therefore higher complexity and maintenance costs, but also shifts the burden of choosing the right variant to the programmer making it again harder to use the library correctly.

### 7.3.2 Compiler selected synchronized/unsynchronized variants

The goal of the synchronization variant selection optimization is to allow programmers to use thread safe implementations of their data structures but reduce the synchronization performance penalty by letting the optimization choose what variant—thread safe or unsafe—to use at a particular program point. This optimization requires the compiler to have knowledge about the available variants of classes and/or methods. The compiler may get this information from different sources: Variants present in the standard JDK may be intrinsics and hard-coded into the compiler; the compiler may also choose to automatically create an unsynchronized version of every **synchronized** method; or the programmer may provide annotations telling the compiler about class and method variants.

Synchronization variants for this optimization come in two granularities: class-level variants and variants on the method-level.

**Class-level variants:** On the class level, a class B may function as an unsynchronized drop-in replacement for another thread-safe class A (that is, B has the same interface as A). This is the case with the java.util.ArrayList and java.lang.StringBuilder JDK classes described above.

112                    CHAPTER 7. OTHER APPLICATIONS IN OPTIMIZATION AND VERIFICATION

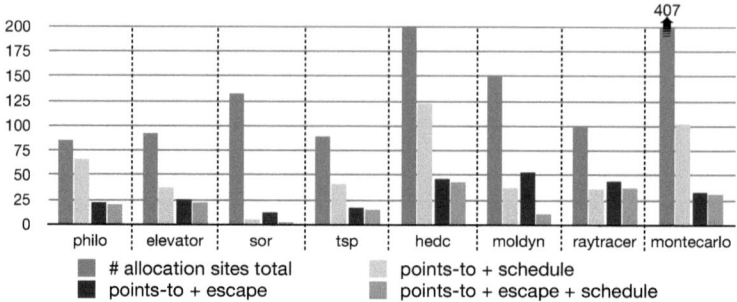

Figure 7.6: Number of allocation sites that may result in shared objects.

**Method-level variants:** Synchronization variants can also be provided on the method level (even though the designers of the JDK did not choose this approach). The java.util.Vector class, for example, may provide unsafe methods such as add_unsafe() and remove_unsave() that are the unsynchronized counterparts of add() and remove(). In this case, the caller can decide whether to use the thread-safe or the unsafe variant. The advantage of the method-level over the class-level granularity is that at runtime, the *same* object can be used in single-threaded phases without synchronization and still be safely synchronized in the multi-threaded phases. When the synchronization variants only exist on the class level, the compiler must conservatively choose the thread-safe variant whenever an object may be used in a multi-threaded phase.

Figure 7.5 shows the synchronization variant selection optimization with class-level and method-level granularity. When choosing variants on the class level, rule USE-SAFE-CLASS-VARIANT checks for each **new** bytecode $BC_{new}$ whether the thread safe variant must be used. If the analysis shows that the object $Obj$ created at $BC_{new}$ will never be accessed in parallel, the compiler can rewrite $BC_{new}$ to use a more performant unsafe variant.

For choosing the right variant on a method level, rule USE-SAFE-METHOD-VARIANT checks every call of the form $v1.m(...)$ represented by bytecode $BC_{call}$. The compiler can rewrite $BC_{call}$ to use the more performant unsafe method if it can show that none of the objects $Obj$ that may directly or indirectly be accessed by the call $v1.m(...)$ may be accessed by a parallel task $B$. Finding all objects that may be accessed by a method call is done by a reachability analysis on the call-graph starting from the node representing $Base.m()$.

### 7.3.3 Experimental data

Figure 7.6 shows the effect of the schedule analysis on the number of allocation sites that may result in shared objects. This experiment does classify all allocation sites, regardless of what type of object is actually created at the allocation site.

The points-to + escape configuration is equivalent to existing thread-escape analyses where only those creation sites are flagged that produce objects that may escape the thread. For most benchmarks, the points-to + escape configuration is very effective in classifying allocation sites that could use thread-unsafe variants. For other benchmarks such as moldyn and raytracer, however, adding the schedule analysis can further reduce the number of shared ob-

## 7.4. HAPPENS-BEFORE ORDER RELAXATION

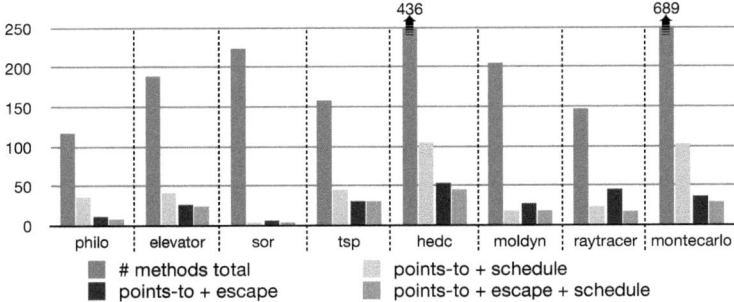

Figure 7.7: Number of methods that may conflict in a parallel context.

jects significantly. In those benchmarks, scheduling information helps to identify cases where an object escapes a task but is only accessed by tasks that are ordered by happens-before relations.

On average, the `points-to + escape` configuration reduces the total number of allocation sites that may result in shared objects by 76%. Adding the schedule analysis, the number is reduced by 83% on average, a 7% improvement over the `points-to + escape` configuration.

Figure 7.7 depicts the number of methods that may conflict when executed in a parallel context. Across the benchmarks, the number of possibly conflicting methods varies between 2% and 30% of all methods executed. For the other methods, a more performant thread-unsafe variant may be chosen. Adding the schedule analysis improves the classification of potentially conflicting method calls from 13% on average with the `points-to + escape` configuration by 4% to 9% on average with the `points-to + escape + schedule` configuration.

## 7.4 Happens-before order relaxation

Programmers as well as automated compiler transformations may introduce unnecessary →-statements in the source code. Happens-before order relaxation aims at removing such superfluous →-statements again. This can be beneficial in two ways:

- Removing a →-statement that creates an ordering between two tasks that are already (transitively) ordered can improve the performance of later analyses as well as improve the generated code. Unnecessary transitive →-statements can be found by looking for transitive edges in the schedule.

- Removing a →-statement between two tasks that are otherwise independent can increase the parallelism in a program. Removing a non-transitive edge between two tasks may be allowed if the read- and write-sets of both tasks are disjoint.

## 7.4.1  Example: Parallel continuation passing style

Many compiler optimizations require a program to be first transformed into a suitable internal representation (IR). The two most common forms of IRs are static single assignment (SSA) and continuation-passing style (CPS). Translating a program into SSA or CPS helps with compiler analyses because both forms make the control flow explicit

While SSA is widely used in compilers for imperative languages, many compilers for functional languages prefer CPS, even though both forms are technically equivalent [11, 56]. In CPS, a function never returns to its caller as in the more familiar direct style. Instead, it expects a continuation function as an additional parameter. When the function has finished its computation, it will call the continuation function and pass it the result value.

As an example for how a program is translated into CPS, consider a method fib() for computing fibonacci numbers:

```
int fib(int k) {
  if (k <= 2) return 1;
  else return fib(k-1) + fib(k-2);
}
```

The **else** case contains two recursive calls to fib(). Because of the +, however, none of these calls is a tail call because the method has to wait until both functions return before the results can be added.

A translation into CPS splits the **else** case into two inner functions generated by the compiler[5]:

```
void fib(int k, #{int -> void} continuation) {
  if (k <= 2)
    continuation(1);
  else
    fib(k-1, #{ int left ->
        fib(k-2, #{int right -> continuation(left+right) })
    });
}
```

This example demonstrates how the translation into CPS adds the additional parameter continuation for the continuation to fib() and changes the return type of fib() to **void**. The return in direct style is translated into a tail call to this continuation function, passing the result as a parameter.

SSA and CPS both have a serious drawback when it comes to multi-threaded systems: Neither one has any support for parallelism. In CPS, for example, the call to the continuation function must be in tail-position; that is, it must be the last thing the function does. Because there can be only one such tail-call, a function cannot fork computation in CPS. This makes CPS inherently single-threaded.

---

[5]In the current version, Java does not contain function pointers and real closures, which are both important for CPS translation. Both could be somewhat simulated with anonymous classes at the expense of much increased verbosity. For the sake of this example, however, we use the lambda expressions for Java proposed by JSR 335 [100]. The notation #{**int** left -> left + 42} represents a closure with one parameter left that computes the value left + 42. The type of the closure is #{**int** -> **int**}.

## 7.4. HAPPENS-BEFORE ORDER RELAXATION

```
1  task fib(int k, Task later) {
2    if(k <= 2) {
3      now.result = 1;
4    } else {
5      Task sum = Task.create(); //forward declarations of sum so that we can use it already
6      Task left = schedule fib(k-1, sum);
7      Task right = schedule fib(k-2, sum);
8
9      Task then = now; //capture now to use it in sum
10     //sum "returns" for fib()
11     sum = schedule #{ -> then.result = left.result + right.result };
12
13     left→right; //left-to-right evaluation order in original program
14     right→sum;
15     sum→later;
16   }
17 }
```

Figure 7.8: Fibonacci numbers translated from CPS to pCPS.

The task model with explicit ordering constraints introduced in Chapter 3 can be used as the basis for a *parallel continuation passing style* (pCPS) form. A transformation similar to CPS can translate the function fib() into the pCPS version with tasks and →-statements shown in Figure 7.8.

The sequential function calls in the expression fib(k-1) + fib(k-2) are translated into code that schedules two tasks left and right to recursively call fib() (lines 6 and 7) and a continuation task sum on line 11 that adds the two results.[6] On line 9 a reference to the current task now is stored in the local variable then. Inside the closure of sum(), the then-variable allows us to set the result slot in behalf of the outer fib() task so that the later task can read it from there.

Because the original program is sequential in nature with a left-to-right evaluation order for the + operator, all scheduled tasks are ordered as a linear list on lines 13 to 15.

### 7.4.2 Removing unnecessary ordering

In the transformed pCPS version of the fib() method from Figure 7.8, the happens-before edge on line 13 is not strictly necessary and can be removed. The edge was introduced by the transformation mainly because of the implicit left-to-right evaluation ordering in the original expression fib(k-1) + fib(k-2). However, a simple analysis can show that the two calls to fib() are independent on the data they use and can therefore be executed in parallel.

When removing a →-statement, the compiler must ensure that the transitive ordering is kept intact. Take, for example, the schedule shown in Figure 7.9(a). Simply removing the

---

[6]Because tasks left and right need a reference to sum and sum needs a reference to left and right, this example uses a *forward declaration* for sum. The expression Task.create() on line 5 creates an empty task object that has no execution target yet; the execution target is set when the compiler sees the corresponding **schedule** statement on line 11.

116                 CHAPTER 7. OTHER APPLICATIONS IN OPTIMIZATION AND VERIFICATION

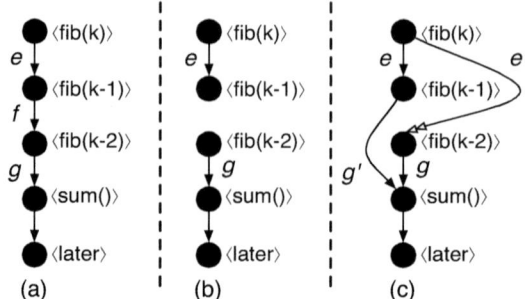

Figure 7.9: Fixing the transitive ordering in the `fib()` schedule after removing the edge `f`.

unnecessary edge `f` results in the schedule shown in Figure 7.9(b). This schedule is broken, however, because by removing `f` the transitive ordering between `fib(k)` and `fib(k-2)` as well as the transitive ordering between `fib(k-1)` and `sum` that was present before the removal is missing.

When deleting an edge $a \to b$, the transitive ordering is maintained by adding additional edges to the schedule: for each incoming edge $x \to a$ into node $a$ the compiler creates a new edge $x \to b$; similarly, for each outgoing edge $b \to y$ from $b$ the compiler creates an edge $a \to y$.

In the example, tasks `fib(k)` and `fib(k-2)` are already ordered by an implicit creation edge and the compiler does not need to explicitly order them. For ordering `fib(k-1)` and `sum`, however, the compiler must add the statement left→sum when it removes left→right. This adds in the additional edge `g'` shown in Figure 7.9(c) and, together with the implicit creation edge `e'`, fixes the transitive ordering. The parallelism has been increased, however, because the `fib(k-1)` and `fib(k-2)` tasks can now be executed in parallel.

### 7.4.3 Related work

A happens-before order relaxation is an automated compiler transformation that increases the parallelism in a sequential part of a program. As such, happens-before order relaxation is related to the techniques for auto scheduling and parallelism extraction of Hierarchical Task Graphs [95, 44] and the Kimble IR [15]. Both approaches are discussed in more detail in Section 3.8.

Another approach for automatically increasing parallelism in a program uses the polyhedral (or polytope) model [46]. The polyhedral model is a mathematical framework that represents $d$ perfectly nested loops as a $d$-dimensional polytope, a mathematical structure where each point of the index space represents one iteration step of the loop nest. By applying a space-time mapping, which are affine coordinate transformations, the polytope is transformed into another equivalent polytope with some dimensions representing space and some dimensions representing time. This target polytope can be translated back into nested loops, where each space dimension becomes a parallel loop and each time dimensions become a sequential loop. The polyhedral model works well for scientific code that works with tight nested loops on matrices. In comparison, the happens-before order relaxation assumes a higher-level program design based on tasks and happens-before relationships.

## 7.5 Verifying programmers' sharing intentions

When writing parallel programs, programmers make assumptions about what objects will be shared between tasks and accessed concurrently. If their assumptions are wrong, the program will not behave as expected. If objects that the programmer assumed to be shared are actually task local, the program takes a performance hit by introducing unnecessary synchronization. If objects that the programmer assumed to be task local are actually accessed concurrently, the program contains (often hard-to-detect) data-races that result in erroneous behavior or even crash the program.

When the programmer has wrong assumptions about what objects are shared, the program is most likely incorrect. More importantly, it is generally impossible to automatically correct a program that was created with wrong sharing assumptions in mind. For example, the argument has been made that even sequential consistency as presented in Chapter 5 fails to prevent many common programming mistakes:

> *"More generally, programmers do not reason about correctness of parallel code in terms of interleavings of individual memory accesses, and sequential consistency does not prevent common sources of concurrency bugs arising from simultaneous access to the same shared data (for example, data races). Even with sequential consistency, such simultaneous accesses can remain dangerous, and should be avoided, or at least explicitly highlighted. Relying on sequential consistency without such highlighting both obscures the code, and greatly complicates the implementation's job."* [2]

The goal of verifying programmers' sharing intentions is to compare programmer-provided sharing annotations with the sharing information computed by the compiler. The programmer may annotate classes, fields, or even individual **new** statements, explicitly highlighting the corresponding objects as being shared. The compiler checks whether the programmer assumptions are compatible with the information from the compiler analysis. If the compiler and the programmer disagree, the compiler generates a warning.

Figure 7.10 shows the rules the compiler can use to decide whether a class, a field, or a **new**-statement should be annotated as being shared.

As an example, consider the compiler checking the sharing intention of a field f. If f is marked as shared but it is not an element in the *sharedField*() relation, the compiler warns the programmer that his sharing assumption is not correct. If, however, f is not annotated, but it is an element in *sharedField*(), the compiler warns about potential data-races.

### 7.5.1 Experimental data

This section presents preliminary experimental data for verifying programmers' sharing intentions for object fields. For verifying sharing annotations on individual **new** statements, the

118     CHAPTER 7. OTHER APPLICATIONS IN OPTIMIZATION AND VERIFICATION

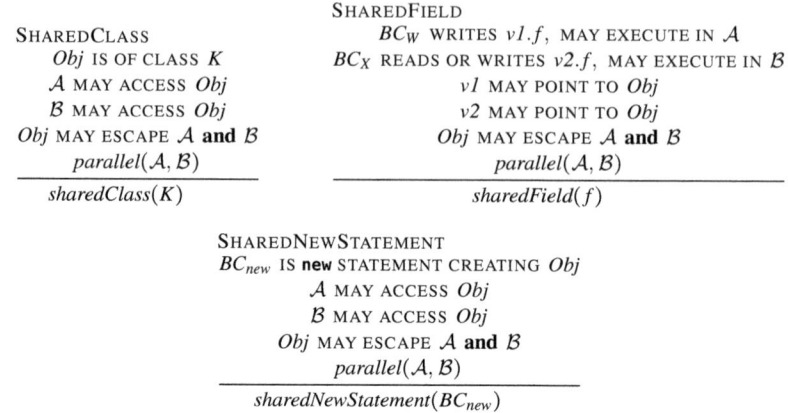

Figure 7.10: Rules to check what classes, fields, and **new**-statements should be annotated as being shared.

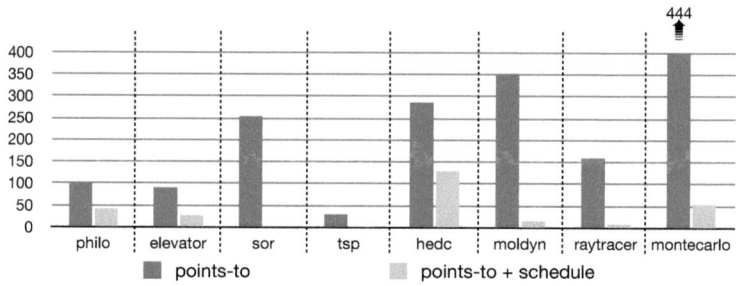

Figure 7.11: Number of pairs of static field accesses that may interfere.

experimental data from Figure 7.6 gives an indication of the effectiveness of the schedule analysis because rule SHAREDNEWSTATEMENT of Figure 7.10 is functionally equivalent to rule USE-SAFE-CLASS-VARIANT of Figure 7.5.

At the core of rule SHAREDFIELD lies the question whether two program points $BC_W$ and $BC_X$ may interfere at runtime by accessing the same object $Obj$ concurrently, where $BC_W$ is a write of field f and $BC_X$ is a read or write of f. We evaluate the precision of the different analysis configurations by looking at the number of pairs of program points $BC_W$ and $BC_X$ that are considered to be interfering. Note that by counting program point pairs, an individual program point $BC_W$ may be counted multiple times if it interferes with more than one other program point. We further distinguish between interferences on instance fields and interferences on static fields.

## 7.6. SUMMARY

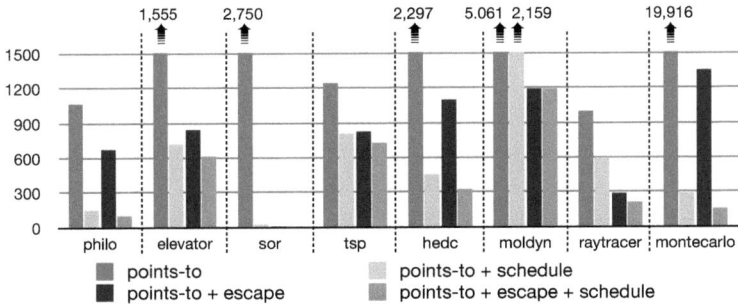

Figure 7.12: Number of pairs of instance field accesses that may interfere.

Figure 7.11 presents the number of program points pairs that may interfere when accessing a static field. Because the escape analysis classifies all objects that are reachable from a static field as escaping, the escape analysis does not have any effect on computing static-field interferences and has been omitted from the results. On average, adding scheduling information reduces the number of potentially interfering static field accesses by 81.8%.

In Figure 7.12 we compare all configurations when computing pairs of interfering instance field accesses. For moldyn and raytracer, the schedule analysis reduces the number of potential interference points more than the escape analysis whereas the escape analysis performs better for hedc and montecarlo. In all cases, however, combining the escape analysis with a schedule analysis is beneficial and reduces the set of interfering program points by on average 79.1% for interfering instance field accesses as compared to 63.4% if only an escape analysis is used.

Table 7.1 presents the overall running time of the sharing intention verification. The verification time contains the individual analyses plus the actual computation of interfering static field accesses and instance field accesses. Looking at the analysis part separately, the escape and schedule analysis together add between 5% and 28% (average 19.79%) overhead to the points-to analysis. However, the additional escape and schedule information has a positive effect on the overall running time of the verification which in all cases makes up for the increased analysis time. This speed-up happens because the additional information quickly reduces the number of program points that have to be checked against the points-to sets. This results in smaller BDDs and speeds up all BDD operations. We did not try to find a good variable ordering for the generic optimization and therefore it is likely that the absolute time reported in Table 7.1 could be significantly improved by simple variable re-ordering. However, the positive effect of reducing the overall search space on the running time of the optimization is clearly visible.

## 7.6 Summary

The case studies from Chapters 5 and 6 introduced optimizations for non-trivial systems and provided detailed evaluations. However, task-schedule information can be applied to various other optimizations and verifications. This chapter gives an overview of a set of optimizations and verifications that have been explored in the scope of this dissertation but that, for time reasons, have not been thoroughly evaluated. However, we report anecdotal and experimental data for those cases where we have a prototypes available.

## 7.6. Summary

|  | philo | elevator | sor | tsp | hedc | mold | ray | monte | average |
|---|---|---|---|---|---|---|---|---|---|
| (1) points-to | 9.40 s | 10.37 s | 14.88 s | 8.51 s | 135.82 s | 19.29 s | 9.98 s | 258.73 s | |
| (2) points-to + escape | 4.58 s | 5.34 s | 5.25 s | 5.19 s | 25.08 s | 7.18 s | 5.06 s | 58.34 s | |
| (3) points-to + schedule | 4.16 s | 4.23 s | 3.56 s | 3.92 s | 9.88 s | 3.70 s | 3.72 s | 5.83 s | |
| (4) points-to + escape + schedule | 3.97 s | 4.12 s | 3.19 s | 3.68 s | 10.47 s | 3.74 s | 3.69 s | 6.32 s | |
| improvement of (4) over (1) | 57.77% | 60.27% | 78.56% | 56.76% | 92.29% | 80.61% | 63.03% | 97.56% | 73.36% |
| improvement of (4) over (2) | 13.32% | 22.85% | 39.24% | 29.09% | 58.25% | 47.91% | 27.08% | 89.17% | 40.86% |
| improvement of (4) over (3) | 4.57% | 2.60% | 10.39% | 6.12% | -5.97% | -1.08% | 0.81% | -8.40% | 1.13% |

Table 7.1: Running time of the sharing intention verification analysis.

# 8

# Future directions

This chapter discusses some possible directions for future work. They can be categorized into improvements to the task model, extensions of the schedule analysis, additional use cases for scheduling information, and integration of schedule analysis with just-in-time compilers.

## 8.1 Task model extensions

**Transforming higher level programs:** The case studies presented in Chapters 5 and 6 have shown that it is feasible for programmers to adapt existing programs to follow the task model presented in Chapter 3. Adapting the benchmarks was relatively straight forward, because the benchmarks are all written with traditional parallel execution patterns in mind. This means, that there are only relatively few points in the benchmarks that actually schedule new tasks and most scheduling of subtasks happens directly in a task's main method and not further down the call chain. Therefore, for the most part transforming the original benchmarks into programs that follow our task model required little more skill than applying syntactic changes.

If the assumption holds, however, that future programs will exhibit much more fine-grained parallelism to make use of multicore processors, the (parallel-)continuation passing style underlying our model makes writing such programs syntactically awkward. Instead, programmers will probably want to use higher-level parallelism constructs and the compiler would do the transformation into the task model automatically for them.

Future work in this area would be to design and implement a pre-processing framework that transforms different parallelism constructs (language constructs or library calls) into a program following our task programming model. We expect this transformation to be similar to a continuation passing style transformation but we have not done any research into this direction.

**Extensions to the model:** One of our design goals was to design a minimal task model that contains as few constructs as possible. However, a feasible alternative to a complex transformation of high-level programs into our minimalist model would be to extend the model with more complex constructs and adapt the schedule analysis accordingly. Extending the task model would make the transformation of existing programs easier but it would add additional complexity to the schedule analysis.

An example for a useful extension to the task model would be a special *happens-within* edge. This edge would tell the analysis that the parent task is suspended while the child tasks are running and then resumes computation in the parent task.

A happens-within edge would allow for a direct translation of fork/join style constructs. Our current model requires the compiler or programmer to cut the parent task into two pieces, one that contains the code that schedules the fork-computation and one that contains the code after the join.

## 8.2 Improving schedule analysis precision

**Directional ordering information:** The schedule analysis presented in this dissertation compresses the scheduling information into the relation *parallel*$(\mathcal{A}, \mathcal{B})$. As the case studies from Chapters 5 and 6 have shown, this relation contains enough information for effectively implementing many optimizations.

Future optimizations, verifications, or analyses, however, may be interested in more detailed information. For example, verifying that a database connection has always been opened before subsequent tasks access it requires directional information in the form of a relation $task1 \rightarrow task2$.

The problem with computing actual happens-before and happens-after information is that at analysis-time the compiler can only work with abstract objects. Imagine that in the above example the program opens a connection, starts some workers, and closes the connection; and it repeats this process multiple times. The static analysis may be forced to abstract the possibly infinite number of Open(), Worker(), and Close() task instances into three single analysis-time objects. This would result in a circular relation:

Open()→Worker()→Close()→Open()→Worker()→...

Here, the fact $Open() \rightarrow Close()$ is not true, because (some) Close() happen before Open(). The problem is, that $Open() \rightarrow Close()$ is a global fact for the whole program; what we would like to verify, however, is that the happens-before property is true within a certain *context*: inside a single iteration, Open()→Close() holds.

A schedule analysis that computes context-dependent, directional scheduling information must therefore take the program flow, execution context, and possibly runtime values into account. This is similar to dependent type systems [47, 82] or polyhedral analysis [19].

For example, by extending the schedule analysis with a notion of loop context $n$ the schedule analysis may be able to deduce the following fact:

$\forall n$ with $n > 0 : Close()_{n-1} \rightarrow Open()_n \wedge Open()_n \rightarrow Close()_n$

This expression states that in every $n^{th}$ iteration (other than the first), the $Close()$ task created in the previous iteration $n-1$ happens-before the $Open()$ task created in the $n^{th}$ iteration and the current $Open()$ task happens before the $Close()$ task of the same iteration. Adding such context sensitivity would require substantial changes to both the model and the analysis presented in this dissertation.

**Task ordering for tasks that were read from fields:** The schedule analysis presented in this dissertation is able to analyze →-statements that reference tasks that were passed as parameters. This ability to analyze the *now happens-before later* pattern provides much of the additional flexibility the schedule analysis allows compared to analyses of syntactic fork/join style parallelism. The schedule analysis loses all of its precision, however, when happens-before relations are created between tasks that have been read from fields. In this case, we conservatively overapproximate the parallelism by simply ignoring the effects of the happens-before edge.

One future direction could be to identify cases where happens-before edges can improve the analysis result even if tasks were read from fields. This would probably require the schedule analysis to be based on more detailed alias information. Another interesting direction could be to embed a linear type system [35, 112] for task objects into an otherwise more traditional type system to avoid aliasing of task objects altogether.

## 8.3 Task-aware program analyses and wellformed-ness checks

This dissertation focusses on using schedule analysis for optimizations. However, it is an open research question whether scheduling information can also help with improving or enabling other program analyses and verification.

**Improving existing analyses** As an example, consider a traditional escape analysis that computes a relation *escapes(object,task)*. An object escapes a task if it is passed to the task, if the task may stores the object in a global field, if the task passes the object to another task, or if the object is reachable through an escaping object.

A scheduling-aware variant of an escape analysis could improve the precision by computing *escapes(fromTask,object,toTask)*. Imagine multiple parallel worker tasks that are scheduled before a common join task where each worker task computes a result object that is passed to the join task. The analysis will conflate the multiple worker task runtime objects into a single analysis-time object. A traditional escape analysis would deduce that the result object escapes the worker task (because it is passed to join) and that multiple tasks may access result in parallel (because the analysis can not distinguish between the individual result objects). A schedule-aware analysis, however, may be able to see that the result object never escapes from one worker task to another but only to the join task. Increasing the precision of the escape analysis may allow the compiler to decrease the precision of a—potentially computationally very expensive—points-to analysis. We have implemented a prototype of a schedule-aware escape analysis but we have not seen any significant improvement in the benchmarks. Future work in that direction would be necessary to find if escape analysis (or other program analyses) can effectively benefit from scheduling information.

**Checking wellformed-ness of task schedules** One common source of errors in parallel programs are deadlocks. [73] In programs that use tasks with explicit happens-before constraints, deadlocks can not only arise from incorrectly using locks but also from circular happens-before relations between two or more tasks. In addition, the execution of a statement a→b can fail if the task b on the right hand side is not guaranteed to be in the future (that is, if not **now**→b). Section 3.7.1 called schedules that do not result in such scheduling conflicts *well-formed*.

Currently there exists no check that can (statically) decide whether a program execution is guaranteed to result in a well-formed schedule. Having such a check would help the programmer to eliminate whole classes of scheduling errors already at compile time. Statically preventing deadlocks may require adding additional constraints to the model, such as disallowing →-statements to reference variables that were read from fields, which would reduce the flexibility of the programming model.

## 8.4 Integration with just-in-time compilers

The schedule analysis presented in this dissertation is a whole-program analysis and therefore operates under a closed-world assumption. The schedule analysis is not a modular analysis—it must inspect the method bodies and cannot simply operate on method interfaces—and therefore requires knowledge about all classes that may be loaded at runtime. To some extend, the lack of modularity is a problem inherent to parallel programs that work on shared memory. This problem manifests itself when a newly created thread brings down a parallel application that was running perfectly fine before. Because the concurrent access to shared state breaks encapsulation, the behavior of a parallel program can only be fully understood by looking at the whole program.

However, while not being truly "modular" the schedule analysis is "additive" in the sense that it analyses one class at a time, adding individual class-information to the final result. This property makes it thinkable to perform a schedule analysis at runtime in a just-in-time compiler (JIT). The JIT has full knowledge of what classes are currently loaded and therefore fulfills the closed-world requirement.

The main concern when integrating schedule analysis with a JIT is runtime overhead. In [67], Lee and Midkiff present a two-phase offline/online interprocedural and inter-task escape analysis that pre-computes summary information at compile-time that is used in a fast but precise interprocedural analysis at runtime. Similar techniques could be applied to transform the offline schedule analysis into an efficient online analysis that can be used in a JIT. For example, the first steps of extracting the abstract schedule from the bytecode could be done by the compiler and stored as a summary in the class file. The evaluation showed that the schedule analysis itself has a relatively small overhead, especially when compared to the points-to analysis. We therefore expect that the feasibility of adding a schedule analysis to a JIT compiler mostly depends on the quality and performance of available points-to analyses in JITs.

Assuming a JIT that includes a schedule analysis, the next open research question would be efficient (but relatively infrequent) re-compilation of large portions of the code. Optimizations of parallel programs can to affect many different parts of the code and are not necessarily local to a single compilation unit. Take, for example, a single-threaded sequentially consistent program in which all field and array accesses were optimized to work without memory fences. If during execution this code loads a class that may start a parallel task, the schedule analysis would notify the JIT that the single-threaded assumption is no longer correct. This may require the JIT to re-compile many of the already loaded and compiled classes. There is a tradeoff between too frequent re-compilation of large code portions and missed optimization opportunities in programs with relatively stable task schedules.

The interplay of class unloading with the schedule analysis opens another possible research direction. Class unloading occurs frequently in systems such as application servers that load (and unload) user-provided plugins and generate classes on-the-fly. If class unloading is simply ignored, the schedule analysis offers a conservative, but maybe unnecessarily imprecise result.

## 8.4. INTEGRATION WITH JUST-IN-TIME COMPILERS

On the other hand, if the JIT must perform a whole-program analysis after each unloading of a class the analysis overhead may become unreasonably high. It is an open question which tasks—if any—can be removed from the *parallel*() relation when a class is unloaded.

# 9
# Conclusions

Fully utilizing the increasing number of cores in modern processors requires finer- and finer-grained parallelism. Fine-grained parallelism is characterized by small tasks with only short pieces of sequential code. Many powerful compiler optimizations for single-threaded code, however, become ineffective when the sequential parts are too short. At the same time, new parallelism-aware optimizations require knowledge about the task scheduling at runtime, but this information is not available in current compilers.

This dissertation presents a programming model for parallel programs where explicit happens-before constraints in the code define a partial ordering of the tasks. This model is flexible enough to express a wide variety of structured and semi-structured parallelism features present in current programming languages and parallelism libraries. As opposed to unstructured threads, however, the proposed model contains enough ordering information to be susceptible to static analysis.

For parallel programs that follow our task model, an optimizing compiler can apply the schedule analysis developed in this dissertation to extract information about what tasks may be executed concurrently and what tasks are always ordered. Together with points-to and escape information, compiler optimizations can use the knowledge about task scheduling to judge whether a transformation in one program point would conflict with another program point. If the transformation may conflict with another part of the program, applying the optimization could potentially change the program semantics and must therefore be prohibited.

In two case studies, we evaluate in detail how effectively optimizing compilers can exploit scheduling information. In both cases, adding schedule analysis to the compiler significantly improves the performance of the optimized programs. The results suggest that scheduling information is important for effective optimizing compilers.

In conclusion, this dissertation has shown that it is possible and beneficial to develop a generic model of parallel execution and accompanying analyses. Instead of each project inventing its own model of concurrency, we therefore propose an independent discipline of schedule analysis. From this, we expect the same beneficial synergies for future parallel optimizations as with the theory of points-to analysis, which allowed optimizations to focus on their optimization problems instead of computing points-to sets.

We believe that static schedule analysis is a necessary step towards efficient next-generation compilers for multicore systems.

# Bibliography

[1] A.-R. Adl-Tabatabai, C. Kozyrakis, and B. Saha. Transactional programming in a multicore environment. In *Proceedings of the 12th ACM SIGPLAN symposium on Principles and practice of parallel programming*, PPoPP '07, pages 272–272, New York, NY, USA, 2007. ACM.

[2] S. V. Adve and H.-J. Boehm. Memory models: a case for rethinking parallel languages and hardware. *Commun. ACM*, 53:90–101, August 2010.

[3] S. V. Adve and K. Gharachorloo. Shared memory consistency models: A tutorial. *Computer*, 29:66–76, December 1996.

[4] S. Agarwal, R. Barik, V. Sarkar, and R. K. Shyamasundar. May-happen-in-parallel analysis of x10 programs. In *Proceedings of the 12th ACM SIGPLAN symposium on Principles and practice of parallel programming*, PPoPP '07, pages 183–193, New York, NY, USA, 2007. ACM.

[5] G. Agha. An overview of actor languages. In *Proceedings of the 1986 SIGPLAN workshop on Object-oriented programming*, OOPWORK '86, pages 58–67, New York, NY, USA, 1986. ACM.

[6] W. Ahn, S. Qi, M. Nicolaides, J. Torrellas, J.-W. Lee, X. Fang, S. Midkiff, and D. Wong. Bulkcompiler: high-performance sequential consistency through cooperative compiler and hardware support. In *Proceedings of the 42nd Annual IEEE/ACM International Symposium on Microarchitecture*, MICRO 42, pages 133–144, New York, NY, USA, 2009. ACM.

[7] J. Aldrich, C. Chambers, E. G. Sirer, and S. J. Eggers. Static analyses for eliminating unnecessary synchronization from java programs. In *Proceedings of the 6th International Symposium on Static Analysis*, SAS '99, pages 19–38, London, UK, 1999. Springer-Verlag.

[8] J. Aldrich, E. G. Sirer, C. Chambers, and S. J. Eggers. Comprehensive synchronization elimination for java. *Sci. Comput. Program.*, 47:91–120, May 2003.

[9] F. D. Anger. On lamport's interprocessor communication model. *ACM Trans. Program. Lang. Syst.*, 11:404–417, July 1989.

[10] C. M. Angerer and T. R. Gross. now happens-before later: static schedule analysis of fine-grained parallelism with explicit happens-before relationships. In *Proceedings of the ACM international conference companion on Object oriented programming systems languages and applications companion*, SPLASH '10, pages 3–10, New York, NY, USA, 2010. ACM.

[11] A. W. Appel. Ssa is functional programming. *SIGPLAN Not.*, 33:17–20, April 1998.

[12] Apple. Grand Central Dispatch: A Better Way to Do Multicore. http://developer.apple.com/technologies/mac/snowleopard/gcd.html, 2011. Last checked: 20/06/2011.

[13] H. Attiya, R. Guerraoui, D. Hendler, P. Kuznetsov, M. M. Michael, and M. Vechev. Laws of order: expensive synchronization in concurrent algorithms cannot be eliminated. In *Proceedings of the 38th annual ACM SIGPLAN-SIGACT symposium on Principles of programming languages*, POPL '11, pages 487–498, New York, NY, USA, 2011. ACM.

[14] R. Barik. Efficient computation of may-happen-in-parallel information for concurrent java programs. In E. Ayguadé, G. Baumgartner, J. Ramanujam, and P. Sadayappan, editors, *Languages and Compilers for Parallel Computing*, volume 4339 of *Lecture Notes in Computer Science*, pages 152–169. Springer Berlin / Heidelberg, 2006.

[15] N. Benoit and S. Louise. Kimble: a hierarchical intermediate representation for multi-grain parallelism. In F. Bouchez, S. Hack, and E. Visser, editors, *Proceedings of the Workshop on Intermediate Representations*, pages 21–28, 2011.

[16] R. D. Blumofe, C. F. Joerg, B. C. Kuszmaul, C. E. Leiserson, K. H. Randall, and Y. Zhou. Cilk: an efficient multithreaded runtime system. In *Proceedings of the fifth ACM SIGPLAN symposium on Principles and practice of parallel programming*, PPOPP '95, pages 207–216, New York, NY, USA, 1995. ACM.

[17] J. Bogda and U. Hölzle. Removing unnecessary synchronization in java. In *Proceedings of the 14th ACM SIGPLAN conference on Object-oriented programming, systems, languages, and applications*, OOPSLA '99, pages 35–46, New York, NY, USA, 1999. ACM.

[18] M. D. Bond, K. E. Coons, and K. S. McKinley. Pacer: proportional detection of data races. In *Proceedings of the 2010 ACM SIGPLAN conference on Programming language design and implementation*, PLDI '10, pages 255–268, New York, NY, USA, 2010. ACM.

[19] U. Bondhugula, A. Hartono, J. Ramanujam, and P. Sadayappan. A practical automatic polyhedral parallelizer and locality optimizer. In *Proceedings of the 2008 ACM SIGPLAN conference on Programming language design and implementation*, PLDI '08, pages 101–113, New York, NY, USA, 2008. ACM.

[20] J. Boyland. Checking interference with fractional permissions. In *Proceedings of the 10th international conference on Static analysis*, SAS'03, pages 55–72, Berlin, Heidelberg, 2003. Springer-Verlag.

[21] J. T. Boyland. Semantics of fractional permissions with nesting. *ACM Trans. Program. Lang. Syst.*, 32:22:1–22:33, August 2010.

[22] E. D. Brooks, III. The butterfly barrier. *Int. J. Parallel Program.*, 15:295–307, October 1986.

[23] D. Callahan, K. Kennedy, and J. Subhlok. Analysis of event synchronization in a parallel programming tool. In *Proceedings of the second ACM SIGPLAN symposium on Principles & practice of parallel programming*, PPOPP '90, pages 21–30, New York, NY, USA, 1990. ACM.

[24] D. Callahan and J. Subhlok. Static analysis of low-level synchronization. In *Proceedings of the 1988 ACM SIGPLAN and SIGOPS workshop on Parallel and distributed debugging*, PADD '88, pages 100–111, New York, NY, USA, 1988. ACM.

[25] L. Ceze, J. Tuck, P. Montesinos, and J. Torrellas. Bulksc: bulk enforcement of sequential consistency. In *Proceedings of the 34th annual international symposium on Computer architecture*, ISCA '07, pages 278–289, New York, NY, USA, 2007. ACM.

[26] S. Chandra and P. M. Chen. Whither generic recovery from application faults? a fault study using open-source software. In *Proceedings of the 2000 International Conference on Dependable Systems and Networks (formerly FTCS-30 and DCCA-8)*, DSN '00, pages 97–106, Washington, DC, USA, 2000. IEEE Computer Society.

[27] P. Charles, C. Grothoff, V. Saraswat, C. Donawa, A. Kielstra, K. Ebcioglu, C. von Praun, and V. Sarkar. X10: an object-oriented approach to non-uniform cluster computing. In *Proceedings of the 20th annual ACM SIGPLAN conference on Object-oriented programming, systems, languages, and applications*, OOPSLA '05, pages 519–538, New York, NY, USA, 2005. ACM.

[28] Z. Chen, B. Xu, and H. Yu. Detecting concurrently executed pairs of statements using an adapted mhp algorithm. In *Proceedings of the 2001 annual ACM SIGAda international conference on Ada*, SIGAda '01, pages 107–114, New York, NY, USA, 2001. ACM.

[29] S. Chiba and M. Nishizawa. An easy-to-use toolkit for efficient java bytecode translators. In *Proceedings of the 2nd international conference on Generative programming and component engineering*, GPCE '03, pages 364–376, New York, NY, USA, 2003. Springer-Verlag New York, Inc.

[30] J.-D. Choi, M. Gupta, M. Serrano, V. C. Sreedhar, and S. Midkiff. Escape analysis for java. In *Proceedings of the 14th ACM SIGPLAN conference on Object-oriented programming, systems, languages, and applications*, OOPSLA '99, pages 1–19, New York, NY, USA, 1999. ACM.

[31] J.-D. Choi, M. Gupta, M. J. Serrano, V. C. Sreedhar, and S. P. Midkiff. Stack allocation and synchronization optimizations for java using escape analysis. *ACM Trans. Program. Lang. Syst.*, 25:876–910, November 2003.

[32] J. Dean and S. Ghemawat. Mapreduce: simplified data processing on large clusters. In *Proceedings of the 6th conference on Symposium on Opearting Systems Design & Implementation - Volume 6*, pages 10–10, Berkeley, CA, USA, 2004. USENIX Association.

[33] E. W. Dijkstra. *Cooperating sequential processes*, pages 65–138. Springer-Verlag New York, Inc., New York, NY, USA, 2002.

[34] E. Duesterwald and M. L. Soffa. Concurrency analysis in the presence of procedures using a data-flow framework. In *Proceedings of the symposium on Testing, analysis, and verification*, TAV4, pages 36–48, New York, NY, USA, 1991. ACM.

[35] M. Fahndrich and R. DeLine. Adoption and focus: practical linear types for imperative programming. *SIGPLAN Not.*, 37:13–24, May 2002.

[36] X. Fang, J. Lee, and S. P. Midkiff. Automatic fence insertion for shared memory multiprocessing. In *Proceedings of the 17th annual international conference on Supercomputing*, ICS '03, pages 285–294, New York, NY, USA, 2003. ACM.

[37] E. Farchi, Y. Nir, and S. Ur. Concurrent bug patterns and how to test them. In *Proceedings of the 17th International Symposium on Parallel and Distributed Processing*, IPDPS '03, pages 286.2–, Washington, DC, USA, 2003. IEEE Computer Society.

[38] M. Feng and C. E. Leiserson. Efficient detection of determinacy races in cilk programs. In *Proceedings of the ninth annual ACM symposium on Parallel algorithms and architectures*, SPAA '97, pages 1–11, New York, NY, USA, 1997. ACM.

[39] J. Ferrante, D. Grunwald, and H. Srinivasan. Compile-time analysis and optimization of explicitly parallel programs*. *Parallel Algorithms Appl.*, 12(1-3):21–56, 1997.

[40] J. Ferrante, K. J. Ottenstein, and J. D. Warren. The program dependence graph and its use in optimization. *ACM Trans. Program. Lang. Syst.*, 9:319–349, July 1987.

[41] C. Flanagan and S. N. Freund. Fasttrack: efficient and precise dynamic race detection. In *Proceedings of the 2009 ACM SIGPLAN conference on Programming language design and implementation*, PLDI '09, pages 121–133, New York, NY, USA, 2009. ACM.

[42] C. Fournet and G. Gonthier. The join calculus: A language for distributed mobile programming. In *Applied Semantics, International Summer School, APPSEM 2000, Caminha, Portugal, September 9-15, 2000, Advanced Lectures*, pages 268–332, London, UK, 2002. Springer-Verlag.

[43] C. Fournet and C. Laneve. Bisimulations in the join-calculus. *Theor. Comput. Sci.*, 266:569–603, September 2001.

[44] M. Girkar and C. D. Polychronopoulos. Automatic extraction of functional parallelism from ordinary programs. *IEEE Trans. Parallel Distrib. Syst.*, 3:166–178, March 1992.

[45] J. Gosling, B. Joy, G. Steele, and G. Bracha. *Java(TM) Language Specification, The (3rd Edition) (Java (Addison-Wesley))*. Addison-Wesley Professional, 2005.

[46] M. Griebl, C. Lengauer, and S. Wetzel. Code generation in the polytope model. In *Proceedings of the 1998 International Conference on Parallel Architectures and Compilation Techniques*, PACT '98, pages 106–, Washington, DC, USA, 1998. IEEE Computer Society.

[47] R. Harper, F. Honsell, and G. Plotkin. A framework for defining logics. *J. ACM*, 40:143–184, January 1993.

[48] T. Harris and K. Fraser. Language support for lightweight transactions. In *Proceedings of the 18th annual ACM SIGPLAN conference on Object-oriented programing, systems, languages, and applications*, OOPSLA '03, pages 388–402, New York, NY, USA, 2003. ACM.

[49] B. Hindman and D. Grossman. Atomicity via source-to-source translation. In *Proceedings of the 2006 workshop on Memory system performance and correctness*, MSPC '06, pages 82–91, New York, NY, USA, 2006. ACM.

[50] C. A. R. Hoare. Communicating sequential processes. *Commun. ACM*, 21:666–677, August 1978.

[51] IBM. T.j. watson libraries for analysis (wala). http://wala.sourceforge.net, June 2011. Last checked: 11/07/2011.

[52] H. Java. Habanero multicore software research project. http://habanero.rice.edu/hj, August 2011. Last checked: 08/20/2011.

[53] P. G. Joisha, R. S. Schreiber, P. Banerjee, H. J. Boehm, and D. R. Chakrabarti. A technique for the effective and automatic reuse of classical compiler optimizations on multithreaded code. In *Proceedings of the 38th annual ACM SIGPLAN-SIGACT symposium on Principles of programming languages*, POPL '11, pages 623–636, New York, NY, USA, 2011. ACM.

[54] G. Kahn. The semantics of a simple language for parallel programming. In J. L. Rosenfeld, editor, *Information processing*, pages 471–475, Stockholm, Sweden, Aug 1974. North Holland, Amsterdam.

[55] R. K. Karmani, A. Shali, and G. Agha. Actor frameworks for the jvm platform: a comparative analysis. In *Proceedings of the 7th International Conference on Principles and Practice of Programming in Java*, PPPJ '09, pages 11–20, New York, NY, USA, 2009. ACM.

[56] R. A. Kelsey. A correspondence between continuation passing style and static single assignment form. In *Papers from the 1995 ACM SIGPLAN workshop on Intermediate representations*, IR '95, pages 13–22, New York, NY, USA, 1995. ACM.

[57] M. Kulkarni, M. Burtscher, C. Cascaval, and K. Pingali. Lonestar: A suite of parallel irregular programs. In *ISPASS'09*, pages 65–76, 2009.

[58] M. Kulkarni, M. Burtscher, R. Inkulu, K. Pingali, and C. Casçaval. How much parallelism is there in irregular applications? In *Proceedings of the 14th ACM SIGPLAN symposium on Principles and practice of parallel programming*, PPoPP '09, pages 3–14, New York, NY, USA, 2009. ACM.

[59] L. Lamport. Time, clocks, and the ordering of events in a distributed system. *Commun. ACM*, 21:558–565, July 1978.

[60] L. Lamport. A new approach to proving the correctness of multiprocess programs. *ACM Trans. Program. Lang. Syst.*, 1:84–97, January 1979.

[61] L. Lamport. The mutual exclusion problem: part i–a theory of interprocess communication. *J. ACM*, 33:313–326, April 1986.

[62] L. Lamport. How to make a correct multiprocess program execute correctly on a multiprocessor. *IEEE Trans. Comput.*, 46:779–782, July 1997.

[63] T. G. P. Language. The go programming language faq. http://golang.org/doc/go_faq.html#csp, August 2011. Last checked: 08/20/2011.

[64] H. Ledgard. *Reference Manual for the ADA Programming Language*. Springer-Verlag New York, Inc., Secaucus, NJ, USA, 1983.

[65] J. Lee, S. P. Midkiff, and D. A. Padua. Concurrent static single assignment form and constant propagation for explicitly parallel programs. In *Proceedings of the 10th International Workshop on Languages and Compilers for Parallel Computing*, LCPC '97, pages 114–130, London, UK, 1998. Springer-Verlag.

[66] J. Lee and D. A. Padua. Hiding relaxed memory consistency with a compiler. *IEEE Trans. Comput.*, 50:824–833, August 2001.

[67] K. Lee and S. P. Midkiff. A two-phase escape analysis for parallel java programs. In *Proceedings of the 15th international conference on Parallel architectures and compilation techniques*, PACT '06, pages 53–62, New York, NY, USA, 2006. ACM.

[68] D. Leijen, W. Schulte, and S. Burckhardt. The design of a task parallel library. In *Proceeding of the 24th ACM SIGPLAN conference on Object oriented programming systems languages and applications*, OOPSLA '09, pages 227–242, New York, NY, USA, 2009. ACM.

[69] L. Li and C. Verbrugge. A practical MHP information analysis for concurrent Java programs. In *Proceedings of the 17th International Workshop on Languages and Compilers for Parallel Computing (LCPC'04)*, number TBA in LNCS. Springer Verlag, Sept. 2004.

[70] S.-T. M. Limited. occam 2.1 reference manual. http://www.wotug.org/occam/documentation/oc21refman.pdf, May 1995. Last checked: 08/20/2011.

[71] C. Lin, V. Nagarajan, and R. Gupta. Efficient sequential consistency using conditional fences. In *Proceedings of the 19th international conference on Parallel architectures and compilation techniques*, PACT '10, pages 295–306, New York, NY, USA, 2010. ACM.

[72] T. Lindholm and F. Yellin. *The Java Virtual Machine Specification*. Addison-Wesley Longman, Amsterdam, 2 edition, April 1999.

[73] S. Lu, S. Park, E. Seo, and Y. Zhou. Learning from mistakes: a comprehensive study on real world concurrency bug characteristics. *SIGOPS Oper. Syst. Rev.*, 42:329–339, March 2008.

[74] B. Lucia, L. Ceze, K. Strauss, S. Qadeer, and H.-J. Boehm. Conflict exceptions: simplifying concurrent language semantics with precise hardware exceptions for data-races. In *Proceedings of the 37th annual international symposium on Computer architecture*, ISCA '10, pages 210–221, New York, NY, USA, 2010. ACM.

[75] J. Manson, W. Pugh, and S. V. Adve. The java memory model. In *Proceedings of the 32nd ACM SIGPLAN-SIGACT symposium on Principles of programming languages*, POPL '05, pages 378–391, New York, NY, USA, 2005. ACM.

[76] D. Marino, M. Musuvathi, and S. Narayanasamy. Literace: effective sampling for lightweight data-race detection. In *Proceedings of the 2009 ACM SIGPLAN conference on Programming language design and implementation*, PLDI '09, pages 134–143, New York, NY, USA, 2009. ACM.

[77] D. Marino, A. Singh, T. Millstein, M. Musuvathi, and S. Narayanasamy. Drfx: a simple and efficient memory model for concurrent programming languages. In *Proceedings of the 2010 ACM SIGPLAN conference on Programming language design and implementation*, PLDI '10, pages 351–362, New York, NY, USA, 2010. ACM.

[78] D. Marino, A. Singh, T. Millstein, M. Musuvathi, and S. Narayanasamy. A case for an sc-preserving compiler. *SIGPLAN Not.*, 46:199–210, June 2011.

[79] M. Martin, C. Blundell, and E. Lewis. Subtleties of transactional memory atomicity semantics. *IEEE Comput. Archit. Lett.*, 5:17–, July 2006.

[80] S. P. Masticola and B. G. Ryder. Non-concurrency analysis. In *Proceedings of the fourth ACM SIGPLAN symposium on Principles and practice of parallel programming*, PPOPP '93, pages 129–138, New York, NY, USA, 1993. ACM.

[81] N. D. Matsakis and T. R. Gross. A time-aware type system for data-race protection and guaranteed initialization. In *Proceedings of the ACM international conference on*

*Object oriented programming systems languages and applications*, OOPSLA '10, pages 634–651, New York, NY, USA, 2010. ACM.

[82] J. McKinna. Why dependent types matter. In *Conference record of the 33rd ACM SIGPLAN-SIGACT symposium on Principles of programming languages*, POPL '06, pages 1–1, New York, NY, USA, 2006. ACM.

[83] A. Miller. The task graph pattern. In *Proceedings of the 2010 Workshop on Parallel Programming Patterns*, ParaPLoP '10, pages 8:1–8:7, New York, NY, USA, 2010. ACM.

[84] R. Milner. *Communicating and mobile systems: the π-calculus*. Cambridge University Press, New York, NY, USA, 1999.

[85] C. Miranda, A. Pop, P. Dumont, A. Cohen, and M. Duranton. Erbium: a deterministic, concurrent intermediate representation to map data-flow tasks to scalable, persistent streaming processes. In *Proceedings of the 2010 international conference on Compilers, architectures and synthesis for embedded systems*, CASES '10, pages 11–20, New York, NY, USA, 2010. ACM.

[86] M. Moir. Transparent support for wait-free transactions. In *Proceedings of the 11th International Workshop on Distributed Algorithms*, WDAG '97, pages 305–319, London, UK, 1997. Springer-Verlag.

[87] S. S. Muchnick. *Advanced compiler design and implementation*. Morgan Kaufmann Publishers Inc., San Francisco, CA, USA, 1997.

[88] M. Musuvathi and S. Qadeer. Iterative context bounding for systematic testing of multi-threaded programs. In *Proceedings of the 2007 ACM SIGPLAN conference on Programming language design and implementation*, PLDI '07, pages 446–455, New York, NY, USA, 2007. ACM.

[89] G. Naumovich and G. S. Avrunin. A conservative data flow algorithm for detecting all pairs of statements that may happen in parallel. In *Proceedings of the 6th ACM SIGSOFT international symposium on Foundations of software engineering*, SIGSOFT '98/FSE-6, pages 24–34, New York, NY, USA, 1998. ACM.

[90] G. Naumovich, G. S. Avrunin, and L. A. Clarke. An efficient algorithm for computing mhp information for concurrent java programs. In *Proceedings of the 7th European software engineering conference held jointly with the 7th ACM SIGSOFT international symposium on Foundations of software engineering*, ESEC/FSE-7, pages 338–354, London, UK, 1999. Springer-Verlag.

[91] D. A. Novillo. *Analysis and optimization of explicitly parallel programs*. PhD thesis, 2000. AAINQ60007.

[92] U. of Kent at Canterbury. Communicating sequential processes for java (jcsp). http://www.cs.kent.ac.uk/projects/ofa/jcsp/, July 2011. Last checked: 08/20/2011.

[93] OpenMP. The openmp api specification for parallel programming. http://www.openmp.org, June 2011. Last checked: 20/06/2011.

[94] Y. G. Park and B. Goldberg. Escape analysis on lists. In *Proceedings of the ACM SIGPLAN 1992 conference on Programming language design and implementation*, PLDI '92, pages 116–127, New York, NY, USA, 1992. ACM.

[95] C. D. Polychronopoulos. The hierarchical task graph and its use in auto-scheduling. In *Proceedings of the 5th international conference on Supercomputing*, ICS '91, pages 252–263, New York, NY, USA, 1991. ACM.

[96] S. Qadeer and D. Wu. Kiss: keep it simple and sequential. In *Proceedings of the ACM SIGPLAN 2004 conference on Programming language design and implementation*, PLDI '04, pages 14–24, New York, NY, USA, 2004. ACM.

[97] R. Raman, J. Zhao, V. Sarkar, M. Vechev, and E. Yahav. Efficient data race detection for async-finish parallelism. In *Proceedings of the First international conference on Runtime verification*, RV'10, pages 368–383, Berlin, Heidelberg, 2010. Springer-Verlag.

[98] K. Randall. Cilk: Efficient multithreaded computing. Technical report, Cambridge, MA, USA, 1998.

[99] J. Reinders. *Intel threading building blocks: outfitting C++ for multi-core processor parallelism*. O'Reilly Series. O'Reilly, 2007.

[100] J. S. Request. Lambda Expressions for the Java Programming Language. http://jcp.org/en/jsr/detail?id=335, 2010. Last checked: 16/08/2011.

[101] E. Ruf. Effective synchronization removal for java. In *Proceedings of the ACM SIGPLAN 2000 conference on Programming language design and implementation*, PLDI '00, pages 208–218, New York, NY, USA, 2000. ACM.

[102] R. Rugina and M. C. Rinard. Pointer analysis for structured parallel programs. *ACM Trans. Program. Lang. Syst.*, 25:70–116, January 2003.

[103] V. Sarkar. Analysis and optimization of explicitly parallel programs using the parallel program graph representation. In *Proceedings of the 10th International Workshop on Languages and Compilers for Parallel Computing*, LCPC '97, pages 94–113, London, UK, 1998. Springer-Verlag.

[104] D. Shasha and M. Snir. Efficient and correct execution of parallel programs that share memory. *ACM Trans. Program. Lang. Syst.*, 10:282–312, April 1988.

[105] T. Shpeisman, V. Menon, A.-R. Adl-Tabatabai, S. Balensiefer, D. Grossman, R. L. Hudson, K. F. Moore, and B. Saha. Enforcing isolation and ordering in stm. In *Proceedings of the 2007 ACM SIGPLAN conference on Programming language design and implementation*, PLDI '07, pages 78–88, New York, NY, USA, 2007. ACM.

[106] L. A. Smith, J. M. Bull, and J. Obdržálek. A parallel java grande benchmark suite. In *Proceedings of the 2001 ACM/IEEE conference on Supercomputing (CDROM)*, Supercomputing '01, pages 8–8, New York, NY, USA, 2001. ACM.

[107] H. Srinivasan, J. Hook, and M. Wolfe. Static single assignment for explicitly parallel programs. In *Proceedings of the 20th ACM SIGPLAN-SIGACT symposium on Principles of programming languages*, POPL '93, pages 260–272, New York, NY, USA, 1993. ACM.

[108] Z. Sura, X. Fang, C.-L. Wong, S. P. Midkiff, J. Lee, and D. Padua. Compiler techniques for high performance sequentially consistent java programs. In *Proceedings of the tenth ACM SIGPLAN symposium on Principles and practice of parallel programming*, PPoPP '05, pages 2–13, New York, NY, USA, 2005. ACM.

[109] T. Terauchi. Checking race freedom via linear programming. In *Proceedings of the 2008 ACM SIGPLAN conference on Programming language design and implementation*, PLDI '08, pages 1–10, New York, NY, USA, 2008. ACM.

[110] T. Terauchi and A. Aiken. A capability calculus for concurrency and determinism. *ACM Trans. Program. Lang. Syst.*, 30:27:1–27:30, September 2008.

[111] C. von Praun and T. R. Gross. Object race detection. *SIGPLAN Not.*, 36:70–82, October 2001.

[112] E. Vries, R. Plasmeijer, and D. M. Abrahamson. Uniqueness typing simplified. In O. Chitil, Z. Horváth, and V. Zsók, editors, *Implementation and Application of Functional Languages*, pages 201–218. Springer-Verlag, Berlin, Heidelberg, 2008.

[113] J. Ševčík and D. Aspinall. On validity of program transformations in the java memory model. In *Proceedings of the 22nd European conference on Object-Oriented Programming*, ECOOP '08, pages 27–51, Berlin, Heidelberg, 2008. Springer-Verlag.

[114] L. Wang and X. Sun. Escape analysis for synchronization removal. In *Proceedings of the 2006 ACM symposium on Applied computing*, SAC '06, pages 1419–1423, New York, NY, USA, 2006. ACM.

[115] J. Whaley and M. S. Lam. Cloning-based context-sensitive pointer alias analysis using binary decision diagrams. In *Proceedings of the ACM SIGPLAN 2004 conference on Programming language design and implementation*, PLDI '04, pages 131–144, New York, NY, USA, 2004. ACM.

[116] J. Whaley and M. Rinard. Compositional pointer and escape analysis for java programs. In *Proceedings of the 14th ACM SIGPLAN conference on Object-oriented programming, systems, languages, and applications*, OOPSLA '99, pages 187–206, New York, NY, USA, 1999. ACM.

[117] Y. Yu, T. Rodeheffer, and W. Chen. Racetrack: efficient detection of data race conditions via adaptive tracking. In *Proceedings of the twentieth ACM symposium on Operating systems principles*, SOSP '05, pages 221–234, New York, NY, USA, 2005. ACM.

[118] Y. Zhang and E. Duesterwald. Barrier matching for programs with textually unaligned barriers. In *Proceedings of the 12th ACM SIGPLAN symposium on Principles and practice of parallel programming*, PPoPP '07, pages 194–204, New York, NY, USA, 2007. ACM.

[119] Y. Zhang, E. Duesterwald, and G. R. Gao. Concurrency analysis for shared memory programs with textually unaligned barriers. In *LCPC*, pages 95–109, 2007.

# A
# Datalog implementation

| | |
|---|---|
| *Variable* | the domain of variables. *Variable* contains all the allocation sites, formal parameters, return values, thrown exceptions, cast operations, and dereferences in the program. |
| *Object* | the domain of heap objects. Heap objects are named by the invocation sites of object creation operations. |
| *Field* | the domain of fields in the program. There is a special field *elements* to denote an array access. |
| *Method* | the domain of implemented methods in the program. It does not include abstract or interface methods. |
| *Selector* | the domain of virtual method names used in invocations. |
| *BC* | the domain of bytecodes in the program. |
| *Type* | the domain of types (classes and interfaces) in the program. |
| *ParamPosition* | an integer domain representing possible parameter positions. |

Figure A.1: The Datalog domains.

This appendix lists the code of the schedule analysis prototype implemented in Datalog. We chose Datalog for the first prototype because it is a concise high-level specification language that has been shown to be well-suited for data-flow analyses and scalable to even large real-world programs [115].

The basis of Datalog are two-dimensional tables called *relations*. In a relation, the columns are the attributes, each of which is associated with a finite domain defining the set of possible values, and the rows are the tuples that are part of this relation. Figure A.1 shows the domains that we use in the implementation of the schedule analysis.

If tuple $(x,y,z)$ is in relation $A$, we say that predicate $A(x,y,z)$ is true. A Datalog program consists of a set of rules that compute new members of relations if the rule body is true. E.g., the rule:

```
D(w, z) :- A(w, x), B(x, y), !C(y, z).
```

says that "tuple $(w,z)$ is added to $D$ if $A(w,x)$, $B(x,y)$, and not $C(y,z)$ are all true." The Datalog runtime will apply rules until a fixed point has been reached and no more tuples can be added to the relations.

Before the analysis (implemented as a Datalog program) starts, a pre-processor extracts information about the analyzed program and generates input tuples that can be read by Datalog.

This set of initial tuples is called the *extensional database*. The pre-processor generates many different relations encoding information about type hierarchies, virtual method calls, object creation, and more.

## A.1 Extensional database

The extensional database consists of relations that are extracted from the program by a pre-processor and that function as the input to the subsequent Datalog programs. The most important relations contain the information about what method contains what statements and the variables that are accessed by each statement. Because Java is a strongly typed language, additional relations model the type hierarchy of the analyzed program.

Type information is used to filter variables (e.g., when passing an actual variable v1 into a formal parameter p or for the implicit **this**). Type-based filtering improves the precision by ruling out spurious aliasing.

```
#*********************
#Root methods of the
#program
#*********************
roots              (method:Method)                                              input

#*********************
#Program statements
#*********************
new                (m:Method, dest:Variable, obj:Object)                        input
schedule           (m:Method, bc:BC, dest:Variable, obj:Object, name:Selector)  input
now                (m:Method, variable:Variable)                                input
constant           (m:Method, variable:Variable, object:Object)                 input
load               (m:Method, variable:Variable, base:Variable, field:Field)    input
primLoad           (m:Method, base:Variable, field:Field)                       input
staticLoad         (m:Method, dest:Variable, field:Field)                       input
staticPrimLoad     (m:Method, field:Field)                                      input
store              (m:Method, base:Variable, field:Field, source:Variable)      input
primStore          (m:Method, base:Variable, field:Field)                       input
staticStore        (m:Method, field:Field, source:Variable)                     input
staticPrimStore    (m:Method, field:Field)                                      input
assign             (m:Method, dest:Variable, source:Variable)                   input
arrow              (m:Method, lhs:Variable, rhs:Variable)                       input
methodReturn       (m:Method, var:Variable)                                     input
methodThrow        (m:Method, var:Variable)                                     input

#*********************
#Monitor enter/exit
#*********************
monitorEnter       (m:Method, variable:Variable)                                input
monitorExit        (m:Method, variable:Variable)                                input

#*********************
#Type information
#*********************
variableType       (method:Method, variable:Variable, type:Type)                input
```

## A.2. RULES FOR THE TASK-SENSITIVE POINTS-TO ANALYSIS

```
objectType              (object:Object, type:Type)                                      input
#NOTE: assignable must be a flattened hierarchy already, including same-type
assignable              (supertype:Type, subtype:Type)                                  input
member                  (type:Type, name:Selector, target:Method)                       input

#*********************
#Intra-procedural
#control flow
#*********************
actual                  (method:Method, invokeBC:BC, param:ParamPosition, var:Variable) input
formal                  (method:Method, param:ParamPosition, var:Variable)              input

#call sites
staticClassInvoke       (m:Method, invokeBC:BC, target:Method)                          input
staticInstanceInvoke    (m:Method, invokeBC:BC, target:Method)                          input
virtualInvoke           (m:Method, invokeBC:BC, name:Selector)                          input
callSiteReturn          (m:Method, invokeBC:BC, var:Variable)                           input

#*********************
#Exception handling
#*********************
#we catch all exceptions by type that can be assigned to var;
catch                   (m:Method, var:Variable)                                        input
```

## A.2   Rules for the task-sensitive points-to analysis

The points-to analysis is a slightly modified version of the points-to analysis described by Whaley and Lam [115]. It is a flow-context insensitive analysis with on-the-fly call graph discovery that uses a 1-call-site and 1-task context sensitivity.

With this sensitivity, an object is always represented as a tuple [objCtxt, obj] where the second element obj represents the creation site (that is, the **new**-statement or the **schedule**-statement) of the object whereas objCtxt represents the creation site of the **this**-object that executes the **new** or **schedule**-statement. In addition, each execution context names the corresponding task object. Because the task object is a normal object, it, too, is represented as a [objCtxt, obj] tuple.

For example, in the clause executionContext(nowCtxt, now, thisCtxt, this, m), the tuple [nowCtxt, now] represents the (contextualized) task object in which method m is executed and [thisCtxt, this] represents the (contextualized) receiver of m.

```
#***************************
#The result relations of the
#points-to analysis
#***************************
#in task [nowCtxt,now], variable v1 of method [thisCtxt,this].m() points to [objCtxt,obj]
variablePT     (nowCtxt:Object, now:Object, \
                thisCtxt:Object, this:Object, \
                method:Method, v1:Variable, \
                objCtxt:Object, object:Object)                              output

#in the heap, [baseCtxt, base].f -> [targetCtxt, target]
```

```
heapPT      (baseCtxt:Object, base:Object, \
                field:Field, \
                targetCtxt:Object, target:Object)              output

#in method [callerThisCtxt,callerThis].callerMethod() executed in [callerNowCtxt,callerNow],
#bytecode invokeBC is a call to
#method [calledThisCtxt,calledThis].calledMethod executed in [calledNowCtxt,calledNow].
#in the end, invocationEdge() represents the context-sensitive call graph
invocationEdge  (callerNowCtxt:Object, callerNow:Object, \
                callerThisCtxt:Object, callerThis:Object, \
                callerMethod:Method, invokeBC:BC, \
                calledNowCtxt:Object, calledNow:Object, \
                caledThisCtxt:Object, calledThis:Object, calledMethod:Method)  output

#**********************
#execution scope
#**********************
#method m on receiver [thisCtxt,this] is executed in task [nowCtxt,now];
#the execution context is just a projection of the invocationEdge relation to simplify some things
executionContext(nowCtxt:Object, now:Object, \
        thisCtxt:Object, this:Object, \
        m:Method)
executionContext(calledNowCtxt, calledNow, calledThisCtxt, calledThis, calledM) :- \
            invocationEdge(_, _, _, _, _, _, calledNowCtxt, calledNow, calledThisCtxt, calledThis,
                calledM).

#**********************
#Root
#**********************
executionContext(0, 0, 0, 0, m) :- \
            roots(m).

#**********************
#type filtering
#**********************
canPointTo(method:Method, variable:Variable, object:Object)
canPointTo(m, v, obj) :- \
            variableType(m, v, varType), \
            objectType(obj, objType), \
            assignable(varType, objType). split

#**********************
#new statements
#**********************
#two options: we could use "this" or "now" as the context for the new object
variablePT(nowCtxt, now, thisCtxt, this, m, v, alsoThis, obj) :-  \
            executionContext(nowCtxt, now, thisCtxt, this, m), \
            new(m, v, obj), \
            this=alsoThis. split

#**********************
#schedule statement
#**********************
variablePT(nowCtxt, now, thisCtxt, this, m, v, alsoNow, obj) :- \
```

## A.2. Rules for the task-sensitive points-to analysis

```
            executionContext(nowCtxt, now, thisCtxt, this, m), \
            schedule(m, _, v, obj, _), \
            now=alsoNow. split

#**********************
#now statement
#**********************
variablePT(nowCtxt, now, thisCtxt, this, m, v, alsoNowCtxt, alsoNow) :- \
            executionContext(nowCtxt, now, thisCtxt, this, m), \
            now(m, v), \
            nowCtxt=alsoNowCtxt, \
            now=alsoNow. split

#**********************
#constants
#**********************
#two options: we could use "this" or "now" as the context for the new object
variablePT(nowCtxt, now, thisCtxt, this, m, v, 0, obj) :- \
            executionContext(nowCtxt, now, thisCtxt, this, m), \
            constant(m, v, obj). split

#**********************
#assignments;
#**********************
variablePT(nowCtxt, now, thisCtxt, this, m, v1, objCtxt, obj) :- \
            executionContext(nowCtxt, now, thisCtxt, this, m), \
            assign(m, v1, v2), \
            variablePT(nowCtxt, now, thisCtxt, this, m, v2, objCtxt, obj), \
            canPointTo(m, v1, obj). split

#**********************
#loads;
#**********************
variablePT(nowCtxt, now, thisCtxt, this, m, v2, targetCtxt, target):- \
            executionContext(nowCtxt, now, thisCtxt, this, m), \
            load(m, v2, v1, f), \
            variablePT(nowCtxt, now, thisCtxt, this, m, v1, baseCtxt, base), \
            heapPT(baseCtxt, base, f, targetCtxt, target), \
            canPointTo(m, v2, target). split

#**********************
#static loads;
#**********************
variablePT(nowCtxt, now, thisCtxt, this, m, v, targetCtxt, target):- \
            executionContext(nowCtxt, now, thisCtxt, this, m), \
            staticLoad(m, v, f), \
            heapPT(0, 0, f, targetCtxt, target), \
            canPointTo(m, v, target). split

#**********************
#stores;
#**********************
heapPT(baseCtxt, base, f, targetCtxt, target):- \
            executionContext(nowCtxt, now, thisCtxt, this, m), \
```

146                                                          APPENDIX A. DATALOG IMPLEMENTATION

```
            store(m, v1, f, v2), \
            variablePT(nowCtxt, now, thisCtxt, this, m, v1, baseCtxt, base), \
            variablePT(nowCtxt, now, thisCtxt, this, m, v2, targetCtxt, target). split

#**********************
#static stores;
#**********************
heapPT(0, 0, f, targetCtxt, target):- \
            executionContext(nowCtxt, now, thisCtxt, this, m), \
            staticStore(m, f, v), \
            variablePT(nowCtxt, now, thisCtxt, this, m, v, targetCtxt, target). split

#**********************
#static calls
#**********************
#statically bound instance methods
invocationEdge(nowCtxt, now, thisCtxt, this, m, invokeBC, alsoNowCtxt, alsoNow, calledThisCtxt,
    calledThis, calledM) :- \
            executionContext(nowCtxt, now, thisCtxt, this, m), \
            staticInstanceInvoke(m, invokeBC, calledM), \
            actual(m, invokeBC, 0, recVar), \
            variablePT(nowCtxt, now, thisCtxt, this, m, recVar, calledThisCtxt, calledThis), \
            nowCtxt=alsoNowCtxt, \
            now=alsoNow. split

#statically bound class methods (do not use actual variable but the global object)
invocationEdge(nowCtxt, now, thisCtxt, this, m, invokeBC, 0, 0, 0, 0, calledM) :- \
            executionContext(nowCtxt, now, thisCtxt, this, m), \
            staticClassInvoke(m, invokeBC, calledM). split

#**********************
#virtual calls
#**********************
invocationEdge(nowCtxt, now, thisCtxt, this, m, invokeBC, alsoNowCtxt, alsoNow, calledThisCtxt,
    calledThis, calledM) :- \
            executionContext(nowCtxt, now, thisCtxt, this, m), \
            virtualInvoke(m, invokeBC, selector), \
            actual(m, invokeBC, 0, recVar), \
            variablePT(nowCtxt, now, thisCtxt, this, m, recVar, calledThisCtxt, calledThis), \
            objectType(calledThis, t), \
            member(t, selector, calledM), \
            nowCtxt=alsoNowCtxt, \
            now=alsoNow. split

#**********************
#schedule statements
#**********************
invocationEdge(nowCtxt, now, thisCtxt, this, m, invokeBC, alsoNow, calledNow, calledThisCtxt,
    calledThis, calledM) :- \
            executionContext(nowCtxt, now, thisCtxt, this, m), \
            schedule(m, invokeBC, _, calledNow, selector), \
            actual(m, invokeBC, 0, recVar), \
            variablePT(nowCtxt, now, thisCtxt, this, m, recVar, calledThisCtxt, calledThis), \
            objectType(calledThis, t), \
```

```
            member(t, selector, calledM), \
            now=alsoNow. split

#**********************
#parameter passing
#**********************
variablePT(calledNowCtxt, calledNow, calledThisCtxt, calledThis, calledM, formalVar, objCtxt, obj) :- \
            invocationEdge(nowCtxt, now, thisCtxt, this, m, invokeBC, calledNowCtxt, calledNow,
                    calledThisCtxt, calledThis, calledM), \
            formal(calledM, z, formalVar), \
            actual(m, invokeBC, z, actualVar), \
            variablePT(nowCtxt, now, thisCtxt, this, m, actualVar, objCtxt, obj). split

#**********************
#returns
#**********************
variablePT(nowCtxt, now, thisCtxt, this, m, callerRetVar, objCtxt, obj) :- \
            invocationEdge(nowCtxt, now, thisCtxt, this, m, invokeBC, calledNowCtxt, calledNow,
                    calledThisCtxt, calledThis, calledM), \
            callSiteReturn(m, invokeBC, callerRetVar), \
            methodReturn(calledM, retVar), \
            variablePT(calledNowCtxt, calledNow, calledThisCtxt, calledThis, calledM, retVar, objCtxt,
                    obj), \
            canPointTo(m, callerRetVar, obj). split

#**********************
#exceptions
#**********************
variablePT(nowCtxt, now, thisCtxt, this, m, caughtExcVar, excCtxt, excObj) :- \
            executionContext(nowCtxt, now, thisCtxt, this, m), \
            catch(m, caughtExcVar), \
            methodThrow(throwingM, thrownExcVar), \
            variablePT(_, _, _, _, throwingM, thrownExcVar, excCtxt, excObj), \
            canPointTo(m, caughtExcVar, excObj). split
```

## A.3 Rules for the task-sensitive escape analysis

The escape analysis first collects escaping variables. A variable v in a method m escapes if v is used as an actual parameter in a **schedule**-statement; if it is used as an actual parameter for a formal parameter that escapes; or if it is stored in a static field. In a second step, the escape analysis collects all escaping objects, starting from the objects referenced by escaping variables and recursively adding all objects that can be reached by an escaping object.

In addition to the escapesTask() relation, the escape analysis computes a taskReaches() relation that can be used by subsequent analyses and optimizations. taskReaches() collects all nodes in the call graph that can be reached from each task entry point.

```
#**********************
#escaping variables
#**********************
#variable v in m escapes if it reaches a schedule statement or
```

```
#a static store directly in m or through method calls
varEscapes(_, _, _, _, m, v) :- \
            schedule(m, invokeBC, _, _, _), \
            actual(m, invokeBC, _, v).

varEscapes(_, _, _, _, m, v) :- \
            staticStore(m, _, v).

varEscapes(nowCtxt, now, thisCtxt, this, m, v2) :- \
            assign(m, v1, v2), \
            varEscapes(nowCtxt, now, thisCtxt, this, m, v1). split

varEscapes(nowCtxt, now, thisCtxt, this, m1, v1) :- \
            invocationEdge(nowCtxt, now, thisCtxt, this, m1, invokeBC, _, _, receiverCtxt, receiver, m2
                ), \
            !schedule(m1, invokeBC, _, _, _) \
            actual(m1, invokeBC, n, v1), \
            formal(m2, n, v2), \
            varEscapes(nowCtxt, now, receiverCtxt, receiver, m2, v2). split

#*********************
#escaping from a task
#*********************
#params flowing into the task are considered escaped
escapesTask(nowCtxt, now, thisCtxt, this, objCtxt, obj) :- \
            invocationEdge(creatorNowCtxt, creatorNow, creatorThisCtxt, creatorThis, m1, invokeBC,
                nowCtxt, now, thisCtxt, this, _), \
            schedule(m1, invokeBC, _, _, _), \
            actual(m1, invokeBC, _, v), \
            variablePT(creatorNowCtxt, creatorNow, creatorThisCtxt, creatorThis, m1, v, objCtxt, obj).
                split

#everything that escapes from the inside is escaped
escapesTask(nowCtxt, now, thisCtxt, this, objCtxt, obj) :- \
            invocationEdge(_, _, _, _, m1, invokeBC, nowCtxt, now, thisCtxt, this, m2), \
            schedule(m1, invokeBC, _, _, _), \
            varEscapes(nowCtxt, now, thisCtxt, this, m2, v), \
            variablePT(nowCtxt, now, thisCtxt, this, m2, v, objCtxt, obj). split

#everything that is reachable through an escaped object escapes
escapesTask(nowCtxt, now, thisCtxt, this, objCtxt2, obj2) :- \
            escapesTask(nowCtxt, now, thisCtxt, this, objCtxt1, obj1), \
            heapPT(objCtxt1, obj1, _, objCtxt2, obj2). split

#*********************
#reachability from task
#methods to nodes in
#the call graph
#*********************
taskReaches(nowCtxt, now, thisCtxt, this, alsoThisCtxt, alsoThis, m) :- \
            invocationEdge(_, _, _, _, m1, invokeBC, nowCtxt, now, thisCtxt, this, m), \
            schedule(m1, invokeBC, _, _, _), \
            thisCtxt=alsoThisCtxt, \
            this=alsoThis. split
```

A.4. RULES FOR THE SCHEDULE ANALYSIS                                            149

```
taskReaches(nowCtxt, now, thisCtxt, this, calledThisCtxt2, calledThis2, m2) :- \
        taskReaches(nowCtxt, now, thisCtxt, this, calledThisCtxt1, calledThis1, m1), \
        invocationEdge(nowCtxt, now, calledThisCtxt1, calledThis1, m1, invokeBC, _, _,
            calledThisCtxt2, calledThis2, m2), \
        !schedule(m1, invokeBC, _, _, _). split
```

## A.4 Rules for the schedule analysis

The Datalog implementation of the schedule analysis expects that the loop-contextualized task-ordering graph for each task method has been extracted beforehand (see Section 4.2.2). Due to the restricted expressiveness of Datalog, the loop-contextualized task-ordering graph extraction had to be implemented in Java and is therefore not presented here. The domains A0 and A1 range over all task variables. Relations that result from this intermediate processing step use the postfix 0.

```
#************************************
#loop-contextualized task-ordering
#graph
#************************************
schedules0(nowCtxt:Object, now:Object, var:A0, resNowCtxt:Object, resNow:Object)
actual0(nowCtxt:Object, now:Object, var:A0, p:ParamPosition, val:A1)
formal0(nowCtxt:Object, now:Object, p:ParamPosition, var:A0)
arrow0(nowCtxt:Object, now:Object, lhs:A0, rhs:A1)

singleton0(nowCtxt:Object, now:Object, a:A0, b:A1)
ordered0(nowCtxt:Object, now:Object, a:A0)
multiple0(nowCtxt:Object, now:Object, a:A0)


#************************************
#ordered-ness of tasks
#************************************

#there can be tasks that are only ordered (in ordered0) but not orderedBefore. mix those into the
    ordered relation
ordered(nowCtxt:Object, now:Object, a:A0, b:A1)
ordered(nowCtxt, now, a, alsoA) :-
        ordered0(nowCtxt, now, a), a=alsoA.
ordered(nowCtxt, now, a, b) :-
        orderedBefore(nowCtxt, now, a, b).
ordered(nowCtxt, now, a, b) :-
        orderedBefore(nowCtxt, now, b, a).
ordered(nowCtxt, now, a, b) :-
        ordered(nowCtxt, now, b, a).


#************************************
#infos about parameter flows
#************************************

#in nowCtxt.now, actual is a direct parameter to a and mapped to formal in a's task resNowCtxt.resNow
param(nowCtxt:Object, now:Object, a:A0, actual:A1, resNowCtxt:Object, resNow:Object, formal:A2)
param(nowCtxt, now, a, actual, resNowCtxt, resNow, formal) :- \
```

```
            actual0(nowCtxt, now, a, n, actual), \
            schedules0(nowCtxt, now, a, resNowCtxt, resNow), \
            formal0(resNowCtxt, resNow, n, formal).
```

#used in negations, where you cannot really use _ (bug in bddbddb? or some concept I don't understand?)
isParam(nowCtxt:Object, now:Object, a:A0, param:A1)
isParam(nowCtxt, now, a, actual) :-
            param(nowCtxt, now, a, actual, _, _, _).

#in t, b is the parameter or ordered after the parameter that is mapped to formal in ta
paramOrAfter(nowCtxt:Object, now:Object, a:A0, b:A1, resNowCtxt:Object, resNow:Object, formal:A2)
paramOrAfter(nowCtxt, now, a, actual, resNowCtxt, resNow, formal) :- \
            param(nowCtxt, now, a, actual, resNowCtxt, resNow, formal).
paramOrAfter(nowCtxt, now, a, after, resNowCtxt, resNow, formal) :- \
            param(nowCtxt, now, a, actual, resNowCtxt, resNow, formal), \
            orderedBefore(nowCtxt, now, actual, after).

isParamOrAfter(nowCtxt:Object, now:Object, a:A0, b:A1)
isParamOrAfter(nowCtxt, now, a, b) :-
            paramOrAfter(nowCtxt, now, a, b, _, _, _).


paramOrBefore(nowCtxt:Object, now:Object, a:A0, b:A1, resNowCtxt:Object, resNow:Object, formal:A2)
paramOrBefore(nowCtxt, now, a, actual, resNowCtxt, resNow, formal) :- \
            param(nowCtxt, now, a, actual, resNowCtxt, resNow, formal).
paramOrBefore(nowCtxt, now, a, before, resNowCtxt, resNow, formal) :- \
            param(nowCtxt, now, a, actual, resNowCtxt, resNow, formal), \
            orderedBefore(nowCtxt, now, before, actual).

isParamOrBefore(nowCtxt:Object, now:Object, a:A0, b:A1)
isParamOrBefore(nowCtxt, now, a, b) :-
            paramOrBefore(nowCtxt, now, a, b, _, _, _).


#************************************
#tasks not ordered computation
#************************************

children(nowCtxt:Object, now:Object, resNowCtxt:Object, resNow:Object)
children(nowCtxt, now, resNowCtxt, resNow) :- \
            schedules0(nowCtxt, now, _, resNowCtxt, resNow).
children(nowCtxt, now, resNowCtxt2, resNow2) :- \
            children(nowCtxt, now, resNowCtxt1, resNow1), \
            children(resNowCtxt1, resNow1, resNowCtxt2, resNow2).

contains(nowCtxt:Object, now:Object, a:A0, b:A1)
contains(nowCtxt, now, a, b) :-
            schedules0(nowCtxt, now, a, _, _), \
            schedules0(nowCtxt, now, b, _, _).
contains(nowCtxt, now, a, b) :-
            formal0(nowCtxt, now, _, a), \
            formal0(nowCtxt, now, _, b).
contains(nowCtxt, now, a, b) :-
            schedules0(nowCtxt, now, a, _, _), \
            formal0(nowCtxt, now, _, b).
contains(nowCtxt, now, a, b) :-
```
```

## A.4. Rules for the Schedule Analysis

```
                contains(nowCtxt, now, b, a).

tasksNotOrderedBefore(nowCtxt:Object, now:Object, b:A0, resNowCtxt:Object, resNow:Object)
tasksNotOrderedBefore(nowCtxt, now, b, resNowCtxt, resNow) :- \
                contains(nowCtxt, now, a, b), \
                !singleton(nowCtxt, now, a, b), \
                !orderedBefore(nowCtxt, now, a, b), \
                schedules0(nowCtxt, now, a, resNowCtxt, resNow).
tasksNotOrderedBefore(nowCtxt, now, b, resNowCtxt, resNow) :- \
                contains(nowCtxt, now, a, b), \
                !singleton(nowCtxt, now, a, b), \
                paramOrAfter(nowCtxt, now, a, b, nCA, nA, formal), \
                tasksNotOrderedBefore(nCA, nA, formal, resNowCtxt, resNow).
tasksNotOrderedBefore(nowCtxt, now, b, resNowCtxt, resNow) :- \
                contains(nowCtxt, now, a, b), \
                !singleton(nowCtxt, now, a, b), \
                !isParamOrAfter(nowCtxt, now, a, b), \
                schedules0(nowCtxt, now, a, nCA, nA), \
                children(nCA, nA, resNowCtxt, resNow).

tasksNotOrderedBefore(nowCtxt, now, b, resNowCtxt, resNow) :- \
                schedules0(nowCtxt, now, b, nCB, nB), \
                children(nCB, nB, resNowCtxt, resNow).

tasksNotOrderedAfter(nowCtxt:Object, now:Object, b:A0, resNowCtxt:Object, resNow:Object)
tasksNotOrderedAfter(nowCtxt, now, b, resNowCtxt, resNow) :- \
                contains(nowCtxt, now, a, b), \
                !singleton(nowCtxt, now, a, b), \
                !orderedBefore(nowCtxt, now, b, a), \
                schedules0(nowCtxt, now, a, resNowCtxt, resNow).
tasksNotOrderedAfter(nowCtxt, now, b, resNowCtxt, resNow) :- \
                contains(nowCtxt, now, a, b), \
                !singleton(nowCtxt, now, a, b), \
                paramOrBefore(nowCtxt, now, a, b, nCA, nA, formal), \
                tasksNotOrderedAfter(nCA, nA, formal, resNowCtxt, resNow).
tasksNotOrderedAfter(nowCtxt, now, b, resNowCtxt, resNow) :- \
                contains(nowCtxt, now, a, b), \
                !singleton(nowCtxt, now, a, b), \
                !isParamOrBefore(nowCtxt, now, a, b), \
                !orderedBefore(nowCtxt, now, b, a), \
                schedules0(nowCtxt, now, a, nCA, nA), \
                children(nCA, nA, resNowCtxt, resNow).

tasksNotOrdered(nowCtxt:Object, now:Object, b:A0, resNowCtxt:Object, resNow:Object)
tasksNotOrdered(nowCtxt, now, b, resNowCtxt, resNow) :- \
                contains(nowCtxt, now, a, b), \
                !singleton(nowCtxt, now, a, b), \
                !ordered(nowCtxt, now, a, b), \
                schedules0(nowCtxt, now, a, resNowCtxt, resNow).
tasksNotOrdered(nowCtxt, now, b, resNowCtxt, resNow) :- \
                contains(nowCtxt, now, a, b), \
                !singleton(nowCtxt, now, a, b), \
                param(nowCtxt, now, a, b, nCA, nA, formal), \
                tasksNotOrdered(nCA, nA, formal, resNowCtxt, resNow).
```

```
tasksNotOrdered(nowCtxt, now, b, resNowCtxt, resNow) :- \
        contains(nowCtxt, now, a, b), \
        !singleton(nowCtxt, now, a, b), \
        !isParam(nowCtxt, now, a, b), \
        paramOrAfter(nowCtxt, now, a, b, nCA, nA, formal), \
        tasksNotOrderedBefore(nCA, nA, formal, resNowCtxt, resNow).
tasksNotOrdered(nowCtxt, now, b, resNowCtxt, resNow) :- \
        contains(nowCtxt, now, a, b), \
        !singleton(nowCtxt, now, a, b), \
        !isParam(nowCtxt, now, a, b), \
        paramOrBefore(nowCtxt, now, a, b, nCA, nA, formal), \
        tasksNotOrderedAfter(nCA, nA, formal, resNowCtxt, resNow).
tasksNotOrdered(nowCtxt, now, b, resNowCtxt, resNow) :- \
        contains(nowCtxt, now, a, b), \
        !singleton(nowCtxt, now, a, b), \
        !isParam(nowCtxt, now, a, b), \
        !isParamOrAfter(nowCtxt, now, a, b), \
        !isParamOrBefore(nowCtxt, now, a, b), \
        !orderedBefore(nowCtxt, now, b, a), \
        schedules0(nowCtxt, now, a, nCA, nA), \
        children(nCA, nA, resNowCtxt, resNow).

#*********************
#The main computation:
#parallel(task1, task2)
#*********************
parallel(nowCtxt1:Object, now1:Object, nowCtxt2:Object, now2:Object) output
parallel(nowCtxt1, now1, nowCtxt2, now2) :- \
        schedules0(nC1, n1, a, nowCtxt1, now1), \
        tasksNotOrdered(nC1, n1, a, nowCtxt2, now2).
#the next clause could be made a little more precise,
#if b is a param to a then b's children are parallel only to all children
#of a that are not ordered before
parallel(nowCtxt1, now1, nowCtxt2, now2) :- \
        contains(nC1, n1, a, b), \
        !singleton(nC1, n1, a, b), \
        schedules0(nC1, n1, a, nCA, nA), \
        schedules0(nC1, n1, b, nCB, nB), \
        children(nCA, nA, nowCtxt1, now1), \
        children(nCB, nB, nowCtxt2, now2).
parallel(nowCtxt1, now1, nowCtxt2, now2) :- \
        parallel(nowCtxt2, now2, nowCtxt1, now1).
```

## A.5 Rules for the synchronization removal optimization

This section presents the rules of the synchronization removal optimization as an example for how a concrete optimization can be implemented using the points-to, escape, and scheduling information computed by the corresponding analyses.

```
#*********************
#interference of
#monitor enters
```

## A.5. Rules for the Synchronization Removal Optimization

```
#**********************
accessesMayInterfere(m1, v1, m2, v2) :- \
        parallel(nowCtxt1, now1, nowCtxt2, now2), \
        executionContext(nowCtxt1, now1, thisCtxt1, this1, m1), \
        executionContext(nowCtxt2, now2, thisCtxt2, this2, m2), \
        monitorEnter(m1, v1), \
        monitorEnter(m2, v2), \
        variablePT(nowCtxt1, now1, thisCtxt1, this1, m1, v1, objCtxt, obj), \
        variablePT(nowCtxt2, now2, thisCtxt2, this2, m2, v2, objCtxt, obj), \
        taskReaches(nowCtxt1, now1, actThisCtxt1, actThis1, thisCtxt1, this1, m1), \
        escapesTask(nowCtxt1, now1, actThisCtxt1, actThis1, objCtxt, obj).    split

#**********************
#filter dead monitor
#enters
#**********************
analyzedMonitorEnters(method:Method, variable:Variable) outputtuples printsize
analyzedMonitorEnters(m, v) :-
        executionContext(_, _, _, _, m), \
        monitorEnter(m, v).

#**********************
#required monitor enters
#**********************
requiredMonitorEnters(method:Method, variable:Variable) outputtuples printsize
requiredMonitorEnters(m, v) :-
        analyzedMonitorEnters(m, v), \
        accessesMayInterfere(m, v, _, _).
requiredMonitorEnters(m, v) :-
        analyzedMonitorEnters(m, v), \
        accessesMayInterfere(_, _, m, v).
```

# i want morebooks!

Buy your books fast and straightforward online - at one of world's fastest growing online book stores! Environmentally sound due to Print-on-Demand technologies.

## Buy your books online at
## www.get-morebooks.com

Kaufen Sie Ihre Bücher schnell und unkompliziert online – auf einer der am schnellsten wachsenden Buchhandelsplattformen weltweit! Dank Print-On-Demand umwelt- und ressourcenschonend produziert.

## Bücher schneller online kaufen
## www.morebooks.de

VDM Verlagsservicegesellschaft mbH
Heinrich-Böcking-Str. 6-8    Telefon: +49 681 3720 174    info@vdm-vsg.de
D - 66121 Saarbrücken       Telefax: +49 681 3720 1749   www.vdm-vsg.de

Printed by Books on Demand GmbH, Norderstedt / Germany